BIGGER THOMAS

Major Literary Characters

**THE ANCIENT WORLD THROUGH
THE SEVENTEENTH CENTURY**

ACHILLES
Homer, *Iliad*

CALIBAN
William Shakespeare, *The Tempest*
Robert Browning, *Caliban upon Setebos*

CLEOPATRA
William Shakespeare, *Antony and
    Cleopatra*
John Dryden, *All for Love*
George Bernard Shaw, *Caesar and
    Cleopatra*

DON QUIXOTE
Miguel de Cervantes, *Don Quixote*
Franz Kafka, *Parables*

FALSTAFF
William Shakespeare, *Henry IV, Part I,
    Henry IV, Part II, The Merry Wives
    of Windsor*

FAUST
Christopher Marlowe, *Doctor Faustus*
Johann Wolfgang von Goethe, *Faust*
Thomas Mann, *Doctor Faustus*

HAMLET
William Shakespeare, *Hamlet*

IAGO
William Shakespeare, *Othello*

JULIUS CAESAR
William Shakespeare, *Julius Caesar*
George Bernard Shaw, *Caesar and
    Cleopatra*

KING LEAR
William Shakespeare, *King Lear*

MACBETH
William Shakespeare, *Macbeth*

ODYSSEUS/ULYSSES
Homer, *Odyssey*
James Joyce, *Ulysses*

OEDIPUS
Sophocles, *Oedipus Rex, Oedipus
    at Colonus*

OTHELLO
William Shakespeare, *Othello*

ROSALIND
William Shakespeare, *As You Like It*

SANCHO PANZA
Miguel de Cervantes, *Don Quixote*
Franz Kafka, *Parables*

SATAN
The Book of Job
John Milton, *Paradise Lost*

SHYLOCK
William Shakespeare, *The Merchant
    of Venice*

THE WIFE OF BATH
Geoffrey Chaucer, *The Canterbury
    Tales*

**THE EIGHTEENTH AND
NINETEENTH CENTURIES**

AHAB
Herman Melville, *Moby-Dick*

ISABEL ARCHER
Henry James, *Portrait of a Lady*

EMMA BOVARY
Gustave Flaubert, *Madame Bovary*

DOROTHEA BROOKE
George Eliot, *Middlemarch*

CHELSEA HOUSE PUBLISHERS

Major Literary Characters

DAVID COPPERFIELD
Charles Dickens, *David Copperfield*

ROBINSON CRUSOE
Daniel Defoe, *Robinson Crusoe*

DON JUAN
Molière, *Don Juan*
Lord Byron, *Don Juan*

HUCK FINN
Mark Twain, *The Adventures of
Tom Sawyer, Adventures of
Huckleberry Finn*

CLARISSA HARLOWE
Samuel Richardson, *Clarissa*

HEATHCLIFF
Emily Brontë, *Wuthering Heights*

ANNA KARENINA
Leo Tolstoy, *Anna Karenina*

MR. PICKWICK
Charles Dickens, *The Pickwick Papers*

HESTER PRYNNE
Nathaniel Hawthorne, *The Scarlet Letter*

BECKY SHARP
William Makepeace Thackeray, *Vanity Fair*

LAMBERT STRETHER
Henry James, *The Ambassadors*

EUSTACIA VYE
Thomas Hardy, *The Return of the Native*

TWENTIETH CENTURY

ÁNTONIA
Willa Cather, *My Ántonia*

BRETT ASHLEY
Ernest Hemingway, *The Sun Also Rises*

HANS CASTORP
Thomas Mann, *The Magic Mountain*

HOLDEN CAULFIELD
J. D. Salinger, *The Catcher in the Rye*

CADDY COMPSON
William Faulkner, *The Sound and the Fury*

JANIE CRAWFORD
Zora Neale Hurston, *Their Eyes Were
Watching God*

CLARISSA DALLOWAY
Virginia Woolf, *Mrs. Dalloway*

DILSEY
William Faulkner, *The Sound and the Fury*

GATSBY
F. Scott Fitzgerald, *The Great Gatsby*

HERZOG
Saul Bellow, *Herzog*

JOAN OF ARC
William Shakespeare, *Henry VI*
George Bernard Shaw, *Saint Joan*

LOLITA
Vladimir Nabokov, *Lolita*

WILLY LOMAN
Arthur Miller, *Death of a Salesman*

MARLOW
Joseph Conrad, *Lord Jim, Heart of
Darkness, Youth, Chance*

PORTNOY
Philip Roth, *Portnoy's Complaint*

BIGGER THOMAS
Richard Wright, *Native Son*

CHELSEA HOUSE PUBLISHERS

Major Literary Characters

BIGGER THOMAS

Edited and with an introduction by
HAROLD BLOOM

CHELSEA HOUSE PUBLISHERS
New York ◇ Philadelphia

Jacket illustration: Canada Lee as Bigger Thomas in the 1941
adaptation of *Native Son* by Paul Green. Courtesy of
The New York Public Library at Lincoln Center Performing
Arts Research Center (Billy Rose Theatre Collection).
Inset: Title page of the first edition of *Native Son*
(New York: Harper & Brothers, 1940).
Courtesy of Harper & Row Publishers, Inc.

Chelsea House Publishers

Editor-in-Chief Nancy Toff
Executive Editor Remmel T. Nunn
Managing Editor Karyn Gullen Browne
Picture Editor Adrian G. Allen
Art Director Maria Epes
Manufacturing Manager Gerald Levine

Major Literary Characters

Managing Editor S. T. Joshi
Copy Chief Richard Fumosa
Designer Maria Epes

Staff for BIGGER THOMAS

Researcher Mary Lawlor
Editorial Assistant Katherine Theodore
Assistant Art Director Loraine Machlin
Production Manager Joseph Romano
Production Assistant Leslie D'Acri

© 1990 by Chelsea House Publishers, a division
of Main Line Book Co.

Introduction © 1990 by Harold Bloom

Printed and bound in the United States of America

Library of Congress Cataloging-in-Publication Data

Bigger Thomas / edited and with an introduction by Harold Bloom.
p.   cm.—(Major literary characters)
Includes bibliographical references.
ISBN 0-7910-0965-3.—ISBN 0-7910-1020-1 (pbk.)
1. Wright, Richard, 1908–1960. Native son.   2. Thomas, Bigger
(Fictitious character)   3. Afro-Americans in Literature.
I. Bloom, Harold.   II. Series.
PS3545.R815N335   1990
813'.52—dc20
89-37692
CIP

CONTENTS

CONTENTS

THE ANALYSIS OF CHARACTER

Harold Bloom

"Character," according to our dictionaries, still has as a primary meaning a graphic symbol, such as a letter of the alphabet. This meaning reflects the word's apparent origin in the ancient Greek *charactēr*, a sharp stylus. *Charactēr* also meant the mark of the stylus' incisions. Recent fashions in literary criticism have reduced "character" in literature to a matter of marks upon a page. But our word "character" also has a very different meaning, matching that of the ancient Greek *ēthos*, "habitual way of life." Shall we say then that literary character is an imitation of human character, or is it just a grouping of marks? The issue is between a critic like Dr. Samuel Johnson, for whom words were as much like people as like things, and a critic like the late Roland Barthes, who told us that "the fact can only exist linguistically, as a term of discourse." Who is closer to our experience of reading literature, Johnson or Barthes? What difference does it make, if we side with one critic rather than the other?

Barthes is famous, like Foucault and other recent French theorists, for having added to Nietzsche's proclamation of the death of God a subsidiary demise, that of the literary author. If there are no authors, then there are no fictional personages, presumably because literature does not refer to a world outside language. Words indeed necessarily refer to other words in the first place, but the impact of words ultimately is drawn from a universe of fact. Stories, poems, and plays are recognizable as such because they are human utterances within traditions of utterances, and traditions, by achieving authority, become a kind of fact, or at least the sense of a fact. Our sense that literary characters, within the context of a fictive cosmos, indeed are fictional personages is also a kind of fact. The meaning and value of every character in a successful work of literary representation depend upon our ideas of persons in the factual reality of our lives.

Literary character is always an invention, and inventions generally are indebted to prior inventions. Shakespeare is the inventor of literary character as we know it; he reformed the universal human expectations for the verbal imitation of personality, and the reformation appears now to be permanent and uncannily inevitable. Remarkable as the Bible and Homer are at representing personages, their characters are relatively unchanging. They age within their stories, but their habitual modes of being do not develop. Jacob and Achilles unfold before us, but without metamorphoses. Lear and Macbeth, Hamlet and Othello severely modify themselves not only by their actions, but by their utterances, and most of all through *overhearing themselves,* whether they speak to themselves or to others. Pondering what they themselves have said, they will to change, and actually do change, sometimes extravagantly yet always persuasively. Or else they suffer change, without willing it, but in reaction not so much to their language as to their relation to that language.

I do not think it useful to say that Shakespeare successfully imitated elements in our characters. Rather, it could be argued that he compelled aspects of character to appear that previously were concealed, or not available to representation. This is not to say that Shakespeare is God, but to remind us that language is not God either. The mimesis of character in Shakespeare's dramas now seems to us normative, and indeed became the accepted mode almost immediately, as Ben Jonson shrewdly and somewhat grudgingly implied. And yet, Shakespearean representation has surprisingly little in common with the imitation of reality in Jonson or in Christopher Marlowe. The origins of Shakespeare's originality in the portrayal of men and women are to be found in the *Canterbury Tales* of Geoffrey Chaucer, insofar as they can be located anywhere before Shakespeare himself. Chaucer's savage and superb Pardoner overhears his own tale-telling, as well as his mocking rehearsal of his own spiel, and through this overhearing he is emboldened to forget himself, and enthusiastically urges all his fellow-pilgrims to come forward to be fleeced by him. His self-awareness, and apocalyptically rancid sense of spiritual fall, are preludes to the even grander abysses of the perverted will in Iago and in Edmund. What might be called the character trait of a negative charisma may be Chaucer's invention, but came to its perfection in Shakespearean mimesis.

The analysis of character is as much Shakespeare's invention as the representation of character is, since Iago and Edmund are adepts at analyzing both themselves and their victims. Hamlet, whose overwhelming charisma has many negative components, is certainly the most comprehensive of all literary characters, and so necessarily prophesies the labyrinthine complexities of the will in Iago and Edmund. Charisma, according to Max Weber, its first codifier, is primarily a natural endowment, and implies a primordial and idiosyncratic power over nature, and so finally over death. Hamlet's uncanniness is at its most suggestive in the scene of his long dying, where the audience, through the mediation of Horatio, itself is compelled to meditate upon suicide, if only because outliving the prince of Denmark scarcely seems an option.

Shakespearean representation has usurped not only our sense of literary character, but our sense of ourselves as characters, with Hamlet playing the part of the largest of these usurpations. Insofar as we have an idea of human disinterestedness, we tend to derive it from the Hamlet of Act V, whose quietism has about it a ghostly authority. Oscar Wilde, in his profound and profoundly witty dialogue, "The Decay of Lying," expressed a permanent insight when he insisted that art shaped every era, far more than any age formed art. Life imitates art, we imitate Shakespeare, because without Shakespeare we would perish for lack of images. Wilde's grandest audacity demystifies Shakespearean mimesis with a Shakespearean vivaciousness: "This unfortunate aphorism about art holding the mirror up to Nature is deliberately said by Hamlet in order to convince the bystanders of his absolute insanity in all art-matters." Of *Hamlet's* influence upon the ages Wilde remarked that: "The world has grown sad because a puppet was once melancholy." "Puppet" is Wilde's own deconstruction, a brilliant reminder that Shakespeare's artistry of illusion has so mastered reality as to have changed reality, evidently forever.

The analysis of character, as a critical pursuit, seems to me as much a Shakespearean invention as literary character was, since much of what we know about how to analyze character necessarily follows Shakespearean procedures. His hero-villains, from Richard III through Iago, Edmund, and Macbeth, are shrewd and endless questers into their own self-motivations. If we could bear to see Hamlet, in his unwearied negations, as another hero-villain, then we would judge him the supreme analyst of the darker recalcitrances in the selfhood. Freud followed the pre-Socratic Empedocles, in arguing that character is fate, a frightening doctrine that maintains the fear that there are no accidents, that overdetermination rules us all of our lives. Hamlet assumes the same, yet adds to this argument the terrible passivity he manifests in Act V. Throughout Shakespeare's tragedies, the most interesting personages seem doom-eager, reminding us again that a Shakespearean reading of Freud would be more illuminating than a Freudian exegesis of Shakespeare. We learn more when we discover Hamlet in the Freudian Death Drive, than when we read *Beyond the Pleasure Principle* into *Hamlet*. In Shakespearean comedy, character achieves its true literary apotheosis, which is the representation of the inner freedom that can be created by great wit alone. Rosalind and Falstaff, perhaps alone among Shakespeare's personages, match Hamlet in wit, though hardly in the metaphysics of consciousness. Whether in the comic or the modern mode, Shakespeare has set the standard of measurement in the balance between character and passion.

In Shakespeare the self is more dramatized than theatricalized, which is why a Shakespearean reading of Freud works out so well. Character-formation after the passing of the Oedipal stage takes the place of fetishistic fragmentings of the self. Critics who now call literary character into question, and who proclaim also the death of the author, invariably also regard all notions, literary and human, of a stable character as being mere reductions of deeper pre-Oedipal desires. It becomes

clear that the fortunes of literary character rise and fall with the prestige of normative conceptions of the ego. Shakespeare's Iago, who wars against being, may be
the first deconstructionist of the self, with his proclamation of "I am not what I am."
This constitutes the necessary prologue to any view that would regard a fixed ego
as a virtual abnormality. But deconstructions of the self are no more modern than
Modernism is. Like literary modernism, the decentered ego came out of the
Hellenistic culture of ancient Alexandria. The Gnostic heretics believed that the
psyche, like the body, was a fallen entity, mechanically fashioned by the Demiurge
or false creator. They held however that each of us possessed also a spark or
pneuma, which was a fragment of the original Abyss or true, alien God. The soul
or psyche within every one of us was thus at war with the self or pneuma, and only
that sparklike self could be saved.

Shakespeare, following after Chaucer in this respect, was the first and remains
still the greatest master of representing character both as a stable soul and a
wavering self. There is a substance that endures in Shakespeare's figures, and there
is also a quicksilver rendition of the unsettling sparks. Racine and Tolstoy, Balzac and
Dickens, follow in Shakespeare's wake by giving us some sense of pre-Oedipal
sparks or drives, and considerably more sense of post-Oedipal character and
personality, stabilizations or sublimations of the fetish-seeking drives. Critics like Leo
Bersani and René Girard argue eloquently against our taking this mimesis as the only
proper work of literature. I would suggest that strong fictions of the self, from the
Bible through Samuel Beckett, necessarily participate in both modes, the sublima-
tion of desire, and the persistence of a primordial desire. The mystery of Hamlet
or of Lear is intimately invested in the tangled mixture of the two modes of
representation.

Psychic mobility is proposed by Bersani as the ideal to which deconstructions
of the literary self may yet guide us. The ideal has its pathos, but the realities of
literary representation seem to me very different, perhaps destructively so. When
a novelist like D. H. Lawrence sought to reduce his characters to Eros and the
Death Drive, he still had to persuade us of his authority at mimesis by lavishing upon
the figures of *The Rainbow* and *Women in Love* all of the vivid stigmata of
normative personality. Birkin and Ursula may represent antithetical and uncanny
drives, but they develop and change as characters pondering their own pronouncements and reactions to self and others. The cost of a non-Shakespearean representation is enormous. Pynchon, in *The Crying of Lot 49* and *Gravity's Rainbow,*
evades the burden of the normative by resorting to something like Christopher
Marlowe's art of caricature in *The Jew of Malta*. Marlowe's Barabas is a marvelous
rhetorician, yet he is a cartoon alongside the troublingly equivocal Shylock. Pynchon's personages are deliberate cartoons also, as flat as comic strips. Marlowe's
achievement, and Pynchon's, are beyond dispute, yet they are like the prelude and
the postlude to Shakespearean reality. They do not wish to engage with our hunger
for the empirical world and so they enter the problematic cosmos of literary
fantasy.

No writer, not even Shakespeare or Proust, alters the available stock that we agree to call reality, but Shakespeare, more than any other, does show us how much of reality we could encounter if only we retained adequate desire. The strong literary representation of character is already an analysis of character, and is part of the healing work of a literary culture, which implicitly seeks to cure violence through a normative mimesis of ego, *as if it were stable,* whether in actuality it is or is not. I do not believe that this is a social quest taken on by literary culture, but rather that we confront here the aesthetic essence of what makes a culture *literary,* rather than metaphysical or ethical or religious. A culture becomes literary when its conceptual modes have failed it, which means when religion, philosophy, and science have begun to lose their authority. If they cannot heal violence, then literature attempts to do so, which may be only a turning inside out of the critical arguments of Girard and Bersani.

I conclude by offering a particular instance or special case as a paradigm for the healing enterprise that is at once the representation and the analysis of literary character. Let us call it the aesthetics of being outraged, or rather of successfully representing the state of being outraged. W. C. Fields was one modern master of such representation, and Nathanael West was another, as was Faulkner before him. Here also the greatest master remains Shakespeare, whose Macbeth, himself a bloody outrage, yet retains our imaginative sympathy precisely because he grows increasingly outraged as he experiences the equivocation of the fiend that lies like truth. The double-natured promises and the prophecies of the weird sisters finally induce in Macbeth an apocalyptic version of the stage actor's anxiety at missing cues, the horror of a phantasmagoric stage fright of missing one's time, of always reacting too late. Macbeth, a veritable monster of solipsistic inwardness but no intellectual, counters his dilemma by fresh murders, that prolong him in time yet provoke him only to a perpetually freshened sense of being outraged, as all his expectations become still worse confounded. We are moved by Macbeth, however estrangedly, because his terrible inwardness is a paradigm for our own solipsism, but also because none of us can resist a strong and successful representation of the human in a state of being outraged.

The ultimate outrage is the necessity of dying, an outrage concealed in a multitude of masks, including the tyrannical ambitions of Macbeth. I suspect that our outrage at being outraged is the most difficult of all our affects for us to represent to ourselves, which is why we are so inclined to imaginative sympathy for a character who strongly conveys that affect to us. The Shrike of West's *Miss Lonelyhearts* or Faulkner's Joe Christmas of *Light in August* are crucial modern instances, but such figures can be located in many other works, since the ability to represent this extreme emotion is one of the tests that strong writers are driven to set for themselves.

However a reader seeks to reduce literary character to a question of marks on a page, she will come at last to the impasse constituted by the thought of death, her death, and before that to all the stations of being outraged that memorialize her own drive towards death. In reading, she quests for evidences that are strong representations, whether of her desire or her despair. Such questings constitute the necessary basis for the analysis of literary character, an enterprise that always will survive every vagary of critical fashion.

EDITOR'S NOTE

This book brings together a representative selection of extracts and essays from the best literary criticism so far devoted to Bigger Thomas, the protagonist of Richard Wright's *Native Son*. I am grateful to Mary Lawlor for her skill and judgment as a researcher for this volume. The extracts and essays are each arranged here in the chronological order of their original publication.

My introduction centers upon the rhetorical pathos of terror that dominates Bigger, and that seems to overdetermine all of his actions.

The critical extracts include important personal statements by James Baldwin and Ralph Ellison, each of whom disengages, Ellison overtly, from the view of the critic Irving Howe that Wright was their prime precursor. A sequence of critical statements follow, in which six notable exegetes of African-American literature work through some of the perplexities provided for most readers by the formidable but alarming figure of Bigger Thomas.

Richard Wright himself fittingly begins the fuller-scale critical essays with an important account of the genesis of Bigger as a literary character. The discussion by Edward Margolies directs itself towards Bigger's Dostoevskian aspect, in which murder is the mode of creativity. Edward A. Watson emphasizes the murder of Bessie Mears by Bigger as being in the rhetorical tradition of the blues, a tradition that forms Bessie's laments. In Keneth Kinnamon's analysis, Wright's politics are seen as imposed upon Bigger's story, rather than unfolding from it.

Dorothy S. Redden absolves Bigger of the category of "guilt," suggesting that "accountability" is more apt to the narrative, while Charles De Arman emphasizes Bigger's final conviction of meaningfulness as being one that acknowledges his guilt yet somehow transcends it. With Ross Pudaloff the focus turns to mass culture, from which Bigger quarries all of his images of self. Bigger's violence again dominates the discussion in Robert James Butler's essay, which sees only a numbing apathy as the alternative to Bigger's murderousness.

The Raskolnikov of Dostoevsky's *Crime and Punishment* is compared to Bigger by Tony Magistrale, after which Laura E. Tanner analyzes the narrator's role in regard to Bigger. Valerie Smith's essay suggests that Bigger's alienation both from blacks and whites is partly redressed by his augmenting expressionism after his consciousness has been freed by his crimes. In this volume's final critical discussion, Alan W. France sees Bigger's story as an instance of male hatred for women combining with the destructive effects of racism. Doubtless such a judgment can be sustained by the relation between Bigger's story and our social reality, but I conclude this editor's note by wondering whether Bigger's authentic force as a literary character is not diminished by our current cultural politics and related resentments.

INTRODUCTION

Writing an introduction to a volume of essays and extracts concerning Richard Wright's "native son," Bigger Thomas, is a sobering experience in the summer of 1989, less than a year after "the Willie Horton election," as future historians may wish to describe the Presidential campaign of 1988. Rereading this manuscript, and returning yet once more to *Native Son,* I am a touch chastened and wish to modify some of my earlier, purely aesthetic reservations about Wright's tormented and now classic work. If our nation were more literate, then the triumph of Lee Atwater and George Bush might as soon be called "the Bigger Thomas election," since a racist campaign demands memorable images, and Richard Wright may be said to have prophesied the image so capably exploited by Chairman Atwater and President Bush.

I am not qualified to judge what are presented to me as African-American aesthetics, and they are in any case still very much in the process of formulation. If there are more universal aesthetics relevant to Wright's representation of Bigger Thomas, and I am by no means certain that there are, then *Native Son* would be an instance of the domination of pathos over logos and ethos. That is, Wright stakes everything upon outrage and shock, upon the terror of feeling. Bigger is so exposed a sensibility that he can be apprehended only as we apprehend Dreiser's Clyde and Carrie, which is under the sign of suffering. Barbara Johnson once suggested that *Native Son* reads differently if we imagine its implied reader as an African-American woman, perhaps even a displacement of Wright's own mother. Whatever one does with that notion, there is something maternal in Wright's stance towards Bigger, even as there was in Dreiser's towards Clyde or Carrie. For all his raw courage, Bigger frequently acts out of terrible and justified fear, and the narrator broods upon that fear with maternal concern.

How well that concern is conveyed to most readers will depend upon their sense of Bigger Thomas as a literary character. Does he persuade as an image of life if we receive him without either guilt or ideology, or is such a reception no longer possible? Can one apprehend Bigger Thomas without patronizing him, which

1

is absurd and irrelevant, and without fearing him in what I will refer to as the Atwater-Bush mode? As a Marxist writer, Wright would have seen his representation of Bigger as a program for social action, but Wright was both a Marxist and a writer without being wholly "a Marxist writer" as such, any more than Dreiser was. Dreiser, at his best, involves us in a pathos so overwhelming that we yield to it even where we find his language inadequate and his procedures awkward. Wright, I would now say, provokes in us the pathos of fear, but a fear too naturalistic to be mistaken as a Gothic pleasure, or an indulgence in nightmare. Any sensitive reader, African-American or whoever, ought to be frightened by Bigger Thomas, because Bigger's is itself the violence of fear. He is driven by solitude, irreality, and superstition to the edge of paranoia, where murder seems to become his only possibility for action, almost his only means of expression. Frantz Fanon famously insisted that Bigger kills in response to the world's anticipation that he must and will commit murder. This may have been an apt political vision, on Fanon's part, but it forgets or does not care that Bigger is a fiction, a man made out of words. A literary character need not do anything; we are there to be held by him, to accept him as another fiction of duration, another postponement of the future.

Even a moral fiction, if that is what Bigger Thomas is, must give pleasure. Dostoevsky's fierce nihilists, Svidrigailov and Stavrogin, have their negative exuberance to recommend them, but Bigger has only his fear and his outrage. No reader should find him tragic, and even the question of pathos alas becomes problematic in the closing pages of the novel. As a naturalistic representation, Bigger Thomas retains force if little enough form, but is the force primarily social? Wright's deliberate error must have been in making Bigger almost totally inarticulate, because speech alone could have made Bigger more vivid to us, and imparted something more than terror to his pathos. But that was Wright's choice, however blindly made; Bigger's plangency was to be mythic, an inarticulate black murderer, full of hatred for nearly everyone. Wright's most savage strike is Bigger's murder of his girl Bessie, a murder intended to make Bigger a figure beyond sympathy. What the slaughter of Bessie does is worse than that, since it calls in doubt the novel's apparent outcry against social injustice.

In certain societies, Bigger could have become a soldier, and prospered thereby. But half a century after the publication of *Native Son*, even a somewhat more enlightened America, the country of Chairman Atwater and President Bush, would not allow an overt sociopath into its armed services. Bigger is a scourge to all, black and pinko-grey (to adapt E. M. Forster's fine term for "white"). An authentic bogeyman, Bigger perhaps represents Wright's deep revenge, not only upon the indubitable racist society of the United States in 1940, but an Oedipal revenge upon black women that so disfigures Wright's work. And there, I suppose, is the clue to what is almost positive in Bigger's pathos. His inarticulateness, rage, fear have compelled him to find dignity and identity only by killing. His final peace before execution, insofar as it is persuasive, comes from his conviction that all men are precisely as he is, no better, no worse. Except for the narrator, we have no link to this ethos that Bigger seems to embody at the close. At some fearful register of being, Bigger's conviction seems also to be Wright's, and expresses resentments in Wright deeper even than his reaction to the societal repression of his people.

I began these remarks by reminding myself that the triumphant Republican use of Willie Horton as a bogeyman returns us to the valid historical justification of Bigger's pathos of terror; Bigger's terror of us, our terror of him. If, half a century after its publication, Bigger's story still survives its aesthetic and human flaws, it must be because that mutual terror retains its relevance. Another time will have to come, if it ever comes, to make Bigger's pathos less terrible for us.

—H. B.

CRITICAL EXTRACTS

JAMES BALDWIN

It must be remembered that the oppressed and the oppressor are bound together within the same society; they accept the same criteria, they share the same beliefs, they both alike depend on the same reality. Within this cage it is romantic, more, meaningless, to speak of a "new" society as the desire of the oppressed, for that shivering dependence on the props of reality which he shares with the *Herrenvolk* makes a truly "new" society impossible to conceive. What is meant by a new society is one in which inequalities will disappear, in which vengeance will be exacted; either there will be no oppressed at all, or the oppressed and the oppressor will change places. But, finally, as it seems to me, what the rejected desire is, is an elevation of status, acceptance within the present community. Thus, the African, exile, pagan, hurried off the auction block and into the fields, fell on his knees before that God in Whom he must now believe; who had made him, but not in His image. This tableau, this impossibility, is the heritage of the Negro in America: *Wash me,* cried the slave to his Maker, *and I shall be whiter, whiter than snow!* For black is the color of evil; only the robes of the saved are white. It is this cry, implacable on the air and in the skull, that he must live with. Beneath the widely published catalogue of brutality—bringing to mind, somehow, an image, a memory of church-bells burdening the air—is this reality which, in the same nightmare notion, he both flees and rushes to embrace. In America, now, this country devoted to the death of the paradox—which may, therefore, be put to death by one—his lot is as ambiguous as a tableau by Kafka. To flee or not, to move or not, it is all the same; his doom is written on his forehead, it is carried in his heart. In *Native Son,* Bigger Thomas stands on a Chicago street corner watching airplanes flown by white men racing against the sun and "Goddamn" he says, the bitterness bubbling up like blood, remembering a million indignities, the terrible, rat-infested house, the humiliation of home-relief, the intense, aimless, ugly bickering, hating it; hatred smoulders through these pages like sulphur fire. All of Bigger's life is controlled, defined by his hatred and his fear. And later, his fear drives him to murder and his hatred to rape; he dies, having come, through this violence, we are told, for the first time, to a kind of life, having for the first time redeemed his manhood. Below the surface of this novel there lies, as it seems to me, a continuation, a complement of that monstrous legend it was written to destroy. Bigger is Uncle Tom's descendant, flesh of his flesh, so exactly opposite a portrait that, when the books are placed together, it seems that the contemporary Negro novelist and the dead New England woman (Harriet Beecher Stowe) are locked together in a deadly, timeless battle; the one uttering merciless exhortations, the other shouting curses. And, indeed, within this web of lust and fury, black and white can only thrust and counter-thrust, long for each other's slow, exquisite death; death by torture, acid, knives and burning; the thrust, the counter-thrust, the longing making the heavier that cloud which blinds and suffocates them both, so that they go down into the pit together. Thus has the cage betrayed us all, this moment, our life, turned to nothing through our terrible attempts to insure it. For Bigger's tragedy is not that he is cold or black or hungry, not even that he is American, black; but that he has accepted a theology that denies him life, that he admits the possibility of his being sub-human and feels constrained, therefore, to battle for his humanity according to those brutal criteria bequeathed him at his birth. But our humanity is our burden, our life; we need not battle for it; we need only to do what is infinitely more difficult—that is, accept it. The failure of the protest novel lies in its rejection of life, the human being, the denial of his beauty, dread, power, in its insistence that it is his categorization alone which is real and which cannot be transcended.

—JAMES BALDWIN, "Everybody's Protest Novel" [1949], *Notes of a Native Son* (Boston: Beacon Press, 1955), pp. 21–23

IRVING HOWE

James Baldwin first came to the notice of the American literary public not through his own fiction but as author of an impassioned criticism of the conventional Negro novel. In 1949 he published in *Partisan Review* an essay called "Everybody's Protest Novel," attacking the kind of fiction, from *Uncle Tom's Cabin* to *Native Son,* that had been written about the ordeal of the American Negroes; and two years later he printed in the same magazine "Many Thousands Gone," a tougher and more explicit polemic against Richard Wright and the school of naturalistic "protest" fiction that Wright represented. The protest novel, wrote Baldwin, is undertaken out of sympathy for the Negro, but through its need to present him merely as a social victim or a mythic agent of sexual prowess, it hastens to confine the Negro to the very tones of violence he has known all his life. Compulsively re-enacting and magnifying his trauma, the protest novel proves unable to transcend it. So choked with rage has this kind of writing become, it cannot show the Negro as a unique person or locate him as a member of a community with its own traditions and values, its own "unspoken recognition of shared experience which creates a way of life." The failure of the protest novel "lies in its insistence that it is [man's] categorization alone which is real and which cannot be transcended."

Like all attacks launched by young writers against their famous elders, Baldwin's essays were also a kind of announcement of his own intentions. He wrote admiringly about Wright's courage ("his work was an immense liberation and revelation for me"), but now, precisely because Wright had prepared the way for all the Negro writers to come, he, Baldwin, would go further, transcending the sterile categories of "Negro-ness," whether those enforced by the white world or those defensively erected by the Negroes themselves. No longer mere victim or rebel, the Negro would stand free in a self-achieved humanity. As Baldwin put it some years later, he hoped "to prevent myself from becoming *merely* a Negro; or even, merely a Negro writer." The world "tends to trap and immobilize you in the role you play," and for the Negro writer, if he is to be a writer at all, it hardly matters whether the trap is sprung from motives of hatred or condescension.

Baldwin's rebellion against the older Negro novelist who had served him as a model and had helped launch his career was not of course an unprecedented event. The history of literature is full of such painful ruptures, and the issue Baldwin raised is one that keeps recurring, usually as an aftermath to a period of "socially engaged" writing. The novel is an inherently ambiguous genre: it strains toward formal autonomy and can seldom avoid being a public gesture. If it is true, as Baldwin said in "Everybody's Protest Novel," that "literature and sociology are not one and the same," it is equally true that such statements hardly begin to cope with the problem of how a writer's own experience affects his desire to represent human affairs in a work of fiction. Baldwin's formula evades, through rhetorical sweep, the genuinely difficult issue of the relationship between social experience and literature. ⟨. . .⟩

The day *Native Son* appeared, American culture was changed forever. No matter how much qualifying the book might later need, it made impossible a repetition of the old lies. In all its crudeness, melodrama and claustrophobia of vision, Richard Wright's novel brought out into the open, as no one ever had before, the hatred, fear and violence that have crippled and may yet destroy our culture.

A blow at the white man, the novel forced him to recognize himself as an oppressor. A blow at the black man, the novel forced him to recognize the cost of his submission. *Native Son* assaulted the most cherished of American vanities: the hope that the accumulated injustice of the past would bring with it no lasting penalties, the fantasy that in his humiliation the Negro somehow retained a sexual potency—or was it a childlike good-nature?—that made it necessary to envy and still more to suppress him. Speaking from the black wrath of retribution, Wright insisted that history can be a punishment. He told us the one thing even the most liberal whites preferred not to hear: that Negroes were far from patient or forgiving, that they were scarred by fear, that they hated every moment of their suppression even when seeming most acquiescent, and that often enough they hated *us,* the decent and cultivated white men who from complicity or neglect shared in the responsibility for their plight. If such younger novelists as Baldwin and Ralph Ellison were to move beyond Wright's harsh naturalism and toward more supple modes of fiction, that was possible only because Wright had been there first, courageous enough to release the full weight of his anger.

In *Black Boy,* the autobiographical narrative he published several years later, Wright would tell of an experience he had while working as a bellboy in the South. Many times he had come into a hotel room carrying luggage or food and seen naked white women lounging about, unmoved by shame at his presence, for "blacks were not considered human beings anyway ... I was a non-man ... I felt doubly cast out." With the publication of *Native Son,* however, Wright forced his readers to acknowledge his anger, and in that way, if none other, he wrested for himself a sense of dignity as a man. He forced his readers to confront the disease of our culture, and to one of its most terrifying symptoms he gave the name of Bigger Thomas.

Brutal and brutalized, lost forever to his unexpended hatred and his fear of the world, a numbed and illiterate black boy stumbling into a murder and never, not even at the edge of the electric chair, breaking through to an understanding of either his plight or himself, Bigger Thomas was a part of Richard Wright, a part even of the James Baldwin who stared with horror at Wright's Bigger, unable either to absorb him into his consciousness or eject him from it. Enormous courage, a discipline of self-conquest, was required to conceive Bigger Thomas, for this was no eloquent Negro spokesman, no admirable intellectual or formidable proletarian. Bigger was drawn—one would surmise, deliberately—from white fantasy and white contempt. Bigger was the worst of Negro life accepted, then rendered a trifle conscious and thrown back at those who had made him what he was. "No American Negro exists," Baldwin would later write, "who does not have his private Bigger Thomas living in the skull."

Wright drove his narrative to the very core of American phobia: sexual fright, sexual violation. He understood that the fantasy of rape is a consequence of guilt, what the whites suppose themselves to deserve. He understood that the white man's notion of uncontaminated Negro vitality, little as it had to do with the bitter realities of Negro life, reflected some ill-formed and buried feeling that our culture has run down, lost its blood, become febrile. And he grasped the way in which the sexual issue has been intertwined with social relationships, for even as the white people who hire Bigger as their chauffeur are decent and charitable, even as the girl he accidentally kills is a liberal of sorts, theirs is the power and the privilege. "We black and they white. They got things and we ain't. They do things and we can't."

The novel barely stops to provision a recognizable social world, often contenting itself with cartoon simplicities and yielding almost entirely to the nightmare incomprehension of Bigger Thomas. The mood is apocalyptic, the tone superbly aggressive. Wright was an existentialist long before he heard the name, for he was committed to the literature of extreme situations both through the pressures of his rage and the gasping hope of an ultimate catharsis.

Wright confronts both the violence and the crippling limitations of Bigger Thomas. For Bigger white people are not people at all, but something more, "a sort of great natural force, like a stormy sky looming overhead." And only through violence does he gather a little meaning in life, pitifully little: "he had murdered and created a new life for himself." Beyond that Bigger cannot go. ⟨. . .⟩

That *Native Son* has grave faults anyone can see. The language is often coarse, flat in rhythm, syntactically overburdened, heavy with journalistic slag. Apart from Bigger, who seems more a brute energy than a particularized figure, the characters have little reality, the Negroes being mere stock accessories and the whites either "agit-prop" villains or heroic Communists whom Wright finds it easier to admire from a distance than establish from the inside. The long speech by Bigger's radical lawyer Max (again a device apparently borrowed from Dreiser) is ill-related to the book itself: Wright had not achieved Dreiser's capacity for absorbing everything, even the most recalcitrant philosophical passages, into a unified vision of things. Between Wright's feelings as a Negro and his beliefs as a Communist there is hardly a genuine fusion, and it is through this gap that a good part of the novel's unreality pours in.

—IRVING HOWE, "Black Boys and Native Sons," *A World More Attractive: A View of Modern Literature and Politics* (New York: Horizon Press, 1963), pp. 98–104

RALPH ELLISON

Wright believed in the much abused idea that novels are "weapons"—the counterpart of the dreary notion, common among most minority groups, that novels are instruments of good public relations. But I believe that true novels, even when most pessimistic and bitter, arise out of an impulse to celebrate human life and therefore are ritualistic and ceremonial at their core. Thus they would preserve as they destroy, affirm as they reject.

In *Native Son*, Wright began with the ideological proposition that what whites think of the Negro's reality is more important than what Negroes themselves know it to be. Hence Bigger Thomas was presented as a near-subhuman indictment of white oppression. He was designed to shock whites out of their apathy and end the circumstances out of which Wright insisted Bigger emerged. Here environment is all—and interestingly enough, environment conceived solely in terms of the physical, the non-conscious. Well, cut off my legs and call me Shorty! Kill my parents and throw me on the mercy of the court as an orphan! Wright could imagine Bigger, but Bigger could not possibly imagine Richard Wright. Wright saw to that.

But without arguing Wright's right to his personal vision, I would say that he was himself a better argument for my approach than Bigger was for his. And so, to be fair and as inclusive as Howe, is James Baldwin. Both are true Negro Americans, and both affirm the broad possibility of personal realization which I see as a saving aspect of American life. Surely, this much can be admitted without denying the injustice which all three of us have protested.

Howe is impressed by Wright's pioneering role and by the "... enormous courage, the discipline of self-conquest required to conceive Bigger Thomas...." And earlier: "If such younger novelists as Baldwin and Ralph Ellison were able to move beyond Wright's harsh naturalism toward more supple modes of fiction, that was only possible because Wright had been there first, courageous enough to release the full weight of his anger."

It is not for me to judge Wright's courage, but I must ask just why it was possible for me to write as I write "only" because Wright released his anger? Can't I be allowed to release my own? What does Howe know of my acquaintance with violence, or the shape of my courage or the intensity of my anger? I suggest that my credentials are at least as valid as Wright's, even though he began writing long before I did, and it is possible that I have lived through and committed even more violence than he. Howe must wait for an autobiography before he can be responsibly certain. Everybody wants to tell us what a Negro is, yet few wish, even in a joke, to be one. But if you would tell me who I am, at least take the trouble to discover what I have been. ⟨...⟩

Howe seems to see segregation as an opaque steel jug with the Negroes inside waiting for some black messiah to come along and blow the cork. Wright is his hero and he sticks with him loyally. But if we are in a jug it is transparent, not opaque, and one is allowed not only to see outside but to read what is going on out there; to make identifications as to values and human quality. So in Macon County, Alabama, I read Marx, Freud, T. S. Eliot, Pound, Gertrude Stein and Hemingway. Books which seldom, if ever, mentioned Negroes were to release me from whatever "segregated" idea I might have had of my human possibilities. I was freed not by propagandists or by the example of Wright—I did not know him at the time and was earnestly trying to learn enough to write a symphony and have it performed by the time I was twenty-six, because Wagner had done so and I admired his music—but by composers, novelists, and poets who spoke to me of more interesting and freer ways of life.

These were works which, by fulfilling themselves as works of art, by being satisfied to deal with life in terms of their own sources of power, were able to give me a broader sense of life and possibility. Indeed, I understand a bit more about myself as Negro because literature has taught me something of my identity as Western man, as political being. It has also taught me something of the cost of being an individual who aspires to conscious eloquence. It requires a real poverty of the imagination to think that this can come to a Negro *only* through the example of *other Negroes*, especially after the performance of the slaves in re-creating themselves, in good part, out of the images and myths of the Old Testament Jews.

No, Wright was no spiritual father of mine, certainly in no sense I recognize—nor did he pretend to be, since he felt that I had started writing too late. It was Baldwin's career, not mine, that Wright proudly advanced by helping him attain the Eugene Saxton Fellowship, and it was Baldwin who found Wright a lion in his path. Being older and familiar with quite different lions in quite different paths, I simply stepped around him.

But Wright was a friend for whose magazine I wrote my first book review and short story, and a personal hero in the same way Hot Lips Paige and Jimmy Rushing were friends and heroes. I felt no need to attack what I considered the limitations of his vision because I was quite impressed by what he had achieved. And in this, although I saw with the black vision of Ham, I was, I suppose, as pious as Shem and Japheth. Still I would write my own books and they would be in themselves, implicitly, criticisms of Wright's; just as all novels of a given historical moment form an argument over the nature of reality and are, to an extent, criticisms each of the other.

While I rejected Bigger Thomas as any *final* image of Negro personality, I recognized *Native Son* as an achievement; as one man's essay in defining the human condition as seen from a specific Negro perspective at a given time in a given place. And I was proud to have known Wright and happy for the impact he had made upon our apathy. But Howe's ideas notwithstanding, history is history, cultural contacts ever mysterious, and taste exasperatingly personal. ⟨. . .⟩

Wright, for Howe, is the genuine article, the authentic Negro writer, and his tone the only authentic tone. But why strip Wright of his individuality in order to criticize other writers. He had his memories and I have mine, just as I suppose Irving Howe has his—or has Marx spoken the final word for him? Indeed, very early in *Black Boy,* Wright's memory and his contact with literature come together in a way revealing, at least to the eye concerned with Wright the literary man, that his manner of keeping faith with the Negroes who remained in the depths is quite interesting:

(After I had outlived the shocks of childhood, after the habit of reflection had been born in me, I used to mull over the strange absence of real kindness in Negroes, how unstable was our tenderness, how lacking in genuine passion we were, how void of great hope, how timid our joy, how bare our traditions, how hollow our memories, how lacking we were in those intangible sentiments that bind man to man and how shallow was even our despair. After I had learned other ways of life I used to brood upon the unconscious irony of those who felt that Negroes led so passional an existence! I saw that what had been taken for our emotional strength was our negative confusions, our flights, our fears, our frenzy under pressure.

(Whenever I thought of the essential bleakness of black life in America, I knew that Negroes had never been allowed to catch the full spirit of Western civilization, that they lived somehow in it but not of it. And when I brooded upon the cultural barrenness of black life, I wondered if clean, positive tenderness, love, honor, loyalty and the capacity to remember were native with man. I asked myself if these human qualities were not fostered, won, struggled and suffered for, preserved in ritual from one generation to another.)

Must I be condemned because my sense of Negro life was quite different? Or because for me keeping faith would never allow me to even raise such a question about any segment of humanity? *Black Boy* is not a sociological case history but an autobiography, and therefore a work of art shaped by a writer bent upon making an ideological point. Doubtlessly, this was the beginning of Wright's exile, the making of a decision which was to shape his life and writing thereafter. And it is precisely at this point that Wright is being what I would call, in Howe's words, "literary to a fault."

For just as *How "Bigger" Was Born* is Wright's Jamesian preface to *Native Son,* the passage quoted above is his paraphrase of Henry James' catalogue of those items of a high civilization which were absent from American life during Haw-thorne's day, and which seemed so necessary in order for the novelist to function. This, then, was Wright's list of those items of high humanity which he found missing among Negroes. Thank God, I have never been quite that literary.

How awful that Wright found the facile answers of Marxism before he learned to use literature as a means for discovering the forms of American Negro humanity. I could not and cannot question their existence, I can only seek again and again to project that humanity as I see it and feel it. To me Wright as *writer* was less interesting than the enigma he personified: that he could so dissociate himself from the complexity of his background while trying so hard to improve the condition of black men everywhere; that he could be so wonderful an example of human possibility but could not for ideological reasons depict a Negro as intelligent, as creative or as dedicated as himself.

In his effort to resuscitate Wright, Irving Howe would designate the role which Negro writers are to play more rigidly than any Southern politician—and for the best of reasons. We must express "black" anger and "clenched militancy"; most of all we should not become too interested in the problems of the art of literature, even though it is through these that we seek our individual identities. And between writing well and being ideologically militant, we must choose militancy.

Well, it all sounds quite familiar and I fear the social order which it forecasts more than I do that of Mississippi. Ironically, during the 1940s it was one of the main sources of Wright's rage and frustration.

—RALPH ELLISON, "The World and the Jug" [1963], *Shadow and Act*
(New York: Random House, 1964), pp. 114–20

HOUSTON A. BAKER, JR.

Bigger's culture is that of the black American race, and he is intelligible as a con-scious literary projection of the folk hero who embodies the survival values of a culture. Tales of the trickster animal who overcomes his stronger opponents, of John, the slave who outwits his master, of the "bad nigger" (Shine, Stackolee, Dupree) who rebels against an oppressive system—all of these contribute to an understanding of Wright's protagonist. Tales of pillage and plunder, accounts of black men inflicting pain and humiliation on white women with impunity, and stories of injustices suffered by black Americans are plentiful in black folklore, and a tale such as the following helps to illuminate the perspective of *Native Son:*

> In a little Southern town, a mob was fixing to lynch a man when a very dignified old judge appeared. "Don't," he pleaded, "put a blot on this fair community by hasty action. The thing to do," he insisted, "is to give the man a fair trial and then lynch him." (Richard M. Dorson, *American Negro Folktales*)

The story is Bigger Thomas's, and if a representative tale from the white-woman genre is considered, the perspective becomes even clearer:

> You take in the South, they always have one strong colored guy on all the plantations. He's given a lot of consideration by the boss—usually he be foreman. Can put two or three of the others in his back pocket.

The story goes on to tell of two such men whose masters arranged for them to fight one another. On the day of the fight, Jim, one of the combatants, in an attempt to frighten John, his adversary, has his boss attach him to an iron chain staked in the ground. But John arrives at the battling grounds, slaps his own boss's wife in the face, and watches Jim run away:

> So the loser, Jim's master, had to pay off John's boss the three or four thousand dollars they'd put in a bag. Still, John's boss got mad about his wife being slapped. He asked John, "What was the idea slapping my wife?" "Well, Jim knowed if I slapped a white woman I'd a killed him, so he run."

John's concluding words bring to mind the fate of Bessie Mears. When we combine tales of injustice and white-woman tales with stories of the bad-man hero, the picture is complete. A white sheriff responds to Billy Lyons's mother:

> Sheriff said, My name might begin with an *s* and end with an *f*,
> But if you want that bad Stackolee you got to get him yourself.

Black folklore includes countless examples of strong black men giving "a faint, wry, bitter smile," or the final, destructive thrust to the revered symbols of white America, and Bigger Thomas's act is simply a continuation of this heritage.

Why, then, have Bigger's character and action, which are built of so many traditional elements, aroused such concern? The answer is not far to seek. Genuine black folklore has seldom been considered valid literary or historical evidence by our cultural custodians. The arts of the black American folk (rural and urban) have been largely ignored, caricatured, or exploited by white America. Black music was transformed into the distorted croons of the minstrel tradition. The forceful idioms of black folk speech were converted into the muddled syntax and thick-lipped jargon of "Negro jokes." Bessie Smith and Louis Armstrong wailing and transcending in the cabarets of Harlem became Paul Whiteman and George Gershwin harmonizing in theatres downtown. In short, the art of black folk culture (like the art of other American subcultures, such as the Irish, Italian, and Jewish) has been adjusted to suit the needs of white America—to reinforce stereotypes and sometimes even to justify the victimization of the black American. America at large has seldom taken an honest look at its black citizenry.

Since black Americans were kept illiterate by the laws of the land during much of their history, they could not challenge the general American view of the black man in poetry or prose. And when black writers did take pen in hand, polemical demands (the need to castigate slavery and caste in America) and the bare formal requirements of their craft exerted pressures that relegated the true folk heritage to a somewhat minor role. This does not mean that the folk heritage was forgotten; James Weldon Johnson's *The Autobiography of an Ex-Colored Man,* Jean Toomer's *Cane,* Langston Hughes's *Not without Laughter,* and Arna Bontemps's *Black Thunder* all rely on the folk experience. But Richard Wright's *Native Son* was the first black novel that captured its full scope and dimension.

Wright's message to America was that black Americans are a unique people who have produced heroes who hate and wish to destroy those contrived symbols of white culture that insure our victimization. Bigger says to his lawyer:

> "What I killed for must've been good! . . . It must have been good! When a man kills, it's for something. . . . I didn't know I was really alive in this world until I felt things hard enough to kill for 'em. . . . It's the truth, Mr. Max. I can say it now, 'cause I'm going to die. I know what I'm saying real good and I know how it sounds. But I'm all right. I feel all right when I look at it that way. . . ."

The voices of David Walker, Nat Turner, Frederick Douglass, Martin Delaney, and a dishevelled group of black forced laborers singing "Lookin' fer Jimbo/ Don' say nothin'/ Go 'head Jimbo/ Don' say nothin' " resound through Bigger's words (quoted from *The Book of Negro Folklore,* ed. Arna Bontemps and Langston Hughes). The message is simple: reverberating through black folk culture it says, "Mean mean mean to be free" (Robert Hayden, "Runagate Runagate"). Wright's theme and his hero were drawn from the folk history to which he was heir. America's attraction to *Native Son* has been the response of the curious to the unknown, the guilty to the reason for guilt, the deceitful to exposure, the sympathetic to the oppressed, the learned to new evidence, and the perceptive to works of genius. No cultural historian (a role that Wright self-consciously assumed the year following *Native Son* in *Twelve Million Black Voices: A Folk History of the Negro in the United States*) could have hoped to evoke more response than *Native Son* did.

—HOUSTON A. BAKER, JR., "Racial Wisdom and Richard Wright's
*Native Son," Long Black Song: Essays in Black American Literature
and Culture* (Charlottesville: University Press of Virginia, 1972),
pp. 131–36

SHERLEY ANNE WILLIAMS

In "Bright and Morning Star" (from the short story collection *Uncle Tom's Children*, 1936), Richard Wright creates a rebel leader, a communist organizer in the rural South, who seeks to unite Black and white workers under the banner of interracial and international brotherhood. Arna Bontemps, in *Black Thunder* (1936) and again in *Drums at Dusk* (1939), tells the story of actual slave revolts; one, *Black Thunder*, deals with the aborted slave rebellion of Gabriel Prosser in 1803; the other is a fictionalized account of the Haitian slave revolt which created a nation.

With the publication of *Native Son* in 1940, Richard Wright turned the impulse to protest in another direction. Rather than showing whites and Blacks what could happen with the help of a strong Black leader, he begins the trend in Black literature whose chief characteristic is its fierce indictment of American society because of the society's brutalizing effect on Black people. Wright and his followers and imitators "protested," as did many other Black writers, against a coercive and racist environment. To label them "protest novelists," however, is to cast a pejorative light on the writers who precede Wright and those who come after him and to limit, unfairly, the range of Wright's own artistry. Most art is, after all, a form of protest against the injustices, the indignities, the cruelties, the uglinesses of life, whether they are perpetrated by whites against Blacks or by fate or God against humanity.

It may seem surprising that Bigger Thomas is not included in the list of rebel heroes, for (Edward) Margolies credits Bigger with being a "metaphysical revolutionary," (Eldridge) Cleaver calls him "a Black rebel of the ghetto" and his creator speaks often of Bigger's "revolt." Bigger is an aborted hustler, a boy too out of touch with himself to understand the yearnings of his own heart, too alienated from his people and their past to find a way of bridging the gap between the rural, religion-haunted South of his family and the seemingly traditionless North. The murders which he commits, the first the inadvertent killing of the rich white girl whose parents employ him as a chauffeur, and the second, the deliberate murder of his Black girl friend, Bessie, are interpreted as rebellious acts whose origins lie in the frustration engendered by the systematic exclusion of Blacks from equal participation in American society. And because Bigger finally breaks through the wall of frustration which has made inarticulate all the longings and desires raging inside of him, and is finally able to give voice to these longings in violence, critics, such as Robert Bone, have applauded his actions. But the nature of his crimes makes suspect the idea that he has expressed anything. Bigger kills Mary accidentally and the macabre method he uses to hide his crime, hacking the girl's body apart and hiding the pieces, stems more from panic than deliberate reasoning. It is only later that calmer reflection shows him a way of capitalizing on his crime. He tries to extort money from the girl's parents who have not yet found her body and believe her kidnapped. This killing is viewed as the liberating action; Bigger breaks free of the stagnant existence in which his family and friends are held. Yet Bigger's next action is to murder Bessie. This crime is deliberate. There is only a difference in degree, rather than kind, between this and the other violent crimes which Black people commit against each other in most Black communities any Saturday night in the year. Had the intention behind the crimes been reversed, the white girl's death a deliberate murder and Bessie's an accident, there would be no need to modify the "revolutionary" aspect of Bigger's character with "metaphysical" or other inactive kinds of adjectives. Another important aspect of Bigger's exclusion from the ranks of rebels in the present context is that none of the people involved in the story see Bigger in this light or his actions from this point of reference. Neither his friends nor his family nor the white lawyer, Max, see Bigger as anything more than a boy who has become entangled in a series of destructive actions. Max and Jan, Mary's white boyfriend, see more penetrating reasons for Bigger's actions and see their relationship to the larger society. The other aspect, if it is there, is lost on them. Bigger remains just as alienated in the end as he was in the beginning and in this he is more akin to anti-heroes in Western literature than to the rebel leader tradition in Black literature. It is obvious that Wright was after something different, that he was not attempting to create a "Black revolutionary," but as he himself has said,

> He [Bigger] was an American, because he was a native son; but he was also a Negro nationalist in a vague sense because he was not allowed to live as an American.
>
> ... his hate had placed him like a wild animal at bay, in a position where he was most symbolic and explainable. In other words, his nationalist complex was for me a concept through which I could grasp more of the total meaning of his life than I could in any other way. I tried to approach Bigger's *snarled* and *confused* nationalist feelings with *conscious* and *informed* ones of my own. Yet Bigger was not nationalist enough to feel the need of religion or the folk culture of his own people. What made Bigger's social consciousness most complex was the fact that he was hovering unwanted between two worlds— between powerful America and his own stunted place in life. . . . The most that I could say of Bigger was that he felt the need for a whole life and *acted* out that need; that was all.

> —SHERLEY ANNE WILLIAMS, "Rebel and Streetman in Black Literature,"
> *Give Birth to Brightness: A Thematic Study in Neo-Black Literature*
> (New York: Dial Press, 1972), pp. 73–77

CHARLES T. DAVIS

It is possible that Wright did not realize completely what he was about in *Uncle Tom's Children*, why a work of such rare power should be so uneven. This claim cannot be made about *Native Son*, as the third book of the novel, "Fate," richly demonstrates. A familiar approach to urban reality dominates the first two books of the novel. That is to day, Bigger Thomas is more or less the product of a defective environment, of a black ghetto in which the potential for violence is considerably heightened by the near presence of a well-to-do white district. I say more or less, because brilliant as Wright's portrayal of this connection is, the environment so described fails to account for all of the elements in Bigger's personality—not, say, for his innocent affection for the symbols of power (resembling the delight with objects of nature found in "Big Boy Leaves Home"), his disproportionate fear of an exposure to sophisticated white society, and his sense of a dim connection with other blacks. These qualities supply an individuality beyond the predictable product of the streets. When the time comes for the humanization of the black ape that Bigger has become, Wright refuses to permit his protagonist a share in Max's vision of the good society that communism would bring into being. Wright does so because he will not violate Bigger's total nature. The artist will make no further concessions to the demand of his public position. No doubt, Wright considered it sufficient to grant Max an opportunity to develop fully the Communist perspective on Bigger's problem. Bigger finds the talk helpful, but concludes, much to the dismay of Wright's comrades, that his salvation lies elsewhere. Though resurrection through the affirmation of one's crimes, a discovery of human identity through murder, seems unlikely and overambitious finally for a young black with Bigger's credentials, it is infinitely preferable to facing with a sense of partial compensation the dawn of a Communist millennium.

—CHARLES T. DAVIS, "Richard Wright: The Artist as Public Figure" [1978], *Black Is the Color of the Cosmos: Essays on Afro-American Literature and Culture 1942–1981*, ed. Henry Louis Gates, Jr. (New York: Garland, 1982), pp. 278–79

NINA KRESSNER COBB

In *Native Son,* Bigger Thomas found meaning in his murders and through them his life had gained significance. In *The Outsider,* Wright rejected this nihilistic form of revolt. Yet signs of discomfort with the conclusions are evident in both novels.

This is clearest in *Native Son,* where the conclusion seems to be at odds with the structure of the novel as a whole. *Native Son* was written in the naturalist tradition, heavily influenced by Theodore Dreiser's *American Tragedy.* In the title of the novel, Wright expressed his belief that Bigger was the product of his environment—racism, poverty, and oppression. The first two sections of the novel detailed the bleak conditions of Bigger's life with the clear implication that they predetermined his attitudes, emotions, actions, and fate. It also seems that Wright had intended to follow the prescriptions of Marxism in this novel. The explicit Marxist analysis of Bigger's situation offered by his lawyer, Boris Max, and the fact that the only characters who had any rapport with Bigger or attempted to understand him were communists lend credence to this interpretation. Furthermore,

naturalism's stress on the influence of environmental conditioning was not incon-
sistent with Marxist economic determinism.

In Book III, Wright shifted his attention to Bigger's acceptance of his imminent
death. Because of the essentially inarticulate and unreflective nature of his protagonist, Wright had had to rely on the device of a narrator or on objective correla-
tives to explain many of Bigger's moods and actions in the first two sections of
Native Son. But in the third section, Bigger became far more introspective and was
able to speak for himself. In prison, Bigger attained a level of self-awareness that
permitted him to come to grips with the meaning of his existence and ultimately to
accept his death. The realization that allowed him to accept his fate was an expression of individual responsibility: "But what I killed for I am."

In the essay "How 'Bigger' Was Born," Wright explained that the novel grew
out of a fascination with what he came to call the Bigger Thomas syndrome. Bigger
was the oppressed man in revolt against the system that denied his humanity.
Wright wanted to depict the conditions that led to Bigger's anger, frustration, fear,
hatred, and, ultimately, to his revolt. In Wright's words, *Native Son* was to be a
sociological case-study. But, in the novel, Bigger rejected his lawyer's sociological
analysis of his actions. Facing death, the only explanation of his life that he found
meaningful was a personal one. Both Wright's sympathy for his hero and his own
experiences had taught him to distrust socio-economic determinism and help explain why Bigger transcended sociological limitations; but they do not account for
the conflict between two different theories of human motivation—environmental
determinism and free will—in *Native Son*.

Critics have generally regarded this dichotomy to be the major flaw in the
novel. In *The Negro Novel in America* (New Haven: Yale University Press, 1958),
pp. 140–52, Robert Bone perceived the flaw as aesthetic: Wright was unable to
integrate Marxism into the artistic fabric of the novel because of his dependence on
the more or less artificial device of the lawyer Boris Max's explanations of Bigger.
On the other hand, Edward Margolies—*Native Sons: A Critical Study of Twentieth
Century Negro American Authors* (Philadelphia: Lippincott, 1968), pp. 73–86—has
argued that Wright was ideologically and philosophically confused. Wright believed
that he was arguing for revolution in communist terms while he actually presented
a more convincing portrayal of Bigger as a nationalist revolutionary and a metaphysical rebel. Both Bone and Margolies agree that Wright had perceived *Native
Son* to be an effective mouthpiece for the communist cause. Their explanation that
Wright had unwittingly refuted economic determinism—though more perceptive
than critics who viewed *Native Son* as a Marxist tract pure and simple—is still
inadequate and does Wright an injustice.

Instead, the dichotomy between environmental determinism and free will in
Native Son should be understood in light of Wright's ambivalence toward individualism itself. His dissatisfaction with individualism accounts for his reliance on a
deterministic explanation that transcends the individual while his intuitive distrust of
this kind of explanation helps explain the ultimate triumph of free will as the mode
of explanation that best accounts for Bigger's transformation. The conflict between

socio-economic determinism and free will in *Native Son* reflects Wright's conflict with and foreshadows his repudiation of the Communist Party while revealing his uneasiness with Western civilization.

—NINA KRESSNER COBB, "Richard Wright: Individualism Reconsidered,"
CLA Journal 21, No. 3 (March 1978): 346–48

HENRY LOUIS GATES, JR.

Ellison's definition of the relation that his works bear to those of Wright constitutes a definition of 'narrative signification', 'pastiche' or 'critical parody', although Ellison employs none of these terms. His explanation of what might be called 'implicit formal criticism', however, comprises what is sometimes called 'troping' and offers a profound definition of 'critical signification' itself:

> I felt no need to attack what I considered the limitations of [Wright's] vision because I was quite impressed by what he had achieved. And in this, although I saw with the black vision of Ham, I was, I suppose, as pious as Shem and Japheth. Still I would write my own books and they would be in themselves, implicitly, criticisms of Wright's; just as all novels of a given historical moment form an argument over the nature of reality and are, to an extent, criticisms each of the other.

Ellison in his fictions signifies upon Wright by parodying Wright's literary structures through repetition and difference. The complexities of the parodying I can readily suggest. The play of language, the signifying, starts with the titles: Wright's *Native Son* and *Black Boy*, titles connoting race, self and presence, Ellison tropes with *Invisible Man*, invisibility an ironic response, of absence, to the would-be presence of 'blacks' and 'natives', while 'man' suggests a more mature and stronger status than either 'son' or 'boy'. Wright's distinctive version of naturalism Ellison signifies upon with a complex rendering of modernism; Wright's reacting protagonist, voiceless to the last, Ellison signifies upon with a nameless protagonist. Ellison's protagonist is nothing but voice, since it is he who shapes, edits and narrates his own tale, thereby combining action with the representation of action to define 'reality' by its representation. This unity of presence and representation is perhaps Ellison's most subtle reversal of Wright's theory of the novel as exemplified in *Native Son*. Bigger's voicelessness and powerlessness to act (as opposed to react) signify an absence, despite the metaphor of presence found in the novel's title; the reverse obtains in *Invisible Man*, where the absence implied by invisibility is undermined by the presence of the narrator as the narrator of his own text.

—HENRY LOUIS GATES, JR., "The Blackness of Blackness: A Critique of
the Sign and the Signifying Monkey," *Black Literature and Literary
Theory*, ed. Henry Louis Gates, Jr. (New York: Methuen, 1984),
pp. 293–94

CHARLES JOHNSON

On black literature, Wright's *Native Son,* an overnight bestseller in 1940, left a large artistic impression. Probably it is one of the two or three best-known novels by black American writers, and it produced many imitators but also a reaction against the brutal "realism" (if we may call it that) of his fiction during and after the depression years, a realism that gained its visceral power at the expense of portraying positive cultural features in black life—in other words, much that is affirmative and joyful in black culture is lost in the literary Lifeworld of Richard Wright.

But it *is* with Wright that something of a watershed is reached in black fiction. Nearly fifty years after its publication, *Native Son* still remains one of our most phenomenologically successful novels, a nightmare as frightening, in its own way, as George Orwell's *1984.* I am at a loss to number all the black authors who were inspired by this work: James Baldwin, Chester Himes, John A. Williams—a full generation of writers, we are forced to say, because as Baldwin once remarked, Wright's "great forte . . . was an ability to convey inward states by means of externals." What I take him to mean by this—or what he should be saying—is that for the first time in black American literature we are presented with a masterfully drawn *Lebenswelt;* we are made to see and experience meaning—the world— from the distorted perspective of a petty thief so mangled by oppression in its many forms that his only possibility for creative action is murder. Like any fully orchestrated, over-rich work of art, *Native Son* resists easy description. It is multi-leveled, exhaustive in detail, layered with existentialist, Marxist, and even religious themes; it echoes Dostoyevsky's *Crime and Punishment* and Dreiser's *An American Tragedy,* conjures the image of Nat Turner, and anticipates the thesis of Frantz Fanon in *The Wretched of the Earth* (1961) as Bigger Thomas finds release from fear and self-hatred through murder. It achieves, in the end, a dimension bordering on racial mythology (the hunt for the killer-slave), yet *Native Son* remains more than anything else a phenomenological description of the black urban experience. Wright forces us to ask, "What is it like to be thoroughly manipulated by others?" He shifts from historical details of black poverty in Chicago to a startling use of poetry and metaphor—the white world, the racial Other, is presented to Bigger's ravaged consciousness as a natural force like snow, or a blizzard, or a storm; he projects himself into innumerable objects littering the black wasteland of his family— for example, the rat killed in the opening scene—and sees his guilt in the red-hot furnace where he has placed Mary Dalton's decapitated body. Page after page, we are forced to *interpret* everyday phenomena from Bigger's unsteady position in the world, a position of powerlessness, of Pavlovian reactions to whites who are godlike but "blind" to his inner life and humanity, a position where black life is experienced as being predestined for tragedy. On yet another level, the "world" of *Native Son* is that of Greek tragedy, and for this I use John M. Anderson's definition: "The hero [of tragedy] symbolizes participation in a process dominated by what is alien to him"; all one must do is replace the gods of Sophocles with modern gods who hide behind such names as "social forces" and "conditioning."

What Wright achieved in *Native Son,* and what no American writer has done quite so well since (including Wright), was the construction of a consistent, coherent, and complete racial universe—Southside Chicago—that is fully shaped by a sensitive if seared black subjectivity. Every prop on the stage of this sustained, brutal thriller reflects *back* to Bigger's mind, to his special, twisted way of seeing. Nothing is neutral. Everything is charged by the broken heart and broken mind of a black boy reduced to a state of thinghood. Everything *means* something; every physical, historical object is a metaphor for feeling. Notice the ontology of Bigger's world. It is Manichean. To *be* is to be white. The Daltons' world is pure Being, a plenum, filled to overflowing with its own whiteness, while Bigger's world has a weedlike contingency—is, in fact, relative being. (Yet the alien white world's ways of seeing are *within* Bigger, like a knot in his belly.) This is Plato's world of the Divided Line and the Cave. Furthermore, Bigger is *stained* (sin) by a black body the coloration of which suggests defilement. And his world before the murder is strangely ahistorical, a shadow realm outside time. If *Native Son* is about anything, it is about the drama of consciousness itself, the effort of this boy to come fully aware of the meaning of his life and those around him. We see the "facts" of black Chicago life for the poor in the 1930s: Wright is meticulous with sociological details; he absorbs the information provided by other authors about political and economic disenfranchisement. The book "teaches." But more important than all this reportage is the fact that Wright reminds us through his method here—eidetic description, or presenting things in their lived essence (meaning) for a historical subject—that the world we live in is, first and foremost, one shaped by the mind. A writer reads him with awe. Nowhere does he cheat by resorting to narrative summary, or "telling," when a full, dramatic scene is required to show Bigger's character in and through action. Indeed, the relentless pace of *Native Son* is fueled precisely because most of the book is unmediated scene, as in a play. We see everything. We are forced to be witnesses to every thought and emotion of a national tragedy two centuries in the making. More: it is *we* whom Wright turns into murderers. Wright is shrewd, very cunning as a craftsman, using various forms of repetition (we are forced to review uneasily the details of Mary's murder at least twenty times as that awful event resurfaces in Bigger's mind) to reinforce the novel's dominant impression in a welter of details about race, class, and sexuality. Every writer dreams of achieving this, I believe—a fictional world so fully rendered that even a single glove, as Prosper Mérimée once said, has its theory and reinforces the unifying vision, the truth, of the novel as a whole.

The completeness of Wright's *Native Son* left black writers with the alternatives of repeating that vision in their fiction or grappling again with the perceptual flux of experience that characterizes the black world—and all worlds—to originate new meaning. This, indeed, was the direction taken, and grandly realized, in Ralph Ellison's *Invisible Man* (1952), which has become something of the modern Ur-text for black fiction. Ellison is indebted to Wright for certain themes (blindness, invisibility) and even, I suspect, for certain characters (his Vet greatly resembles the madman in Bigger's cell in book three of *Native Son*); but Ellison conceives his novel in an exuberant Hegelian spirit that traces a nameless black student from one "posture" of twentieth-century black life to another in prose both bewitching and (at times) prolix. And, as if this were not enough, he gives our age a new metaphor for alienation. Every chapter is structured according to the principle of "rising conflict to resolution." The book brims with stylish set pieces: the eviction scene in which every object reveals black history; Ras's monologue to Todd Clifton, which captures the essential thought of Black Nationalism; and allusions to James Joyce's *Portrait of the Artist as a Young Man*, Sigmund Freud, Booker T. Washington, and concerns spanning the Harlem Renaissance and the years following it. Almost everything one could want in a novel or vision is here: humor, suspense, black history from which Ellison's vivid imagination teases forth truth beneath mere facts, and a rogues' gallery of grotesques—Ellison is, one must admit, a sort of intellectual cartoonist when it comes to characterization; his people are, for the most part, principles.

—CHARLES JOHNSON, "Being and Race," *Being and Race: Black Writing since 1970* (Bloomington: Indiana University Press, 1988), pp. 12–15

CRITICAL ESSAYS

Richard Wright

HOW ''BIGGER'' WAS BORN

I am not so pretentious as to imagine that it is possible for me to account completely for my own book, *Native Son*. But I am going to try to account for as much of it as I can, the sources of it, the material that went into it, and my own years' long changing attitude toward that material.

In a fundamental sense, an imaginative novel represents the merging of two extremes; it is an intensely intimate expression on the part of a consciousness couched in terms of the most objective and commonly known events. It is at once something private and public by its very nature and texture. Confounding the author who is trying to lay his cards on the table is the dogging knowledge that his imagination is a kind of community medium of exchange: what he has read, felt, thought, seen, and remembered is translated into extensions as impersonal as a worn dollar bill.

The more closely the author thinks of why he wrote, the more he comes to regard his imagination as a kind of self-generating cement which glued his facts together, and his emotions as a kind of dark and obscure designer of those facts. Always there is something that is just beyond the tip of the tongue that could explain it all. Usually, he ends up by discussing something far afield, an act which incites skepticism and suspicion in those anxious for a straight-out explanation.

Yet the author is eager to explain. But the moment he makes the attempt his words falter, for he is confronted and defied by the inexplicable array of his own emotions. Emotions are subjective and he can communicate them only when he clothes them in objective guise; and how can he ever be so arrogant as to know when he is dressing up the right emotion in the right Sunday suit? He is always left with the uneasy notion that maybe *any* objective drapery is as good as *any* other for any emotion.

And the moment he does dress up an emotion, his mind is confronted with the riddle of that "dressed up" emotion, and he is left peering with eager dismay

From *How "Bigger" Was Born* (New York: Harper & Brothers, 1940), pp. 1–39.

23

back into the dim reaches of his own incommunicable life. Reluctantly, he comes to the conclusion that to account for his book is to account for his life, and he knows that that is impossible. Yet, some curious, wayward motive urges him to supply the answer, for there is the feeling that his dignity as a living being is challenged by something within him that is not understood.

So, at the outset, I say frankly that there are phases of *Native Son* which I shall make no attempt to account for. There are meanings in my book of which I was not aware until they literally spilled out upon the paper. I shall sketch the outline of how I *consciously* came into possession of the materials that went into *Native Son,* but there will be many things I shall omit, not because I want to, but simply because I don't know them.

The birth of Bigger Thomas goes back to my childhood, and there was not just one Bigger, but many of them, more than I could count and more than you suspect. But let me start with the first Bigger, whom I shall call Bigger No. 1.

When I was a bareheaded, barefoot kid in Jackson, Mississippi, there was a boy who terrorized me and all of the boys I played with. If we were playing games, he would saunter up and snatch from us our balls, bats, spinning tops, and marbles. We would stand around pouting, sniffling, trying to keep back our tears, begging for our playthings. But Bigger would refuse. We never demanded that he give them back; we were afraid, and Bigger was bad. We had seen him clout boys when he was angry and we did not want to run that risk. We never recovered our toys unless we flattered him and made him feel that he was superior to us. Then, perhaps, if he felt like it, he condescended, threw them at us and then gave each of us a swift kick in the bargain, just to make us feel his utter contempt.

That was the way Bigger No. 1 lived. His life was a continuous challenge to others. At all times he *took* his way, right or wrong, and those who contradicted him had him to fight. And never was he happier than when he had someone cornered and at his mercy; it seemed that the deepest meaning of his squalid life was in him at such times.

I don't know what the fate of Bigger No. 1 was. His swaggering personality is swallowed up somewhere in the amnesia of my childhood. But I suspect that his end was violent. Anyway, he left a marked impression upon me; maybe it was because I longed secretly to be like him and was afraid. I don't know.

If I had known only one Bigger I would not have written *Native Son.* Let me call the next one Bigger No. 2; he was about seventeen and tougher than the first Bigger. Since I, too, had grown older, I was a little less afraid of him. And the hardness of this Bigger No. 2 was not directed toward me or the other Negroes, but toward the whites who ruled the South. He bought clothes and food on credit and would not pay for them. He lived in the dingy shacks of the white landlords and refused to pay rent. Of course, he had no money, but neither did we. We did without the necessities of life and starved ourselves, but he never would. When we asked him why he acted as he did, he would tell us (as though we were little children in a kindergarten) that the white folks had everything and he had nothing.

Further, he would tell us that we were fools not to get what we wanted while we were alive in this world. We would listen and silently agree. We longed to believe and act as he did, but we were afraid. We were Southern Negroes and we were hungry and we wanted to live, but we were more willing to tighten our belts than risk conflict. Bigger No. 2 wanted to live and he did; he was in prison the last time I heard from him.

There was Bigger No. 3, whom the white folks called a "bad nigger." He carried his life in his hands in a literal fashion. I once worked as a ticket-taker in a Negro movie house (all movie houses in Dixie are Jim Crow; there are movies for whites and movies for blacks), and many times Bigger No. 3 came to the door and gave my arm a hard pinch and walked into the theater. Resentfully and silently, I'd nurse my bruised arm. Presently, the proprietor would come over and ask how things were going. I'd point into the darkened theater and say: "Bigger's in there." "Did he pay?" the proprietor would ask. "No, sir," I'd answer. The proprietor would pull down the corners of his lips and speak through his teeth: "We'll kill that goddamn nigger one of these days." And the episode would end right there. But later on Bigger No. 3 was killed during the days of Prohibition: while delivering liquor to a customer he was shot through the back by a white cop.

And then there was Bigger No. 4, whose only law was death. The Jim Crow laws of the South were not for him. But as he laughed and cursed and broke them, he knew that some day he'd have to pay for his freedom. His rebellious spirit made him violate all the taboos and consequently he always oscillated between moods of intense elation and depression. He was never happier than when he had outwitted some foolish custom, and he was never more melancholy than when brooding over the impossibility of his ever being free. He had no job, for he regarded digging ditches for fifty cents a day as slavery. "I can't live on that," he would say. Ofttimes I'd find him reading a book; he would stop and in a joking, wistful, and cynical manner ape the antics of the white folks. Generally, he'd end his mimicry in a depressed state and say: "The white folks won't let us do nothing." Bigger No. 4 was sent to the asylum for the insane.

Then there was Bigger No. 5, who always rode the Jim Crow streetcars without paying and sat wherever he pleased. I remember one morning his getting into a streetcar (all streetcars in Dixie are divided into two sections: one section is for whites and is labeled—FOR WHITES; the other section is for Negroes and is labeled—FOR COLORED) and sitting in the white section. The conductor went to him and said: "Come on, nigger. Move over where you belong. Can't you read?" Bigger answered: "Naw, I can't read." The conductor flared up: "Get out of that seat!" Bigger took out his knife, opened it, held it nonchalantly in his hand, and replied: "Make me." The conductor turned red, blinked, clenched his fists, and walked away, stammering: "The goddamn scum of the earth!" A small angry conference of white men took place in the front of the car and the Negroes sitting in the Jim Crow section overheard: "That's that Bigger Thomas nigger and you'd better leave 'im alone." The Negroes experienced an intense flash of pride and the

streetcar moved on its journey without incident. I don't know what happened to
Bigger No. 5. But I can guess.

The Bigger Thomases were the only Negroes I know of who consistently
violated the Jim Crow laws of the South and got away with it, at least for a sweet
brief spell. Eventually, the whites who restricted their lives made them pay a
terrible price. They were shot, hanged, maimed, lynched, and generally hounded
until they were either dead or their spirits broken.

There were many variations to this behavioristic pattern. Later on I encountered other Bigger Thomases who did not react to the locked-in Black Belts with
this same extremity and violence. But before I use Bigger Thomas as a springboard
for the examination of milder types, I'd better indicate more precisely the nature
of the environment that produced these men, or the reader will be left with the
impression that they were essentially and organically bad.

In Dixie there are two worlds, the white world and the black world, and they
are physically separated. There are white schools and black schools, white churches
and black churches, white businesses and black businesses, white graveyards and
black graveyards, and, for all I know, a white God and a black God. . . .

This separation was accomplished after the Civil War by the terror of the Ku
Klux Klan, which swept the newly freed Negro through arson, pillage, and death out
of the United States Senate, the House of Representatives, and many state legis-
latures, and out of the public, social, and economic life of the South. The motive for
this assault was simple and urgent. The imperialistic tug of history had torn the
Negro from his African home and had placed him ironically upon the most fertile
plantation areas of the South; and, when the Negro was freed, he outnumbered the
whites in many of these fertile areas. Hence, a fierce and bitter struggle took place
to keep the ballot from the Negro, for had he had a chance to vote, he would have
automatically controlled the richest lands of the South and with them the social,
political, and economic destiny of a third of the Republic. Though the South is
politically a part of America, the problem that faced her was peculiar and the
struggle between the whites and the blacks after the Civil War was in essence a
struggle for power, ranging over thirteen states and involving the lives of tens of
millions of people.

But keeping the ballot from the Negro was not enough to hold him in check;
disfranchisement had to be supplemented by a whole panoply of rules, taboos, and
penalties designed not only to insure peace (complete submission), but to guarantee
that no real threat would ever arise. Had the Negro lived upon a common territory, separate from the bulk of the white population, this program of oppression
might not have assumed such a brutal and violent form. But this war took place
between people who were neighbors, whose homes adjoined, whose farms had
common boundaries. Guns and disfranchisement, therefore, were not enough to
make the black neighbor keep his distance. The white neighbor decided to limit the
amount of education his black neighbor could receive; decided to keep him off the
police force and out of the local national guards; to segregate him residentially; to
Jim Crow him in public places; to restrict his participation in the professions and

jobs; and to build up a vast, dense ideology of racial superiority that would justify any act of violence taken against him to defend white dominance; and further, to condition him to hope for little and to receive that little without rebelling.

But, because the blacks were so *close* to the very civilization which sought to keep them out, because they could not *help* but react in some way to its incentives and prizes, and because the very tissue of their consciousness received its tone and timbre from the strivings of that dominant civilization, oppression spawned among them a myriad variety of reactions, reaching from outright blind rebellion to a sweet, other-worldly submissiveness.

In the main, this delicately balanced state of affairs has not greatly altered since the Civil War, save in those parts of the South which have been industrialized or urbanized. So volatile and tense are these relations that if a Negro rebels against rule and taboo, he is lynched and the reason for the lynching is usually called "rape," that catchword which has garnered such vile connotations that it can raise a mob anywhere in the South pretty quickly, even today.

Now for the variations in the Bigger Thomas pattern. Some of the Negroes living under these conditions got religion, felt that Jesus would redeem the void of living, felt that the more bitter life was in the present the happier it would be in the hereafter. Others, clinging still to that brief glimpse of post–Civil War freedom, employed a thousand ruses and stratagems of struggle to win their rights. Still others projected their hurts and longings into more naïve and mundane forms— blues, jazz, swing—and, without intellectual guidance, tried to build up a compensatory nourishment for themselves. Many labored under hot suns and then killed the restless ache with alcohol. Then there were those who strove for an education, and when they got it, enjoyed the financial fruits of it in the style of their bourgeois oppressors. Usually they went hand in hand with the powerful whites and helped to keep their groaning brothers in line, for that was the safest course of action. Those who did this called themselves "leaders." To give you an idea of how completely these "leaders" worked with those who oppressed, I can tell you that I lived the first seventeen years of my life in the South without so much as hearing of or seeing one act of rebellion from *any* Negro, save the Bigger Thomases.

But why did Bigger revolt? No explanation based upon a hard and fast rule of conduct can be given. But there were always two factors psychologically dominant in his personality. First, through some quirk of circumstance, he had become estranged from the religion and the folk culture of his race. Second, he was trying to react to and answer the call of the dominant civilization whose glitter came to him through the newspapers, magazines, radios, movies, and the mere imposing sight and sound of daily American life. In many respects his emergence as a distinct type was inevitable.

As I grew older, I became familiar with the Bigger Thomas conditioning and its numerous shadings no matter where I saw it in Negro life. It was not, as I have already said, as blatant or extreme as in the originals; but it was there, nevertheless, like an undeveloped negative.

Sometimes, in areas far removed from Mississippi, I'd hear a Negro say: "I wish

I didn't have to live this way. I feel like I want to burst." Then the anger would pass; he would go back to his job and try to eke out a few pennies to support his wife and children.

Sometimes I'd hear a Negro say: "God, I wish I had a flag and a country of my own." But that mood would soon vanish and he would go his way placidly enough.

Sometimes I'd hear a Negro ex-soldier say: "What in hell did I fight in the war for? They segregated me even when I was offering my life for my country." But he, too, like the others, would soon forget, would become caught up in the tense grind of struggling for bread.

I've even heard Negroes, in moments of anger and bitterness, praise what Japan is doing in China, not because they believed in oppression (being objects of oppression themselves), but because they would suddenly sense how empty their lives were when looking at the dark faces of Japanese generals in the rotogravure supplements of the Sunday newspapers. They would dream of what it would be like to live in a country where they could forget their color and play a responsible role in the vital processes of the nation's life.

I've even heard Negroes say that maybe Hitler and Mussolini are all right; that maybe Stalin is all right. They did not say this out of any intellectual comprehension of the forces at work in the world, but because they felt that these men "did things," a phrase which is charged with more meaning than the mere words imply. There was in the back of their minds, when they said this, a wild and intense longing (wild and intense because it was suppressed!) to belong, to be identified, to feel that they were alive as other people were, to be caught up forgetfully and exultingly in the swing of events, to feel the clean, deep, organic satisfaction of doing a job in common with others.

It was not until I went to live in Chicago that I first thought seriously of writing of Bigger Thomas. Two items of my experience combined to make me aware of Bigger as a meaningful and prophetic symbol. First, being free of the daily pressure of the Dixie environment, I was able to come into possession of my own feelings. Second, my contact with the labor movement and its ideology made me see Bigger clearly and feel what he meant.

I made the discovery that Bigger Thomas was not black all the time; he was white, too, and there were literally millions of him, everywhere. The extension of my sense of the personality of Bigger was the pivot of my life; it altered the complexion of my existence. I became conscious, at first dimly, and then later on with increasing clarity and conviction, of a vast, muddied pool of human life in America. It was as though I had put on a pair of spectacles whose power was that of an x-ray enabling me to see deeper into the lives of men. Whenever I picked up a newspaper, I'd no longer feel that I was reading of the doings of whites alone (Negroes are rarely mentioned in the press unless they've committed some crime!), but of a complex struggle for life going on in my country, a struggle in which I was involved. I sensed, too, that the Southern scheme of oppression was but an appendage of a far vaster and in many respects more ruthless and impersonal commodity-profit machine.

Trade-union struggles and issues began to grow meaningful to me. The flow of goods across the seas, buoying and depressing the wages of men, held a fascination. The pronouncements of foreign governments, their policies, plans, and acts were calculated and weighed in relation to the lives of people about me. I was literally overwhelmed when, in reading the works of Russian revolutionists, I came across descriptions of the "holiday energies of the masses," "the locomotives of history," "the conditions prerequisite for revolution," and so forth. I approached all of these new revelations in the light of Bigger Thomas, his hopes, fears, and despairs; and I began to feel far-flung kinships, and sense, with fright and abashment, the possibilities of *alliances* between the American Negro and other people possessing a kindred consciousness.

As my mind extended in this general and abstract manner, it was fed with even more vivid and concrete examples of the lives of Bigger Thomas. The urban environment of Chicago, affording a more stimulating life, made the Negro Bigger Thomases react more violently than even in the South. More than ever I began to see and understand the environmental factors which made for this extreme conduct. It was not that Chicago segregated Negroes more than the South, but that Chicago had more to offer, that Chicago's physical aspect—noisy, crowded, filled with the sense of power and fulfillment—did so much more to dazzle the mind with a taunting sense of possible achievement that the segregation it did impose brought forth from Bigger a reaction more obstreperous than in the South.

So the concrete picture and the abstract linkages of relationships fed each other, each making the other more meaningful and affording my emotions an opportunity to react to them with success and understanding. The process was like a swinging pendulum, each to and fro motion throwing up its tiny bit of meaning and significance, each stroke helping to develop the dim negative which had been implanted in my mind in the South.

During this period the shadings and nuances which were filling in Bigger's picture came, not so much from Negro life, as from the lives of whites I met and grew to know. I began to sense that they had their own kind of Bigger Thomas behavioristic pattern which grew out of a more subtle and broader frustration. The waves of recurring crime, the silly fads and crazes, the quicksilver changes in public taste, the hysteria and fears—all of these had long been mysteries to me. But now I looked back of them and felt the pinch and pressure of the environment that gave them their pitch and peculiar kind of being. I began to feel with my mind the inner tensions of the people I met. I don't mean to say that I think that environment *makes* consciousness (I suppose God makes that, if there is a God), but I do say that I felt and still feel that the environment supplies the instrumentalities through which the organism expresses itself, and if that environment is warped or tranquil, the mode and manner of behavior will be affected toward deadlocking tensions or orderly fulfillment and satisfaction.

Let me give examples of how I began to develop the dim negative of Bigger. I met white writers who talked of their responses, who told me how whites reacted to this lurid American scene. And, as they talked, I'd translate what they said in terms of Bigger's life. But what was more important still, I read their novels. Here, for the first time, I found ways and techniques of gauging meaningfully the effects of American civilization upon the personalities of people. I took these techniques, these ways of seeing and feeling, and twisted them, bent them, adapted them, until they became *my* ways of apprehending the locked-in life of the Black Belt areas. This association with white writers was the life preserver of my hope to depict Negro life in fiction, for my race possessed no fictional works dealing with such problems, had no background in such sharp and critical testing of experience, no novels that went with a deep and fearless will down to the dark roots of life.

Here are examples of how I culled information relating to Bigger from my reading:

There is in me a memory of reading an interesting pamphlet telling of the friendship of Gorky and Lenin in exile. The booklet told of how Lenin and Gorky were walking down a London street. Lenin turned to Gorky and, pointing, said: "Here is *their* Big Ben." "There is *their* Westminster Abbey." "There is *their* library." And at once, while reading that passage, my mind stopped, teased, challenged with the effort to remember, to associate widely disparate but meaningful experiences in my life. For a moment nothing would come, but I remained convinced that I had heard the meaning of those words sometime, somewhere before. Then, with a sudden glow of satisfaction of having gained a little more knowledge about the world in which I lived, I'd end up by saying: "That's Bigger. That's the Bigger Thomas reaction."

In both instances the deep sense of exclusion was identical. The feeling of looking at things with a painful and unwarrantable nakedness was an experience, I learned, that transcended national and racial boundaries. It was this intolerable sense of feeling and understanding so much, and yet living on a plane of social reality where the look of a world which one did not make or own struck one with a blinding objectivity and tangibility, that made me grasp the revolutionary impulse in my life and the lives of those about me and far away.

I remember reading a passage in a book dealing with old Russia which said: "We must be ready to make endless sacrifices if we are to be able to overthrow the Czar." And again I'd say to myself: "I've heard that somewhere, sometime before." And again I'd hear Bigger Thomas, far away and long ago, telling some white man who was trying to impose upon him: "I'll kill you and go to hell and pay for it." While living in America I heard from far away Russia the bitter accents of tragic calculation of how much human life and suffering it would cost a man to live as a man in a world that denied him the right to live with dignity. Actions and feelings of men ten thousand miles from home helped me to understand the moods and impulses of those walking the streets of Chicago and Dixie.

I am not saying that I heard any talk of revolution in the South when I was a kid there. But I did hear the lispings, the whispers, the mutters which some day, under one stimulus or another, will surely grow into open revolt unless the conditions which produce Bigger Thomases are changed.

In 1932 another source of information was dramatically opened up to me and I saw data of a surprising nature that helped to clarify the personality of Bigger. From the moment that Hitler took power in Germany and began to oppress the Jews, I tried to keep track of what was happening. And on innumerable occasions I was startled to detect, either from the side of the Fascists or from the side of the oppressed, reactions, moods, phrases, attitudes that reminded me strongly of Bigger, that helped to bring out more clearly the shadowy outlines of the negative that lay in the back of my mind.

I read every account of the Fascist movement in Germany I could lay my hands on, and from page to page I encountered and recognized familiar emotional pat terns. What struck me with particular force was the Nazi preoccupation with the construction of a society in which there would exist among all people (*German* people, of course!) *one* solidarity of ideals, *one* continuous circulation of funda-mental beliefs, notions, and assumptions. I am not now speaking of the popular idea of regimenting people's thought; I'm speaking of the implicit, almost unconscious, or pre-conscious, assumptions and ideals upon which whole nations and races act and live. And while reading these Nazi pages I'd be reminded of the Negro preacher in the South telling of a life beyond this world, a life in which the color of men's skins would not matter, a life in which each man would know what was deep down in the hearts of his fellow man. And I could hear Bigger Thomas standing on a street corner in America expressing his agonizing doubts and chronic suspicions, thus: "I ain't going to trust nobody. Everything is a racket and everybody is out to get what he can for himself. Maybe if we had a true leader, we could do something." And I'd know that I was still on the track of learning about Bigger, still in the midst of the modern struggle for solidarity among men.

When the Nazis spoke of the necessity of a highly ritualized and symbolized life, I could hear Bigger Thomas on Chicago's South Side saying: "Man, what we need is a leader like Marcus Garvey. We need a nation, a flag, an army of our own. We colored folks ought to organize into groups and have generals, captains, lieu-tenants, and so forth. We ought to take Africa and have a national home." I'd know, while listening to these childish words, that a white man would smile derisively at them. But I could not smile, for I knew the truth of those simple words from the facts of my own life. The deep hunger in those childish ideas was like a flash of lightning illuminating the whole dark inner landscape of Bigger's mind. Those words told me that the civilization which had given birth to Bigger contained no spiritual sustenance, had created no culture which could hold and claim his allegiance and faith, had sensitized him and had left him stranded, a free agent to roam the streets of our cities, a hot and whirling vortex of undisciplined and unchannelized impulses. The results of these observations made me feel more than ever estranged from the civilization in which I lived, and more than ever resolved toward the task of creating with words a scheme of images and symbols whose direction could enlist the sympathies, loyalties, and yearnings of the millions of Bigger Thomases in every land and race. . . .

But more than anything else, as a writer, I was fascinated by the similarity of the emotional tensions of Bigger in America and Bigger in Nazi Germany and Bigger in old Russia. All Bigger Thomases, white and black, felt tense, afraid, nervous, hysterical, and restless. From far away Nazi Germany and old Russia had come to me items of knowledge that told me that certain modern experiences were creating types of personalities whose existence ignored racial and national lines of demarcation, that these personalities carried with them a more universal drama-element than anything I'd ever encountered before; that these personalities were mainly imposed upon men and women living in a world whose fundamental assumptions could no longer be taken for granted: a world ridden with national and class strife; a world whose metaphysical meanings had vanished; a world in which God no longer existed as a daily focal point of men's lives; a world in which men could no longer retain their faith in an ultimate hereafter. It was a highly geared world whose nature was conflict and action, a world whose limited area and vision imperiously urged men to satisfy their organisms, a world that existed on a plane of animal sensation alone.

It was a world in which millions of men lived and behaved like drunkards, taking a stiff drink of hard life to lift them up for a thrilling moment, to give them a quivering sense of wild exultation and fulfillment that soon faded and let them down. Eagerly they took another drink, wanting to avoid the dull, flat look of things, then still another, this time stronger, and then they felt that their lives had meaning. Speaking figuratively, they were soon chronic alcoholics, men who lived by violence, through extreme action and sensation, through drowning daily in a perpetual nervous agitation.

From these items I drew my first political conclusions about Bigger: I felt that Bigger, an American product, a native son of this land, carried within him the potentialities of either Communism or Fascism. I don't mean to say that the Negro boy I depicted in *Native Son* is either a Communist or a Fascist. He is not either. But he is product of a dislocated society; he is a dispossessed and disinherited man; he is all of this, and he lives amid the greatest possible plenty on earth and he is looking and feeling for a way out. Whether he'll follow some gaudy, hysterical leader who'll promise rashly to fill the void in him, or whether he'll come to an understanding with the millions of his kindred fellow workers under trade-union or revolutionary guidance depends upon the future drift of events in America. But, granting the emotional state, the tensity, the fear, the hate, the impatience, the sense of exclusion, the ache for violent action, the emotional and cultural hunger, Bigger Thomas, conditioned as his organism is, will not become an ardent, or even a lukewarm, supporter of the *status quo*.

The difference between Bigger's tensity and the German variety is that Bigger's, due to America's educational restrictions on the bulk of her Negro population, is in a nascent state, not yet articulate. And the difference between Bigger's longing for self-identification and the Russian principle of self-determination is that Bigger's, due to the effects of American oppression, which has not allowed for the forming of deep ideas of solidarity among Negroes, is still in a state of individual anger and hatred. Here, I felt, was *drama!* Who will be the first to touch off these Bigger Thomases in America, white and black?

For a long time I toyed with the idea of writing a novel in which a Negro Bigger Thomas would loom as a symbolic figure of American life, a figure who would hold within him the prophecy of our future. I felt strongly that he held within him, in a measure which perhaps no other contemporary type did, the outlines of action and feeling which we would encounter on a vast scale in the days to come. Just as one sees when one walks into a medical research laboratory jars of alcohol containing abnormally large or distorted portions of the human body, just so did I see and feel that the conditions of life under which Negroes are forced to live in America contain the embryonic emotional prefigurations of how a large part of the body politic would react under stress.

So, with this much knowledge of myself and the world gained and known, why should I not try to work out on paper the problem of what will happen to Bigger? Why should I not, like a scientist in a laboratory, use my imagination and invent test-tube situations, place Bigger in them, and, following the guidance of my own hopes and fears, what I had learned and remembered, work out in fictional form an emotional statement and resolution of this problem?

But several things militated against my starting to work. Like Bigger himself, I felt a mental censor—product of the fears which a Negro feels from living in America—standing over me, draped in white, warning me not to write. This censor's warnings were translated into my own thought processes thus: "What will white people think if I draw the picture of such a Negro boy? Will they not at once say: 'See, didn't we tell you all along that niggers are like that? Now, look, one of their own kind has come along and drawn the picture for us!' " I felt that if I drew the picture of Bigger truthfully, there would be many reactionary whites who would try to make of him something I did not intend. And yet, and this was what made it difficult, I knew that I could not write of Bigger convincingly if I did not depict him as he *was:* that is, resentful toward whites, sullen, angry, ignorant, emotionally unstable, depressed and unaccountably elated at times, and unable even, because of his own lack of inner organization which American oppression has fostered in him, to unite with the members of his own race. And would not whites misread Bigger and, doubting his authenticity, say: "This man is preaching hate against the whole white race"?

The more I thought of it the more I became convinced that if I did not write of Bigger as I saw and felt him, if I did not try to make him a living personality and at the same time a symbol of all the larger things I felt and saw in him, I'd be reacting as Bigger himself reacted: that is, I'd be acting out of *fear* if I let what I thought whites would say constrict and paralyze me.

As I contemplated Bigger and what he meant, I said to myself: "I must write this novel, not only for others to read, but to free *myself* of this sense of shame and fear." In fact, the novel, as time passed, grew upon me to the extent that it became a necessity to write it; the writing of it turned into a way of living for me.

Another thought kept me from writing. What would my own white and black comrades in the Communist party say? This thought was the most bewildering of all. Politics is a hard and narrow game; its policies represent the aggregate desires and aspirations of millions of people. Its goals are rigid and simply drawn, and the minds of the majority of politicians are set, congealed in terms of daily tactical maneuvers. How could I create such complex and wide schemes of associational thought and feeling, such filigreed webs of dreams and politics, without being mistaken for a "smuggler of reaction," "an ideological confusionist," or "an individ- ualistic and dangerous element"? Though my heart is with the collectivist and proletarian ideal, I solved this problem by assuring myself that honest politics and honest feeling in imaginative representation ought to be able to meet on common healthy ground without fear, suspicion, and quarreling. Further, and more impor- tantly, I steeled myself by coming to the conclusion that whether politicians ac- cepted or rejected Bigger did not really matter; my task, as I felt it, was to free myself of this burden of impressions and feelings, recast them into the image of Bigger and make him *true*. Lastly, I felt that a right more immediately deeper than that of politics or race was at stake; that is, a *human* right, the right of a man to think and feel honestly. And especially did this personal and human right bear hard upon me, for temperamentally I am inclined to satisfy the claims of my own ideals rather than the expectations of others. It was this obscure need that had pulled me into the labor movement in the beginning and by exercising it I was but fulfilling what I felt to be the laws of my own growth.

There was another constricting thought that kept me from work. It deals with my own race. I asked myself: "What will Negro doctors, lawyers, dentists, bankers, school teachers, social workers and business men, think of me if I draw such a picture of Bigger?" I knew from long and painful experience that the Negro middle and professional classes were the people of my own race who were more than others ashamed of Bigger and what he meant. Having narrowly escaped the Bigger Thomas reaction pattern themselves—indeed, still retaining traces of it within the confines of their own timid personalities—they would not relish being publicly reminded of the lowly, shameful depths of life above which they enjoyed their bourgeois lives. Never did they want people, especially *white* people, to think that their lives were so much touched by anything so dark and brutal as Bigger.

Their attitude toward life and art can be summed up in a single paragraph: "But, Mr. Wright, there are so many of us who are *not* like Bigger. Why don't you portray in your fiction the *best* traits of our race, something that will show the white people what we have done in *spite* of oppression? Don't represent anger and bitterness. Smile when a white person comes to you. Never let him feel that you are so small that what he has done to crush you has made you hate him! Oh, above all, save your *pride!*"

But Bigger won over all these claims; he won because I felt that I was hunting on the trail of more exciting and thrilling game. What Bigger meant had claimed me because I felt with all of my being that he was more important than what any person, white or black, would say or try to make of him, more important than any political analysis designed to explain or deny him, more important, even, than my own sense of fear, shame, and diffidence.

But Bigger was still not down upon paper. For a long time I had been writing of him in my mind, but I had yet to put him into an image, a breathing symbol draped out in the guise of the only form of life my native land had allowed me to know intimately, that is, the ghetto life of the American Negro. But the basic reason for my hesitancy was that another and far more complex problem had risen to plague me. Bigger, as I saw and felt him, was a snarl of many realities; he had in him many levels of life.

First, there was his personal and private life, that intimate existence that is so difficult to snare and nail down in fiction, that elusive core of being, that individual data of consciousness which in every man and woman is like that in no other. I had to deal with Bigger's dreams, his fleeting, momentary sensations, his yearning, visions, his deep emotional responses.

Then I was confronted with that part of him that was dual in aspect, dim, wavering, that part of him which is so much a part of *all* Negroes and *all* whites that I realized that I could put it down upon paper only by feeling out its meaning first within the confines of my own life. Bigger was attracted and repelled by the American scene. He was an American, because he was a native son; but he was also a Negro nationalist in a vague sense because he was not allowed to live as an American. Such was his way of life and mine; neither Bigger nor I resided fully in either camp.

Of this dual aspect of Bigger's social consciousness, I placed the nationalistic side first, not because I agreed with Bigger's wild and intense hatred of white people, but because his hate had placed him, like a wild animal at bay, in a position where he was most symbolic and explainable. In other words, his nationalist complex was for me a concept through which I could grasp more of the total meaning of his life than I could in any other way. I tried to approach Bigger's *snarled* and *confused* nationalist feelings with *conscious* and *informed* ones of my own. Yet, Bigger was not nationalist enough to feel the need of religion or the folk culture of his own people. What made Bigger's social consciousness most complex was the fact that he was hovering unwanted between two worlds—between powerful America and his own stunted place in life—and I took upon myself the task of trying to make the reader feel this No Man's Land. The most that I could say of Bigger was that he felt the *need* for a whole life and *acted* out of that need; that was all.

Above and beyond all this, there was that American part of Bigger which is the heritage of us all, that part of him which we get from our seeing and hearing, from school, from the hopes and dreams of our friends; that part of him which the common people of America never talk of but take for granted. Among millions of people the deepest convictions of life are never discussed openly; they are felt, implied, hinted at tacitly and obliquely in their hopes and fears. We live by an idealism that makes us believe that the Constitution is a good document of government, that the Bill of Rights is a good legal and humane principle to safeguard our civil liberties, that every man and woman should have the opportunity to realize himself, to seek his own individual fate and goal, his own peculiar and untranslatable destiny. I don't say that Bigger knew this in the terms in which I'm speaking of it; I don't say that any such thought ever entered his head. His emotional and intellectual life was never that articulate. But he knew it emotionally, intuitively, for his emotions and his desires were developed, and he caught it, as most of us do, from the mental and emotional climate of our time. Bigger had all of this in him, dammed up, buried, implied, and I had to develop it in fictional form.

There was still another level of Bigger's life that I felt bound to account for and render, a level as elusive to discuss as it was to grasp in writing. Here again, I had to fall back upon my own feelings as a guide, for Bigger did not offer in his life any articulate verbal explanations. There seems to hover somewhere in that dark part of all our lives, in some more than in others, an objectless, timeless, spaceless element of primal fear and dread, stemming, perhaps, from our birth (depending upon whether one's outlook upon personality is Freudian or non-Freudian!), a fear and dread which exercises an impelling influence upon our lives all out of proportion to its obscurity. And, accompanying this *first fear,* is, for the want of a better name, a reflex urge toward ecstasy, complete submission, and trust. The springs of religion are here, and also the origins of rebellion. And in a boy like Bigger, young, unschooled, whose subjective life was clothed in the tattered rags of American "culture," this primitive fear and ecstasy were naked, exposed, unprotected by religion or a framework of government or a scheme of society whose final faiths would gain his love and trust; unprotected by trade or profession, faith or belief; opened to every trivial blast of daily or hourly circumstance.

There was yet another level of reality in Bigger's life: the impliedly political. I've already mentioned that Bigger had in him impulses which I had felt were present in the vast upheavals of Russia and Germany. Well, somehow, I had to make these political impulses felt by the reader in terms of Bigger's daily actions, keeping in mind as I did so the probable danger of my being branded as a propagandist by those who would not like the subject matter.

Then there was Bigger's relationship with white America, both North and South, which I had to depict, which I had to make known once again, alas; a relationship whose effects are carried by every Negro, like scars, somewhere in his body and mind.

I had also to show what oppression had done to Bigger's relationships with his own people, how it had split him off from them, how it had baffled him; how oppression seems to hinder and stifle in the victim those very qualities of character which are so essential for an effective struggle against the oppressor.

Then there was the fabulous city in which Bigger lived, an indescribable city, huge, roaring, dirty, noisy, raw, stark, brutal; a city of extremes: torrid summers and sub-zero winters, white people and black people, the English language and strange tongues, foreign born and native born, scabby poverty and gaudy luxury, high idealism and hard cynicism! A city so young that, in thinking of its short history, one's mind, as it travels backward in time, is stopped abruptly by the barren stretches of wind-swept prairie! But a city old enough to have caught within the homes of its long, straight streets the symbols and images of man's age-old destiny, of truths as old as the mountains and seas, of dramas as abiding as the soul of man itself! A city which has become the pivot of the Eastern, Western, Northern, and Southern poles of the nation. But a city whose black smoke clouds shut out the sunshine for seven months of the year; a city in which, on a fine balmy May morning, one can sniff the stench of the stockyards; a city where people have grown so used to gangs and murders and graft that they have honestly forgotten that government can have a pretense of decency!

With all of this thought out, Bigger was still unwritten. Two events, however, came into my life and accelerated the process, made me sit down and actually start work on the typewriter, and just stop the writing of Bigger in my mind as I walked the streets.

The first event was my getting a job in the South Side Boys' Club, an institution which tried to reclaim the thousands of Negro Bigger Thomases from the dives and the alleys of the Black Belt. Here, on a vast scale, I had an opportunity to observe Bigger in all of his moods, actions, haunts. Here I felt for the first time that the rich folk who were paying my wages did not really give a good goddamn about Bigger, that their kindness was prompted at bottom by a selfish motive. They were paying me to distract Bigger with ping-pong, checkers, swimming, marbles, and baseball in order that he might not roam the streets and harm the valuable white property which adjoined the Black Belt. I am not condemning boys' clubs and ping-pong as such; but these little stopgaps were utterly inadequate to fill up the centuries-long chasm of emptiness which American civilization had created in these Biggers. I felt that I was doing a kind of dressed-up police work, and I hated it.

I would work hard with these Biggers, and when it would come time for me to go home I'd say to myself, under my breath so that no one could hear: "Go to it, boys! Prove to the bastards that gave you these games that life is stronger than ping-pong. . . . Show them that full-blooded life is harder and hotter than they suspect, even though that life is draped in a black skin which at heart they despise. . . ."

They did. The police blotters of Chicago are testimony to how *much* they did. That was the only way I could contain myself for doing a job I hated; for a moment I'd allow myself, vicariously, to feel as Bigger felt—not much, just a little, just a *little*—but, still, there it was.

The second event that spurred me to write of Bigger was more personal and subtle. I had written a book of short stories which was published under the title of *Uncle Tom's Children*. When the reviews of that book began to appear, I realized that I had made an awfully naïve mistake. I found that I had written a book which even bankers' daughters could read and weep over and feel good about. I swore to myself that if I ever wrote another book, no one would weep over it; that it would be so hard and deep that they would have to face it without the consolation of tears. It was this that made me get to work in dead earnest.

Now, until this moment I did not stop to think very much about the plot of

Native Son. The reason I did not is because I was not for one moment ever worried about it. I had spent years learning about Bigger, what had made him, what he meant; so, when the time came for writing, *what had made him and what he meant* constituted my plot. But the far-flung items of his life had to be couched in imaginative terms, terms known and acceptable to a common body of readers, terms which would, in the course of the story, manipulate the deepest held notions and convictions of their lives. That came easy. The moment I began to write, the plot fell out, so to speak. I'm not trying to oversimplify or make the process seem oversubtle. At bottom, what happened is very easy to explain.

Any Negro who has lived in the North or the South knows that times without number he has heard of some Negro boy being picked up on the streets and carted off to jail and charged with "rape." This thing happens so often that to my mind it had become a representative symbol of the Negro's uncertain position in America. Never for a second was I in doubt as to what kind of social reality or dramatic situation I'd put Bigger in, what kind of test-tube life I'd set up to evoke his deepest reactions. Life had made the plot over and over again, to the extent that I knew it by heart. So frequently do these acts recur that when I was halfway through the first draft of *Native Son* a case paralleling Bigger's flared forth in the newspapers of Chicago. (Many of the newspaper items and some of the incidents in *Native Son* are but fictionalized versions of the Robert Nixon case and rewrites of news stories from the *Chicago Tribune.*) Indeed, scarcely was *Native Son* off the press before Supreme Court Justice Hugo L. Black gave the nation a long and vivid account of the American police methods of handling Negro boys.

Let me describe this stereotyped situation: A crime wave is sweeping a city and citizens are clamoring for police action. Squad cars cruise the Black Belt and grab the first Negro boy who seems to be unattached and homeless. He is held for perhaps a week without charge or bail, without the privilege of communicating with anyone, including his own relatives. After a few days this boy "confesses" anything that he is asked to confess, any crime that handily happens to be unsolved and on the calendar. Why does he confess? After the boy has been grilled night and day, hanged up by his thumbs, dangled by his feet out of twenty-story windows, and beaten (in places that leave no scars—cops have found a way to do that), he signs the papers before him, papers which are usually accompanied by a verbal promise to the boy that he will not go to the electric chair. Of course, he ends up by being executed or sentenced for life. If you think I'm telling tall tales, get chummy with some white cop who works in a Black Belt district and ask him for the lowdown.

When a black boy is carted off to jail in such a fashion, it is almost impossible to do anything for him. Even well-disposed Negro lawyers find it difficult to defend him, for the boy will plead guilty one day and then not guilty the next, according to the degree of pressure and persuasion that is brought to bear upon his frightened personality from one side or the other. Even the boy's own family is scared to death; sometimes fear of police intimidation makes them hesitate to acknowledge that the boy is a blood relation of theirs.

Such has been America's attitude toward these boys that if one is picked up and confronted in a police cell with ten white cops, he is intimidated almost to the point of confessing anything. So far removed are these practices from what the average American citizen encounters in his daily life that it takes a huge act of his imagination to believe that it is true; yet, this same average citizen, with his kindness, his American sportsmanship and good will, would probably act with the mob if a self-respecting Negro family moved into his apartment building to escape the Black Belt and its terrors and limitations. . . .

Now, after all of this, when I sat down to the typewriter, I could not work; I could not think of a good opening scene for the book. I had definitely in mind the kind of emotion I wanted to evoke in the reader in that first scene, but I could not think of the type of concrete event that would convey the motif of the entire scheme of the book, that would sound, in varied form, the note that was to be resounded throughout its length, that would introduce to the reader just what kind of an organism Bigger's was and the environment that was bearing hourly upon it. Twenty or thirty times I tried and failed; then I argued that if I could not write the opening scene, I'd start with the scene that followed. I did. The actual writing of the book began with the scene in the pool room.

Now, for the writing. During the years in which I had met all of those Bigger Thomases, those varieties of Bigger Thomases, I had not consciously gathered material to write of them; I had not kept a notebook record of their sayings and doings. Their actions had simply made impressions upon my sensibilities as I lived from day to day, impressions which crystallized and coagulated into clusters and configurations of memory, attitudes, moods, ideas. And these subjective states, in turn, were automatically stored away somewhere in me. I was not even aware of the process. But, excited over the book which I had set myself to write, under the stress of emotion, these things came surging up, tangled, fused, knotted, entertaining me by the sheer variety and potency of their meaning and suggestiveness.

With the whole theme in mind, in an attitude almost akin to prayer, I gave myself up to the story. In an effort to capture some phase of Bigger's life that would not come to me readily, I'd jot down as much of it as I could. Then I'd read it over and over, adding each time a word, a phrase, a sentence until I felt that I had caught all the shadings of reality I felt dimly were there. With each of these rereadings and rewritings it seemed that I'd gather in facts and facets that tried to run away. It was an act of concentration, of trying to hold within one's center of attention all of that bewildering array of facts which science, politics, experience, memory, and imagination were urging upon me. And then, while writing, a new and thrilling relationship would spring up under the drive of emotion, coalescing and telescoping alien facts into a known and felt truth. That was the deep fun of the job: to feel within my body that I was pushing out to new areas of feeling, strange landmarks of emotion, tramping upon foreign soil, compounding new relationships of perceptions, making new and—until that very split second of time!—unheard-of and unfelt effects with words. It had a buoying and tonic impact upon me; my senses would strain and seek for more and more of such relationships; my temperature would rise as I worked. That is writing as I feel it, a kind of significant living.

The first draft of the novel was written in four months, straight through, and ran to some 576 pages. Just as a man rises in the mornings to dig ditches for his bread, so I'd work daily. I'd think of some abstract principle of Bigger's conduct and at once my mind would turn it into some act I'd seen Bigger perform, some act which I hoped would be familiar enough to the American reader to gain his credence. But in the writing of scene after scene I was guided by but one criterion: to tell the truth as I saw it and felt it. That is, to objectify in words some insight derived from my living in the form of action, scene, and dialogue. If a scene seemed improbable to me, I'd not tear it up, but ask myself: "Does it reveal enough of what I feel to stand in spite of its unreality?" If I felt it did, it stood. If I felt that it did not, I ripped it out. The degree of morality in my writing depended upon the degree of felt life and truth I could put down upon the printed page. For example, there is a scene in *Native Son* where Bigger stands in a cell with a Negro preacher, Jan, Max, the State's Attorney, Mr. Dalton, Mrs. Dalton, Bigger's mother, his brother, his sister, Al, Gus, and Jack. While writing that scene, I knew that it was unlikely that so many people would ever be allowed to come into a murderer's cell. But I wanted those people in that cell to elicit a certain important emotional response from Bigger. And so the scene stood. I felt that what I wanted that scene to say to the reader was *more important than its surface reality or plausibility.*

Always, as I wrote, I was both reader and writer, both the conceiver of the action and the appreciator of it. I tried to write so that, in the same instant of time, the objective and subjective aspects of Bigger's life would be caught in a focus of prose. And always I tried to *render, depict,* not merely to tell the story. If a thing was cold, I tried to make the reader *feel* cold, and not just tell about it. In writing in this fashion, sometimes I'd find it necessary to use a stream of consciousness technique, then rise to an interior monologue, descend to a direct rendering of a dream state, then to a matter-of-fact depiction of what Bigger was saying, doing, and feeling. Then I'd find it impossible to say what I wanted to say without stepping in and speaking outright on my own; but when doing this I always made an effort to retain the mood of the story, explaining everything only in terms of Bigger's life and, if possible, in the rhythms of Bigger's thought (even though the words would be mine). Again, at other times, in the guise of the lawyer's speech and the newspaper items, or in terms of what Bigger would overhear or see from afar, I'd give what others were saying and thinking of him. But always, from the start to the finish, it was Bigger's story, Bigger's fear, Bigger's flight, and Bigger's fate that I tried to depict. I wrote with the conviction in mind (I don't know if this is right or wrong; I only know that I'm temperamentally inclined to feel this way) that the main burden of all serious fiction consists almost wholly of character-destiny and the items, social, political, and personal, of that character-destiny.

As I wrote I followed, almost unconsciously, many principles of the novel which my reading of the novels of other writers had made me feel were necessary for the building of a well-constructed book. For the most part the novel is rendered in the present; I wanted the reader to feel that Bigger's story was happening *now,* like a play upon the stage or a movie unfolding upon the screen. Action follows action, as in a prize fight. Wherever possible, I told of Bigger's life in close-up, slow-motion, giving the feel of the grain in the passing of time. I had long had the feeling that this was the best way to "enclose" the reader's mind in a new world, to blot out all reality except that which I was giving him.

Then again, as much as I could, I restricted the novel to what Bigger saw and felt, to the limits of his feeling and thoughts, even when I was conveying *more* than that to the reader. I had the notion that such a manner of rendering made for a sharper effect, a more pointed sense of the character, his peculiar type of being and consciousness. Throughout there is but one point of view: Bigger's. This, too, I felt, made for a richer illusion of reality.

I kept out of the story as much as possible, for I wanted the reader to feel that there was nothing between him and Bigger; that the story was a special *première* given in his own private theater.

I kept the scenes long, made as much happen within a short space of time as possible; all of which, I felt, made for greater density and richness of effect.

In a like manner I tried to keep a unified sense of background throughout the story; the background would change, of course, but I tried to keep before the eyes of the reader at all times the forces and elements against which Bigger was striving.

And, because I had limited myself to rendering only what Bigger saw and felt, I gave no more reality to the other characters than that which Bigger himself saw.

This, honestly, is all I can account for in the book. If I attempted to account for scenes and characters, to tell why certain scenes were written in certain ways, I'd be stretching facts in order to be pleasantly intelligible. All else in the book came from my feelings reacting upon the material, and any honest reader knows as much about the rest of what is in the book as I do; that is, if, as he reads, he is willing to let his emotions and imagination become as influenced by the materials as I did. As I wrote, for some reason or other, one image, symbol, character, scene, mood, feeling evoked its opposite, its parallel, its complementary, and its ironic counterpart. Why? I don't know. My emotions and imagination just like to work that way. One can account for just so much of life, and then no more. At least, not yet.

With the first draft down, I found that I could not end the book satisfactorily. In the first draft I had Bigger going smack to the electric chair; but I felt that two murders were enough for one novel. I cut the final scene and went back to worry about the beginning. I had no luck. The book was one-half finished, with the opening and closing scenes unwritten. Then, one night, in desperation—I hope that I'm not disclosing the hidden secrets of my craft!—I sneaked out and got a bottle. With the help of it, I began to remember many things which I could not remember before. One of them was that Chicago was overrun with rats. I recalled that I'd seen many rats on the streets, that I'd heard and read of Negro children being bitten by rats in their beds. At first I rejected the idea of Bigger battling a rat in his room; I was afraid that the rat would "hog" the scene. But the rat would not leave me; he presented himself in many attractive guises. So, cautioning myself to allow the rat scene to disclose *only* Bigger, his family, their little room, and their relationships, I let the rat walk in, and he did his stuff.

Many of the scenes were torn out as I reworked the book. The mere re-reading of what I'd written made me think of the possibility of developing themes which had been only hinted at in the first draft. For example, the entire guilt theme that runs through *Native Son* was woven in *after* the first draft was written.

At last I found out how to end the book; I ended it just as I had begun it, showing Bigger living dangerously, taking his life into his hands, accepting what life had made him. The lawyer, Max, was placed in Bigger's cell at the end of the novel to register the moral—or what *I* felt was the moral—horror of Negro life in the United States.

The writing of *Native Son* was to me an exciting, enthralling, and even a romantic experience. With what I've learned in the writing of this book, with all of its blemishes, imperfections, with all of its unrealized potentialities, I am launching out upon another novel, this time about the status of women in modern American society. This book, too, goes back to my childhood just as Bigger went, for, while I was storing away impressions of Bigger, I was storing away impressions of many other things that made me think and wonder. Some experience will ignite some-where deep down in me the smoldering embers of new fires and I'll be off again to write yet another novel. It is good to live when one feels that such as that will happen to one. Life becomes sufficient unto life; the rewards of living are found in living.

I don't know if *Native Son* is a good book or a bad book. And I don't know if the book I'm working on now will be a good book or a bad book. And I really don't care. The mere writing of it will be more fun and a deeper satisfaction than any praise or blame from anybody.

I feel that I'm lucky to be alive to write novels today, when the whole world is caught in the pangs of war and change. Early American writers, Henry James and Nathaniel Hawthorne, complained bitterly about the bleakness and flatness of the American scene. But I think that if they were alive, they'd feel at home in modern America. True, we have no great church in America; our national traditions are still of such a sort that we are not wont to brag of them; and we have no army that's above the level of mercenary fighters; we have no group acceptable to the whole of our country upholding certain humane values; we have no rich symbols, no colorful rituals. We have only a money-grubbing, industrial civilization. But we do have in the Negro the embodiment of a past tragic enough to appease the spiritual hunger of even a James; and we have in the oppression of the Negro a shadow athwart our national life dense and heavy enough to satisfy even the gloomy broodings of a Hawthorne. And if Poe were alive, he would not have to invent horror; horror would invent him.

Edward Margolies

NATIVE SON AND THREE KINDS OF REVOLUTION

Richard Wright's *Native Son* (1940) represents a watershed in Negro letters. It seized the imagination of readers and catapulted its author into fame, making him a source of controversy for years to come—a controversy that has not yet subsided. The initial reaction was shock. Wright's account of a shiftless, seemingly apathetic slum boy who harbored an obsessive hatred of whites came as a startling revelation even to the most liberal of white readers—who, when they thought of Negroes at all, tended to regard them benignly as persons just like themselves in black skins. Perhaps even more shocking was Wright's apparent view that the brutal murders Bigger commits in celebration of his hatred are, after all, the logical outcome of his absurd position in American life. Wright was not, of course, condoning violence, but he *was* saying that the alternative behavior, for the majority of slum Negroes, was dumb submission to a dehumanizing lot. Moreover, Wright further startled white (and Negro) readers by taking as his central figure the stereotyped "nigger" (the name Bigger is suggestive), whose crimes against a white girl were vaguely sexual in origin. That any Negro author should want to aggravate the paranoid fantasies of racist extremists seemed to some readers almost beyond belief.

Needless to say, white and Negro critics rushed to print, praising or condemning the novel, and still do. And it is not surprising that some of Wright's harshest critics were Negroes. He did not give a true picture of the Negro, they said, but rather a monstrous version of the stereotype that has condemned the vast majority of law-abiding members of their race to live in subhuman conditions (this was precisely Wright's point—that subhuman conditions produce subhuman persons). They protested additionally that Wright's determinism or communism (he was a Party member at the time) distorted reality, since whites and Negroes have often in history transcended their debased environments. Was not Wright himself

From *Native Sons: A Critical Study of Twentieth Century Negro American Authors* (Philadelphia: J. B. Lippincott, 1968), pp. 65–66, 71–86.

born into grinding poverty? Here the critics may have had a point, but Wright was writing not about those "transcended" Negroes, but rather about the many more who had remained mired in the despair and hopelessness of the ghettos. ⟨. . .⟩

Native Son has as much impact now as it did when it was first published, in spite of the fact that its flaws are more obvious today than they could have been in the last years of the Depression, when proletarian literature still enjoyed a vogue. Nearly all the weaknesses and embarrassments we have come to recognize in proletarian fiction are present in *Native Son,* yet somehow the reader is not so conscious of them. One reason, of course, is that Bigger Thomas, unlike the usual array of proletarian victims, is thoroughly the antihero. He is not simply weak, he is an outright coward. He is incapable of warmth, love, or loyalty, he is a sullen bully, and he enjoys his first sense of humanity and freedom only after he commits two brutal murders.

Still, *Native Son* possesses many of the characteristic failings of proletarian literature. It is transparently propagandistic, arguing for a humane, socialist society where such crimes as Bigger committed could not conceivably take place. Wright builds up rather extensive documentation to prove that Bigger's actions, behavior, values, attitudes, and fate are determined by his status and place in American life. Bigger's immediate Negro environment is depicted as being unrelentingly bleak and empty, while the white world that stands just beyond his reach remains cruelly indifferent or hostile to his needs. With the exception of Bigger, none of the characters is portrayed in any depth, and most are depicted as representative "types" of the social class to which they belong. Despite his brutally conditioned psychology, there are moments in the novel when Bigger, like the heroes of other proletarian fiction, appears to be on the verge of responding to the stereotyped Communist vision of black and white workers marching together in the sunlight of fraternal friendship. Finally, Wright succumbs too often to the occupational disease of proletarian authors by hammering home sociological points in didactic expository prose when they could be understood just as clearly in terms of the organic development of the novel.

Yet if *Native Son* illustrates some of the conventional flaws of proletarian fiction, it also reveals Wright exploring new problems of character portrayal, prose style, and theme. As has already been suggested, there is the sympathetic presentation of perhaps one of the most disagreeable characters in fiction. And although *Native Son* makes its obvious sociological points, for well over two thirds of the novel Wright dwells on the peculiar states of mind of his protagonist, Bigger, which exist somehow outside the realm of social classes or racial issues. Indeed, Wright himself frequently makes the point that Bigger hangs psychologically suspended somewhere between the white world and the black.

> He felt he had no physical existence at all right then; he was something he hated, the badge of shame which he knew was attached to a black skin. It was a shadowy region, a No Man's Land, the ground that separated the white world from the black that he stood upon. He felt naked, transparent. . . .

Hence if categorizing terms are to be used, *Native Son* is as much a psychological novel as it is sociological, with Wright dwelling on various intensities of shame, fear and hate. Finally, there is the style. Since the viewpoint throughout is that of the illiterate and inarticulate Bigger, Wright had to discover a means of communicating thoughts and feelings Bigger is unable to express. At times Wright frankly interprets them to his readers, but often he reveals them in objectified images of Bigger's environment—the way the streets look to him, the feel of the sleet and the snow against his skin, the sounds of a rat rustling in the darkness of a tenement—and in dispassionate, unadorned accounts of Bigger's movements which in themselves give an accurate picture of Bigger's emotions.

To make his readers identify with the violent emotions and behavior of an illiterate Negro boy is no mean feat—but Wright goes beyond the mere shock of reader recognition, and the subsequent implications of shared guilt and social responsibility, and raises questions regarding the ultimate nature of man. What are man's responsibilities in a world devoid of meaning and purpose? That Wright couched these questions in what one critic has called the "linguistics" of Marxism has perhaps deterred readers from examining *Native Son* in the light of its other philosophical values. Since moral responsibility involves choice, can Wright's deterministic Marxism be reconciled with the freedom of action that choice implies? The contradiction is never resolved, and it is precisely for this reason that the novel fails to fulfill itself, for the plot, the structure, even the portrayal of Bigger himself, are often at odds with Wright's official determinism. But when on occasion the novel transcends its Marxist and proletarian limitations the reading becomes magnificent.

The structure of *Native Son* is classically simple. The book divides into three parts, the first two covering a little less than seventy-two hours, the third perhaps a little more than a month.

Book I, "Fear," traces a day in the life of twenty-year-old Bigger Thomas, from the time he wakes up in the morning and kills a rat in the squalid one room tenement he shares with his mother, sister, and brother, to the time he creeps back into bed twenty-one hours later, having just murdered a white girl. Bigger's day thus symbolically begins and ends in death. But Wright shows that all of Bigger's waking existence is a kind of meaninglessness—a kind of death. In the morning Bigger loiters on the street with members of his gang and plots (fearfully) to rob a white man's store. Later he goes to a movie and sits through a banal Hollywood double bill. Wright here shows how the glitter of the great white world beyond titillates Bigger and, at the same time, frustrates him all the more. When Bigger returns from the movie he has a savage fight in a pool room with one of the co-conspirators in the proposed robbery. Next he goes off to a job interview that has been arranged for him by the relief authorities. Mr. Dalton, the prospective employer, is a rich white man philanthropically inclined toward Negroes. He also owns considerable real estate in Chicago's South Side and has a controlling interest in the house in which Bigger's family lives. Bigger is hired as a chauffeur, and his first assignment is to drive Dalton's daughter, Mary, to the University. Once in the car, however, Mary redirects Bigger to another address where she is joined by her lover, Jan. Mary and

Jan are Communists and want to befriend Bigger; they sit up front with him in the car and ask all sorts of intimate questions to which Bigger reacts with suspicion and fear. It is women like Mary, he reasons, who have made things hard for Negroes. They make Bigger take them to a Negro restaurant where they embarrass him by forcing him to join them at a table. Later Bigger drives them around the park while Mary and Jan drink from a bottle and make love in the back seat. After Jan leaves, Bigger discovers Mary is much too drunk to walk to the house by herself, so he carries her to her bedroom and places her on the bed. He finds himself somewhat sexually stimulated, but just at that moment Mary's blind mother enters the room and calls to her daughter. Bigger, fearing what Mrs. Dalton will think, places a pillow over Mary's head so that she cannot respond. After Mrs. Dalton leaves, Bigger discovers he has accidentally smothered Mary to death. He throws the corpse into a trunk and takes the trunk downstairs to the cellar where he thrusts Mary's body into the furnace. Then he carries the trunk out to the car, since Mary had said she wanted him to take it to the railroad station the following morning. Thus ends Bigger's day—he goes home.

Wright forecasts Bigger's doom from the very start. Bigger knows deep in his heart that he is destined to bear endless days of dreary poverty, abject humiliation, and tormenting frustration, for this is what being a Negro means. Yet should he admit these things to himself, he may well commit an act of unconscionable violence. "He knew that the moment he allowed what his life meant to enter fully into his consciousness, he would either kill himself or someone else." And he knows he will not always be able to delude himself. He tells his friend, Gus, early in the novel, "Sometimes I feel like something awful's going to happen to me." Hence, Bigger's principal fear is self-knowledge—and this, of course, is the theme and title of Book I. The other fears that make up Bigger's life are by-products of this basic terror.

All Bigger's actions stem from his fear. He hates whites because he fears them. He knows they are responsible for his immobility, his frustration, yet to admit even this would be admitting simultaneously a profound self-hatred. So he channels his hatred and aggression toward other Negroes, and thereby, momentarily at least, assuages his ego. He is afraid, for example, to steal from a white store keeper, and terrified that his friends can read his heart—so he attacks them in order to prove his courage to himself. He hates Mary Dalton because he fears she will jeopardize his job, and he regards all her overtures as efforts to humiliate him. He kills her because he fears the help he has given her will be misunderstood. Bigger's nature, then, is composed of dread and hate. He hates what he fears—and his bravado and violence are merely illusory compensations for his terror.

The second book, "Flight," describes Bigger's awakening sense of life at a time, paradoxically, when his life is most in danger. Although his killing of Mary was an accident, Bigger decides that he must assume full responsibility for her death. Hence, for once in his life he will know the consequences of an action he has "voluntarily" taken. In killing Mary, he feels, he has destroyed symbolically all the oppressive forces that have made his life a misery. Thus perhaps her death was not so accidental as it seemed at the time. He enjoys a sense of potency and freedom that he has never before experienced. He knows something, has done something, that the whites do not know—and proceeds now to act with new-found dignity. Ironically the dignity takes the form of acts compounding his crime. He plans to lay the blame for Mary's disappearance on Jan. Jan was, after all, the last white person to see Mary alone; he is also a Communist, and Bigger knows most Communists are hated. He succeeds in implying Jan's guilt and Jan is arrested and held for questioning. Meanwhile Bigger has revealed to his girl, Bessie, that he is involved in Mary's disappearance—which is now front page news—and Bessie reluctantly agrees to help him extort ransom from the Daltons under the pretense that their daughter has been kidnaped. This plan falls through when reporters discover Mary's charred bones in the furnace, and Bigger is forced to flee. He and Bessie conceal themselves in a vacated tenement, but Bigger realizes Bessie is at best an unenthusiastic co-conspirator, and decides he must kill her or she will some day reveal his whereabouts to the police. He makes love to her and after she has gone to sleep he smashes her head in with a brick. The monstrousness of the second murder exhilarates Bigger all the more:

> And, yet, out of it all, over and above all that had happened, impalpable but real, there remained to him a queer sense of power. *He* had done this. *He* had brought all this about. In all his life these two murders were the most meaningful things that had ever happened to him. He was living, truly and deeply, no matter what others might think, looking at him with their blind eyes. Never had he had the chance to live out the consequence of his actions; never had his will been so free as in this night and day of fear and murder and flight.

Hence Bigger has *opted* to become a murderer, and freely chosen this identity. In an absurd, hostile world that denies his humanity and dichotomizes his personality, he has made a choice that somehow integrates his being:

> There was something he *knew* and something he *felt;* something the *world* gave him and something he *himself* had; something spread out in *front* of him and something spread out in *back;* and never in all his life, with this black skin of his, had the two worlds, thought and feeling, will and mind, aspiration and satisfaction, been together; never had he felt a sense of wholeness.
>
>   . . .
>
> He had committed murder twice and had created a new world for himself.

Ironically, Bigger has assumed exactly the role the white world thrusts upon the Negro in order to justify his oppression. If the Negro is a beast who must be caged in order to protect the purity of the white race, that is at least an identity—preferable to that of someone obsequious, passive, and happily acquiescent to his exploitation. Bigger's choices are moral and metaphysical, not political or racial. He has the choice, as Esther Merle Jackson has pointed out, between force and submission, love and hate, life and death. He elects force as a sign of his being, and by rebelling against established authority—despite the impossibility of success—he acquires a measure of freedom.

None of the above is intended to deny that oppressive environmental factors limit the modes of Bigger's actions; nonetheless, environment by itself does not explain Bigger. Bigger's original alienation from the Negro community was made of his own free choice. His mother, his sister, his girl—each has made an individual adjustment of some sort to the conditions of Negro life. But Bigger cannot accept his mother's religiosity, his sister's Y.W.C.A. virtue, or Bessie's whisky. All seem to him evasions of reality. Though his rejection of Negro life was only a negative choice, his acts of murder are positive—thus in a degree humanizing—since he is quite prepared to accept the consequences.

The remainder of Book II has a taut, tense rhythm corresponding to the quickening pace of flight and pursuit. As the police inexorably close in, Bigger flies from one street to the next, one tenement to the next; he is chased across roofs—until finally he is flung down from the chimney to which he has been clinging by the pressure of the water directed at him from the hoses of firemen.

Book III, "Fate," draws together all the significant strands of Bigger's life, and shows how all society, white and black, has a stake in his crimes. The newspapers, the police, and the politicians use Bigger for their own self-aggrandizement. The Communists defend him, although even they do not altogether understand him. Futile attempts are made to convert him to Christianity. Philanthropists and the business community are implicated, since both are exploiters of the Negro. Racists burn crosses in various parts of the city; outside the courtroom in which Bigger is tried, a howling white mob cries for his blood. Bigger's attorney, Max, in a useless but eloquent address to the jury, tries to explain Bigger's crimes in terms of the devastating psychological blows of slavery and racial exploitation.

Immediately after his capture, Bigger reverts to his pose of sullen apathy. But Max's genuine efforts to help and understand him awaken in Bigger a vague sense of hope and trust in men. He needs Max and looks forward to his visits. He knows the jury will doom him, but this does not disturb him very much. Throughout the agony of his trial, Bigger has been trying to puzzle through the meaning of his life and world. He has always lived so isolated from other human beings that he is no longer sure. He asks Max, but even Max can only respond in historical and socio-economic terms. Some day, Max tells him, men might be able to express their beings in terms other than struggle and exploitation. But although moved, Bigger cannot ultimately accept this. For him the essence of life is violence and power.

"I didn't want to kill!" Bigger shouted. "But what I killed for, I *am!* . . . What I killed for must have been good!" Bigger's voice was full of frenzied anguish. "It must have been good! When a man kills, it's for something. . . . I didn't know I was really alive in this world until I felt things hard enough to kill for 'em. . . ."

Bigger elects to face death on the same principles that have finally made his life meaningful.

The chief philosophical weakness of *Native Son* is not that Bigger does not surrender his freedom to Max's determinism, or that Bigger's Zarathustrian principles do not jibe with Max's socialist visions; it is that Wright himself does not seem to be able to make up his mind. The reader feels that Wright, although intellectually committed to Max's views, is more emotionally akin to Bigger's. And somehow Bigger's impassioned hatred comes across more vividly than Max's eloquent reasoning. Indeed, the very length of Max's plea to the jury (sixteen pages in the Harper edition) suggests that Wright, through Max, is endeavoring to convince himself.

The whole of Book III seems out of key with the first two-thirds of the novel. Where Books I and II confine themselves to a realistic account of Bigger's thoughts and actions, Book III tries to interpret these in a number of rather dubious symbolic sequences. In one scene Bigger, in his cell, confronts all the people with whom he has previously been involved: the Daltons, Jan, a Negro preacher, his mother, brother, and sister, three members of his street gang, Max, and the district attorney. Everything is highly contrived—as if Wright is placing before Bigger's eyes all the major influences that have made up his life. In another scene of transparently "symbolic" significance, Bigger, after a trying day in court, flings a wooden crucifix out of the cell door, thereby suggesting his rejection of Christianity.

Perhaps the most flagrant violation of verisimilitude is Max's plea to the jury. Although it undoubtedly makes good sociological sense and is possibly even a sound assessment of Bigger's character, it is not the sort of thing that would ordinarily persuade a jury. A more realistic approach to the intensely hysterical courtroom atmosphere would have been for Max to plead some sort of insanity— rather than to depict Bigger as a helpless victim of American civilization.

Finally, Book III contains a number of improbable colloquies between Bigger and Max. Here Bigger is almost unbelievable. After twenty years of conditioning to mistrust every human being, especially whites, he suddenly opens up and bares his soul to Max. The point Wright is making is a good one: no one has ever before cared to understand Bigger as a human being and not as a symbol; no one has ever before granted him his dignity. Nonetheless, to suggest that Bigger would respond so quickly to Max, under such circumstances, is to make excessive demands on the credulity of the reader.

The inconsistency of Wright's ideologies and philosophical attitudes prevents Bigger and the other characters from developing properly, adulterates the structure of the novel, and occasionally clouds an otherwise lucid prose style.

There are three kinds of revolutionism in *Native Son*—and none of them altogether engages the reader as representing Wright's point of view. Max's communism is of course what Wright presumes his novel is expressing—yet this kind of revolutionism is, as we have seen, imposed from without and not an integral element of Bigger's being. Revolutionism of a Negro nationalist variety is far more in keeping with Bigger's character. Bigger hates all whites with such an intensity that it gives him extreme pleasure to think he killed Mary deliberately. His is a reverse racism. As Max puts it:

> Every time he comes in contact with us, he kills! It is a physiological and psychological reaction, embedded in his being. Every thought he thinks is potential murder. Excluded from, and unassimilated in our society, yet longing to gratify impulses akin to our own ... every sunrise and sunset make him guilty of subversive actions. Every movement of his body is an unconscious protest. Every desire, every dream, no matter how intimate or personal, is a plot or a conspiracy. Every hope is a plan for insurrection. Every glance of the eye is a threat. *His very existence is a crime against the state!*

Sometimes Bigger's racism takes more of a political form:

> There were rare moments when a feeling and longing for solidarity with other black people would take hold of him. He would dream of making a stand against that white force. ... He felt that some day there would be a black man who would whip the black people into a tight band and together they would act. ...

But as Camus has written, "Human rebellion ends in metaphysical revolution"—and it is in the role of the metaphysical revolutionary that Bigger looms most significantly for modern readers. The metaphysical revolutionary challenges the very conditions of being—the needless suffering, the absurd contrast between his inborn sense of justice and the amorality and injustice of the external world. He tries to bring the world into accord with his sense of justice, but if this fails he will attempt to match in himself its injustice and chaos. In either case the principle is the same: "He attacks a shattered world in order to demand unity from it."

In *How "Bigger" Was Born* (a piece Wright produced afterward, describing the genesis of the novel), Wright describes it thus:

> [It was] a world whose fundamental assumptions could no longer be taken for granted, a world ridden with class and national strife, a world whose metaphysical meanings had vanished ... a world in which men could no longer retain their faith in an ultimate hereafter.

By rejecting these "fundamental assumptions" and identifying himself with the world of violence and strife he knows to be true, Bigger gives his life meaning and clarity:

> He felt that he had his destiny in his grasp. He was more alive than he could ever remember having been; his mind and attention were pointed, focused toward a goal. For the first time in his life he moved consciously between two sharply defined poles: he was moving away from the threatening

penalty of death, from the death-like times that brought him that tightness and hotness in his chest; and he was moving toward that sense of fullness. . . .

Compare Camus's description of the romantic criminal, Satan:

> Since violence is at the root of all creation, deliberate violence shall be its answer. The fact that there is an excess of despair adds to the causes of despair and brings rebellion to that state of indignant frustration which follows the long experience of injustice and where the distinction between good and evil finally disappears.

Perhaps it is Bigger's Satanic election of violence, rather than his continued undying hatred of whites, that so terrifies Max at the close of the novel. Max senses that as a Communist he too has dispensed with the old social order—but the metaphysical vacuum that has been created does not necessarily lead men like Bigger to communism; it may just as easily lead to the most murderous kind of nihilism. Max's horror was to become Wright's own dilemma two years after the publication of *Native Son*, when he himself left the Party. He could no longer accept the assumptions of communism, yet the prospects of a new world of positive meaning and value seemed very distant indeed. It is, then, in the roles of a Negro nationalist revolutionary and a metaphysical rebel that Wright most successfully portrays Bigger. And it is from these aspects of Bigger's character rather than from any Marxist interpretation that Wright's sociology really emerges.

The metaphor that Wright uses best to illustrate the relationship between the races is "blindness"—and blindness is one result of Bigger's racist nationalist pride. Prior to his conversion by murder, Bigger has blinded himself to the realities of Negro life (as well as to the humanity of whites—he is unable to accept Jan's offer of friendship, for example, because he blindly regards all whites as symbols of oppression). It is only after his metaphysical rebellion has been effected by the death of the two girls that Bigger acquires sight. When he looks at his family, he realizes they are as blind as he had been; he understands what it means to be a Negro. Buddy, his brother, "was blind . . . Buddy, too, went round and round in a groove and did not see things. Buddy's clothes hung loosely compared with the way Jan's hung. Buddy seemed aimless, lost, with no sharp or hard edges, like a chubby puppy . . . he saw in Buddy a certain stillness, an isolation, meaninglessness." When he looks at his mother he sees "how soft and shapeless she was. . . . She moved about slowly, touching objects with her fingers as she passed them, using them for support. . . . There was in her heart, it seemed, a heavy and delicately balanced burden whose weight she did not want to assume by disturbing it one whit." His sister, Vera, "seemed to be shrinking from life in every gesture she made. The very manner in which she sat showed a fear so deep as to be an organic part of her. . . ."

Bigger's new vision also enables him to see how blind whites are to his humanity, his existence. Whites prefer to think of Negroes in easily stereotyped images of brute beast or happy minstrel. They are incapable of viewing black men as possessing sensitivity and intelligence. It is this blindness that Bigger counts on as the means of getting away with his crimes. When he schemes with Bessie to collect ransom money from the Daltons, he tells her: "They think the Reds is doing it. They won't think *we* did. They don't think we got enough guts to do it. They think niggers is too scared. . . ." Even well-meaning people like Mr. and Mrs. Dalton are blind to the sufferings of Negroes. Believing that acts of charity can somehow miraculously banish in Negroes feelings of shame, fear, and suspicion, the Daltons lavish millions of dollars on Negro colleges and welfare organizations—while at the same time they continue to support the rigid caste system that is responsible for the Negroes' degradation in the first place. Mrs. Dalton's blindness is symbolic of the blindness of the white liberal philanthropic community.

Finally, the Communists, Mary, Jan, and Max, are just as blind to the humanity of Negroes as the others—even though they presumably want to enlist Negroes as equals in their own cause. For Mary and Jan, Bigger is an abstraction—a symbol of exploitation rather than someone whose feelings they have ever really tried to understand. Although he does not know it, this is really the reason Bigger hates them. Even when Mary concedes her blindness she has no idea how condescending her statements sound:

> "You know, Bigger, I've long wanted to go into those houses," she said, pointing to the tall, dark apartment buildings looming to either side of them, "and just *see* how your people live. You know what I mean? I've been to England, France and Mexico, but I don't know how people live ten blocks from me. We know so *little* about each other. I just want to *see*. I want to *know* these people. Never in my life have I been inside of a Negro home. Yet they *must* live like we live. They're human. . . . There are twelve million of them. . . . They live in our country. . . . In the same city with us. . . ." her voice trailed off wistfully.

In the final analysis, *Native Son* stands on shifting artistic grounds. Had Wright only managed to affix a different ending, more in accord with the character of Bigger and the philosophical viewpoint he seeks to embody, the novel might have emerged a minor masterpiece. Yet, for all its faults, *Native Son* retains surprising power. The reasons are still not clearly understood, even by present-day critics.

It is not simply that the "Negro problem" has once more intruded itself onto the national consciousness, if not the national conscience—although "sociology" should certainly not be discounted as an important factor. Nor is it merely the sensational nature of the crimes Bigger committed, compounded as they were with racial and sexual overtones. In part, of course, it is the terrible excitement, the excruciating suspense of flight and pursuit that Wright invests in his best prose. In part, too, it is the shock of unembellished hatred in Wright's portrayal of a seemingly nondescript, apathetic Negro boy.

James Baldwin, writing of *Native Son,* says every Negro carries about within him a Bigger Thomas—but that the characterization by itself is unfair in that there are complexities, depths to the Negro psychology and life, that Wright has left unexplored. To depict Bigger exclusively in terms of unsullied rage and hatred is to do the Negro a disservice. In Baldwin's view, Bigger is a "monster."

This, of course, is precisely the point Wright wishes to make—and herein lies its most terrible truth for the reader. Wright is obviously not describing the "representative" Negro—although he makes clear that what has happened to Bigger can more easily befall Negroes than whites. He is describing a person so alienated from traditional values, restraints, and civilized modes of behavior, that he feels free to construct his own ethics—that for him an act of murder is an act of creation.

But can such a person exist? Yes, if his actual experiences contradict the interpretations that civilization ordinarily puts on human action. Although Bigger dreams the American dreams, he knows he can never realize them because he is a Negro. If the civilization rejects him out of hand, he will reject the traditional and acceptable means and values for achieving the rewards that civilization has to offer. This is not a conscious rationalizing process on the part of Bigger—it is almost second nature. How else can he do more than survive? Such "monsters," as Baldwin calls them, exist. Our tabloids could not exist without them. But even supposing they do not commit murder, their sense of isolation and alienation is growing in the face of an increasingly impersonal mass society. And in mass, the isolated, the alienated, are capable of consent or indifference to napalm bombs, nuclear holocaust, or extermination camps.

It is perhaps in this respect that *Native Son* is so much more disturbing today than when it was first published. It is not that Bigger Thomas is so different from us; it is that he is so much like us.

Edward A. Watson

BESSIE'S BLUES

Although *Native Son* encompasses a multifaceted attack on almost every American cultural stereotype, from the impersonality of the big-business machinery of ghetto real-estate to frenetic cross-burning Klansmen, from the blind altruism of the millionaire philanthropic "liberal" to the knife-wielding darkie, no reference is made to jazz or jazz-oriented music throughout the entire novel. Once, during Bigger's self-searching conversation with Boris Max in the Cook County Jail, where he tries to explain the very tenuous nature of his early church affiliation, is some mention made of the Negro's escape into music:

> "Did you ever go to church, Bigger?"
> "Yeah; when I was little. But that was a long time ago."
> "Your folks were religious?"
> "Yeah; they went to church all the time."
> "Why did you stop going?"
> "I didn't like it. There was nothing in it. As, all they did was sing and shout and pray all the time. And it didn't get 'em nothing. All the colored folks do that, but it don't get 'em nothing. The white folks got everything" (*Native Son*, Harper and Row, Paperback edition, p. 329).

On two other occasions Wright mentions music or singing: when he returns home to get his gun on the first day, Bigger hears his mother singing: "Lord, I want to be a Christian,/ In my heart, in my heart...." And at Ernie's Kitchen Shack, "Somebody put a nickel in an automatic phonograph and they listened to the music."

The lack of reference to music, dancing, inherent rhythm, and the hand-clapping soul-searing hymn-singing of the Negro seems odd in a book of the calibre of *Native Son* which explores and explodes all of the stereotypes of the Negro held by white America. However, it seems that Wright achieved a subtle yet

From *New Letters* 38, No. 2 (Winter 1971): 64–70.

powerful imaginative success through Bessie Mears, Bigger's girl, whose speech and life-style embodies in no simple way the spirit of the *blues.*

Unlike Mrs. Thomas, whose medium of escape from the trials of life is religion, Bessie's anodyne is alcohol and sex. Except that she is Bigger's girl, there is nothing special about Bessie: she works as a maid in a white neighborhood, is easily coaxed into compromises by the scent of money, loves her "no-good" man, and delights in the passionate euphoria of sex. Nevertheless, when she speaks, there always emerges that incredulous, searching pessimism of the forlorn heroine whom the *blues* apotheosizes. Her two plaintive "songs" on pages 169–170 and 215–216 are, in my estimation, literary variations on the extemporaneous blues shout.

The first speech which Bessie "sings" immediately after Bigger confesses to having murdered Mary Dalton is fraught with the despair, fear, and pain of the lost lover implicated in guilt by association:

> "Bigger, please! Don't do this to me! *Please!* All I do is work, work like a dog! From morning till night. I ain't got no happiness. I ain't never had none. I ain't got nothing and you do this to me. After how good I been to you. Now you just spoil my whole life. I've done everything for you I know how and you do this to me. *Please,* Bigger. . . ." She turned her head away and stared at the floor. "Lord, don't let this happen to me! I ain't done nothing for this to come to me! I just work! I ain't had no happiness, no nothing. I just work. I'm black and I work and don't bother nobody. . . ."

Clearly, Bessie's blues are an extension of the earthly complaint in the tradition of Ma Rainey and Bessie Smith. The elements of jazz lyrics prior to 1930 were more cynical and distrusting, and specifically condemned those motivated by self-interest—usually, the hard-hearted lover (male or female)—who ran roughshod over the less fortunate partner. In this respect, Wright probably looked back to Bessie Smith and Ma Rainey rather than to Billie Holiday who, singing between 1936 and 1939, came more directly under the influence of the optimistic lyricism of Tin Pan Alley. The gulf between "Sing Sing Blues," "Sinful Blues," and "Bleeding Hearted Blues" (Bessie Smith) and "A Sailboat in the Moonlight," "The Man I Love" and "Yesterdays"—("Yesterdays, Yesterdays, / Days I knew as happy, sweet, sequestered days, / Olden days, golden days, / Days of mad romance and love") by Billie Holiday, is rather extreme and points to a decreasing emphasis of the elements of fear, pain and brutality of the earlier blues. Wright, of course, was concerned with exactly that fear, pain, and brutality which is the logical consequence of the dehumanization of the black man. Hence, Bessie's *blues* is a poignant reminder of the suffering woman caught up in a web of uncontrollable destructive forces.

With something akin to both editorial and poetic license, I have attempted to reconstruct Bessie's first speech into a medium which, more or less, approximates the more traditional and extemporaneous blues voice:

BESSIE'S BLUES #1

[Lover,] please! Don't do this to me! Please!
All I do is work, work like a dog!
From morning till night.
I ain't got no happiness, I ain't never had none,
I ain't got nothing and you do this to me
After how good I been to you.

Now you just spoil my whole life
[And] I've done everything for you I know how,
And you do this to me;
Please, [Lover] . . .
[I ain't done nothing for this to come to me.]

Lord [up above], don't let this happen to me!
['Cause] I ain't done nothing for this to come to me!
I just work, [work like a dog];
I ain't had no happiness, no nothing
[And I ain't never had none],
I just work, [work like a dog];
[For] I'm black and I work and don't bother nobody.
[Lord up above, don't let this happen to me,
Lord up above, don't let this happen to me. . . .]

All the traditional elements are here: hard-hearted lover, lack of worldly
goods, lack of happiness, hard work, comparison to a dog, the "sin" of blackness,
docility, and the appeal to God. Bessie's first *blues* is conditioned by both fear and
despair and results in an aching consciousness summing up the brutal experience of
her life.

The second speech which appears on pages 215 and 216 is much longer than
the first and adds two additional dimensions to the first *blues:* flight from justice
(which, in *Native Son* is synonymous with death) and recognition of fate. Bessie
speaks:

"Oh Lord," she moaned. "What's the use of running? They'll catch us
anywhere. I should've known this would happen." She clenched her hands in
front of her and rocked to and fro with her eyes closed upon gushing tears.
"All my life's been full of hard trouble. If I wasn't hungry, I was sick. And if I
wasn't sick, I was in trouble. I ain't never bothered nobody. I just worked hard
every day as long as I can remember, till I was tired enough to drop; then I had
to get drunk to forget it. I had to get drunk to sleep. That's all I ever did. And
now I'm in this. They looking for me and when they catch me they'll kill me."
She bent her head to the floor. "God only knows why I ever let you treat me
this way. I wish to God I never seen you. I wish one of us had died before we
was born. God knows I do! All you ever caused me was trouble. . . . All you

ever did since we been knowing each other was to get me drunk so's you could have me. That was all! I see it now. I ain't drunk now. I see everything you ever did to me. I didn't want to see it before. I was too busy thinking about how good I felt when I was with you. I thought I was happy, but deep down in me I knew I wasn't. But you got me into this murder and I see it all now. I been a fool, just a blind dumb black drunk fool. Now I got to run away and I know deep down in your heart you really don't care."

This speech is more intense and revealing than the first, and, in keeping with traditional blues, reveals a pathetic autobiography which is flashed across the screen, as it were, in a moment of personal catastrophe. Here, nothing is tragic; there is no resolution. Bessie's confession is a confession of failure, and she has no hope of conquering life since she has not really lived.

For purposes of upholding the structural divisions of the novel, I have divided this second speech into two *blues,* the first of which contemplates the inevitability of death despite attempts to flee (Flight), and the second, the fateful consequences of Bessie's association with her hard-hearted lover (Fate). Thus, the three songs which Bessie sings correspond with, and form a counterpoint to the three divisions of the book—Fear, Flight, Fate. Admittedly, I have forced the speeches to fit a pre-established structural pattern; nevertheless, the point to be made is that the "songs" treat characteristic blues themes which fall naturally under the three divisions of the book. Again, with some license, I have *constructed* Bessie's Blues #2:

Oh, Lord, what's the use of running?
They'll catch us anywhere;
I should've known this would happen.
                    (Repeat)

All my life's been full of hard trouble:
If I wasn't hungry, I was sick
And if I wasn't sick, I was in trouble.
I ain't never bothered nobody,
I just worked hard every day
(As long as I can remember)
Till I was tired enough to drop.
Then I had to get drunk to forget it,
I had to get drunk to sleep;
That's all I ever did

And now I'm in this.
They looking for me
And when they catch me they'll kill me.

[Oh, Lord, what's the use of running
Oh, Lord, what's the use of running. . . .]

Bessie's anguish is not directed to Bigger but to an inscrutable God who Bigger, at a later moment, believes is capable of creating an "obscene joke" on the black man. Bessie's confession is to an implacable God and she senses doom with the extreme conviction of the pessimist. Part of the *pathos* of the *blues* is its recurring sense of doom. The speaker always recognizes the conflict between life and death but is powerless to guide the self into any alternate condition which even vaguely suggests a promise of Life. In short, the *blues* is a futile gasp in time, a perpetual and unredeeming sorrow. (The current practice of singing *spirituals* with the intonations and tonalities of the *blues* is an attempt, conscious or unconscious, to fuse two philosophically incompatible complaints.) This sense of futility is carried over into the third song where Bessie sees the culmination of her life etched in sharp strokes of blackness:

BESSIE'S BLUES #3

God only knows why I ever let you treat me this way;
I wish to God I had never seen you.
I wish one of us had died before we was born
God knows I do.

All you ever caused me was trouble
Just plain black trouble;
All you ever did since we been knowing each other
Was to get me drunk so's you could have me.
That was all; I see it now. . . .

But I ain't drunk now,
I see everything you ever did to me;
I didn't want to see it before
['Cause] I was busy thinking
How good I felt when I was with you.

I thought I was happy
But deep down in me, I knew I wasn't
But you got me in this [thing] murder,
[And I see it all now].

I been a fool,
Just a blind dumb black drunk fool
Now I got to run away and I know
Deep down in your heart
You really don't care.

[I see it now,
I see it all now,
God knows I do
'Cause deep down in your heart
You really don't care.]

Bessie's recognition of her plight must be seen as the final step to oblivion from the release of her meaningless life. Her life has been spent in toil, an unrelenting pain which is only momentarily relieved by drink. Even sex, we now discover, had no real meaning for her. (This fact is further substantiated when Bigger rapes her before he kills her.) Now, when she recognizes that the man she loves "really don't care," life is over for her, and the *blues* is her testimony that she paid her dues. Bessie's song recalls all of the forlorn sentiments of the blues singer, and her wailing is the private anguish of the self as scapegoat.

There is some possibility that Wright avoided the explicit in depicting the *blues* because he recognized it as the subtle art it is. And since *Native Son* treated all the prejudices, stereotypes and cultural prejudgments as art, it seems only fitting that Wright should have treated the blues as a very sensitive and vibrant art form. In this sense, *Native Son* is one extended blues the spirit of which is particularized in Bessie. Wright chose Bessie, perhaps because of another soulful Bessie, and, perhaps, because she was the only black woman in the novel who could sing of broken hearts and broken dreams, of Fear and Flight and Fate; of a life full of "just plain black trouble."

Keneth Kinnamon

NATIVE SON

The structure of *Native Son* is a simple one, indicated in its broad outline by the titles Wright gave to the three parts of the novel—"Fear," "Flight," and "Fate." It is Bigger's fear that precipitates the chain of events leading to his inevitable fate. In a sense, the narrative action can be considered the externalization of Bigger's psychic instability, itself the result of his racial status. Living with his mother and younger brother and sister in a sordid, one-room "kitchenette" apartment in a South Side slum during the Depression, Bigger recognizes his own propensity for violence very early in Book One: "He knew that the moment he allowed himself to feel to its fullness how they lived, the shame and misery of their lives, he would be swept out of himself with fear and despair. . . . He knew that the moment he allowed what his life meant to enter fully into his consciousness, he would either kill himself or someone else." Shortly afterward when he is talking to Gus, he expresses this same sense of foreboding: " 'Sometimes I feel like something awful's going to happen to me. . . . Naw; it ain't like something going to happen to me. It's . . . It's like I was going to do something I can't help. . . .' "[1] This feeling of inevitability not only affirms the determinism of Wright's naturalistic and Marxist vision, but also increases the coherence and tension of the novel.

The chief device employed to create a sense of fate is a careful foreshadowing of subsequent events. In the opening scene in the Thomas flat, Bigger kills a terrified black rat that ceases its flight and turns desperately on its antagonists when all avenues of escape are closed. This scene prefigures Bigger's own fate. When Bigger takes his girl friend, Bessie Mears, to the deserted building where she is to wait for the ransom money, "something with dry whispering feet flitted across his path, emitting as the rush of its flight died a thin, piping wail of lonely *fear*." Another rat appears when they enter another building as they flee from Bigger's fate. Bigger encounters still another one as he is searching for a vacant apartment in which to

From *The Emergence of Richard Wright: A Study in Literature and Society* (Urbana: University of Illinois Press, 1972), pp. 126–143.

hide. The final "rat," of course, is Bigger himself, who likewise fights his pursuers when further flight is hopeless. Rats contribute to the naturalistic verisimilitude of the South Side setting, but more important, they forecast Bigger's fate and help tighten the coherence of the work. When Bigger attends the movies with Jack, he sees a film entitled *The Gay Woman,* which depicts the life of the leisure class. The thoughts stimulated in Bigger by this film foreshadow, rather too accurately for plausibility, what is to happen a few hours later: "Maybe Mr. Dalton was a million-aire. Maybe he had a daughter who was a hot kind of girl; maybe she spent lots of money; maybe she'd like to come to the South Side and see the sights sometimes. Or maybe she had a secret sweetheart and only he would know about it because he would have to drive her around; maybe she would give him money not to tell." Still another example of the same device is Bigger's response to Bessie's first suspicion that something has happened to Mary Dalton: "He stiffened with fear. He felt suddenly that he wanted something in his hand, something solid and heavy: his gun, a knife, a *brick.*"[2] It is with a brick, of course, that he later bashes in Bessie's head.

In addition to such prefiguring of subsequent events, Wright increases the cohesion of the novel by repetition of key phrases. One of Bigger's most typical reactions to adverse circumstances is a desire to "blot out" whatever offends him: "He wanted to wave his hand and blot out the white man who was making him feel like this."[3] The phrase "blot out" occurs at least eight times in the novel. When moments of extreme fear drive him to the point of violence, he sees or recalls a real (Mrs. Dalton) or imaginary "white blur"[4] approaching him. Such repetition helps to relate one event or scene to another through the medium of Bigger's sensibility, and thus concentrates and unifies the effect of the action on the reader.

This concentrated emotional tension also inheres in the rapid movement of events in the short time span of the first part of the plot. Books One and Two take place in a period of some sixty hours, from the battle with the rat in the Thomas flat on Saturday morning to the capture of Bigger late Monday night. The reader's attention, furthermore, focuses constantly on the developing action; there are no flashbacks to interrupt the relentless forward momentum of the narrative.

The first two parts of *Native Son,* then, form a tight fictional structure created by the rapid pace of the narrative, a brief time span, the focus on Bigger's actions and reactions, the repetition of key phrases, and the foreshadowing of subsequent events in the plot. The tension relaxes and the pace slows in Book Three as the center of emphasis shifts somewhat from Bigger the individual to Bigger the social symbol. In contrast to his earlier frenzy, Bigger is now passive, withdrawn, almost catatonic. The action of Book Three, Bigger's imprisonment and trial, is analytical, verbal, and psychological, not dramatic, physical, and psychological as in Books One and Two. Kenneth Burke used the terms "imagistic" and "conceptual" in describing the novel before and after Bigger's capture.[5] The central question of Book Three is whether Bigger can be reached by anyone, whether he can derive some meaning from his nightmarish experiences. To the extent that he is representative of black people in America, this question of the meaning of his individual "fate" relates to the polemic intent of the novel as a whole, which is concerned with the collective racial situation and destiny of American blacks. If the account of Bigger's imprisonment and trial seems pallid after the earlier action, the reader should remember that Wright's intention was not merely to write gripping melodrama but to confront in his fiction the meaning, as well as to express the agony, of black experience in America. To do so he found it necessary to speak through Boris Max, a more sophisticated mouthpiece than Bigger could possibly be. To the objection that the meaning of the novel should have been embodied in the main action, one may reply that it is; the final section, though perhaps too static and essayistic, recapitulates explicitly the implicit meaning of Books One and Two.

"But always, from the start to the finish," Wright explains in How "Bigger" Was Born, "it was Bigger's story, Bigger's fear, Bigger's flight, and Bigger's fate that I tried to depict. I wrote with the conviction in mind . . . that the main burden of all serious fiction consists almost wholly of character-destiny and the items, social, political, and personal, of that character-destiny."[6] To a quite remarkable degree, Native Son is Bigger's book; it is difficult to recall another modern American novel that focuses so sharply on the mind and emotions of its protagonist and that at the same time analyzes so carefully the "social, political, and personal" soil out of which they grew.

The emotional complex of Bigger's personality comprises fear, shame, and hatred as its primary elements. His name, suggesting "nigger" or "big nigger,"[7] indicates the origin of his fear, which is created by racial oppression from a white world so vast and powerful that he is helpless before it. His consciousness of his fear creates a sense of shame at his own inadequacy, equated by whites with his racial status. The combination of this fear and shame produces hatred, both self-hatred and hatred for the inequities of his life and the whites responsible for those inequities and his consequent humiliation. Unable to cope with his dilemma in any rational way, he can respond only by withdrawal or by aggression, by brooding or by violence: "These were the rhythms of his life: indifference and violence; periods of abstract brooding and periods of intense desire; moments of silence and moments of anger. . . ."[8]

Bigger's emotional pattern precludes any viable human relationship. He is profoundly alone. His father was killed in racial strife when Bigger was a small child. Toward his remaining family, Mrs. Thomas, Vera, and Buddy, he feels hatred "because he knew that they were suffering and that he was powerless to help them."[9] His conflict with his mother is intensified because of her nagging and because her religious resignation contrasts sharply with his own rebellious instincts. With Vera he is constantly bickering. Only his younger brother, Buddy, can evoke some feeling of tenderness, but even he is not entirely exempt from Bigger's surge of murderous fear and rage when he finds Mary's money that Bigger has dropped on the floor of the Thomas flat.

Nor does Bigger find friendship or love with his companions or his mistress.

With Gus he can articulate his bitter frustration in a racist society, but he can also a few hours later vent that frustration on his "friend" with furious violence. Bessie is, as Max points out at the trial, merely a means of sexual release. Her life, as well as Bigger's, is too blighted for their relationship to develop any further dimension. When it seems necessary, Bigger crushes her skull and disposes of her body, as if it were nothing more than an object, by throwing it down an air shaft. Such are his relations with other blacks.

His relations with whites are of course even more distant and fearful. He at least partially understands other blacks, however alienated from them, but white people are strange as well as threatening, and at the same time enticing. They represent to Bigger a world both fascinating and forbidden, a world of power and wealth but also of cruelty and danger. Bigger and his companions have committed numerous crimes against blacks, but robbing a white delicatessen is quite a different matter: "They had the feeling that the robbing of Blum's would be a violation of ultimate taboo; it would be trespassing into territory where the full wrath of an alien white world would be turned loose upon them; in short, it would be a symbolic challenge of the white world's rule over them; a challenge which they yearned to make, but were afraid to." At the Dalton house Bigger replies to his white interlocutors in monosyllables; communication across the racial barrier is almost impossible. Bigger's reactions to whites, it should be emphasized, are determined more by the total configuration of his crippled personality than by the specific circumstances of his encounters with them or by their actual attitudes toward him. He is so conditioned by the racial situation that he cannot respond to individual whites as separate persons, but only as abstract embodiments of white power—"that white looming mountain of hate."[10] In Book One of *Native Son* white people are kind to Bigger. Mr. and Mrs. Dalton hope to improve the economic condition of Bigger and his family. Mary and Jan offer him, however awkwardly, egalitarian friendship and political enlightenment. Even the Daltons' Irish maid, Peggy, gives him good food, kindness, and, in her own way, understanding.[11] But to all of these well-meant advances Bigger responds with his familiar emotional pattern of fear, shame, and hatred, just as he does later to the overt hostility of whites like Britten and Buckley. Eventually Jan and Boris Max are able to elicit from Bigger some dawning sense of his solidarity with oppressed whites. Their personal goodwill is so persistent, too, that it finally begins to melt Bigger's hostility. But their success in these efforts in Book Three has seemed to many readers, including this one, rather too contrived.

In order to achieve such an intense realization of Bigger's character, Wright has written, it was necessary to restrict point of view in the novel "to what Bigger saw and felt, to the limits of his feeling and thoughts, even when I was conveying *more* than that to the reader."[12] Wright was not entirely consistent in carrying out this limitation, which does not take the form of first-person narrative, but it does account for an important difference in the characterization of other persons in the novel. The depiction of blacks, whom Bigger understands, is sharp and realistic. The depiction of whites, whom Bigger cannot fathom, is deliberately vague and one-dimensional, for his perception of them is imperfect: they are all, in a sense, "white blurs" to his vision.

The members of Bigger's family are vividly particularized. Mrs. Thomas toils and worries to keep her family together, but in her submissiveness and blind, compensatory piety she is quite unable to understand Bigger's rebellious spirit. Vera is a nervous and self-conscious adolescent. Buddy sides with his elder brother, but he is still too young to muster enough courage to rebel, like Bigger, against his mother's values. Bessie too is a thoroughly convincing character. Her monotonous days of toil in the kitchens of white people are relieved only by the few hours of alcohol and sex that she seizes when she can. The aimlessness of her life makes her helpless before the hard concentration of Bigger's purpose:

> "Bigger, please! Don't do this to me! *Please!* All I do is work, work like a dog! From morning till night. I ain't got no happiness. I ain't never had none. I ain't got nothing and you do this to me. After how good I been to you. Now you just spoil my whole life. I've done everything for you I know how and you do this to me. *Please,* Bigger. . . ." She turned her head away and stared at the floor. "Lord, don't let this happen to me!. . . I just work! I ain't had no happiness, no nothing. I just work. I'm black and I work and don't bother nobody. . . ."[13]

Her plea is a valid one, but it does not move either Bigger or the Lord.

Even the minor black characters in *Native Son* are sketched vividly. Gus, G.H., and Jack are primarily foils to Bigger, but the quality of their life is imparted to the reader with economic precision. The corpulent poolroom-owner, Doc, "who held a half-smoked, unlit cigar in his mouth and leaned on the front counter,"[14] is roused from boredom to lazy mirth by Bigger's sadistic assault on Gus, but then flies into a rage when Bigger cuts the felt cloth on a pool table. Reverend Hammond, pitiable in the helpless sincerity of his religious convictions, is also memorable, as is the crazed university student in Bigger's cellblock.

The white characters in *Native Son,* on the other hand, are vague stereotypes, for our sense of them is filtered through Bigger's sensibility. Mr. Dalton is a South Side slumlord who fails to recognize the inconsistency and futility of his philanthropic activities on behalf of blacks. The blind Mrs. Dalton is so vague as a person, in her flowing white clothes and accompanied by her white cat, that she operates almost wholly as a symbol. Mary Dalton is sophomoric in her parlor radicalism. Her thoughtless efforts toward camaraderie with Bigger induce terror rather than trust. Such overt racists as Britten, the Daltons' private detective, and State's Attorney Buckley, of course, are simply typical spokesmen for the pervasive white hatred that is responsible for Bigger's plight. Bigger sees both of these men as official representatives of the dominant white society, instinctively recognizing their hostility. The reader, too, sees them solely in this role.

The case of two other white characters, Jan Erlone and Boris Max, is somewhat different. Wright obviously wished to present these Communists favorably. If Jan's goodwill is expressed in a bumbling and insensitive manner in his initial approach to Bigger, he more than compensates for this mistake by his heroic support of Bigger after Mary's death. Jan's nobility, indeed, is too pure to be entirely credible. The point is not that Jan's attitude is unmotivated, for such a devout Communist would be fully capable of suppressing personal grief for a higher ideological cause. The difficulty is rather that we are given hardly a glimpse of the inner conflict, so fraught with opportunities for emotional dishonesty, that would issue in such a decision as Jan's. The reason, again, is that we know Jan primarily through Bigger, but whereas white foolishness or malice may be so presented, white sacrificial love—given the general emotional tone of the novel—cannot be. The accord and fraternity which Jan and Bigger achieve is not emotionally convincing, though it may be ideologically necessary. Insofar as attorney Max is a person in the novel, he serves as a kindly father surrogate to Bigger. Clearly his main function, however, is that of authorial mouthpiece. But as shown below, even as sympathetic and knowledgeable a white man as Max at last shrinks from the final truth about Bigger Thomas.

Characterization in *Native Son,* then, is sharply vivid for the black characters, vague and one-dimensional for the rather stereotyped whites. The reason for this difference, which is an artistic achievement rather than a liability, is the restriction of point of view mainly to Bigger. One may argue, of course, that Wright was simply incapable of the imaginative projection necessary for the creation of rounded white characters, but that is to ignore the necessary concentration on Bigger's sensibility. Furthermore, in such later works as *The Outsider, Savage Holiday,* and *The Long Dream,* Wright was to show his ability to present convincing white characters in fiction.

Characterization, action, and overt statement convey most of the meaning of *Native Son,* but Wright's naturalism is by no means so thorough as to preclude the use of symbols to enrich that meaning. The opening scene of the rat at bay, as has been noted, foreshadows symbolically Bigger's own destiny. His aspirations, fed by an American social system that both stimulates them and denies the opportunities for their fulfillment, soar to the heavens. Early in the novel Bigger gazes longingly at a skywriting airplane:

> "Looks like a little bird," Bigger breathed with childlike wonder.
> "Them white boys sure can fly," Gus said. . . .
> "I could fly one of them things if I had a chance," Bigger mumbled reflectively, as though talking to himself. . . .
> "If you wasn't black and if you had some money and if they'd let you go to that aviation school, you *could* fly a plane," Gus said.[15]

Instead, white society consigns him to the hell of the Dalton basement to maintain the glowing, searing, fiery furnace. Like Big Boy in his kiln, like the protagonist of "The Man Who Lived Underground," and like Wright himself in the subterranean corridors of the Chicago hospital where he once worked, Bigger is an underground man. The nearest he comes to the heights, ironically, is his ascent of the water tank on the tenement roof, but the white mob quickly brings him down.

The color white in *Native Son,* as is often the case in Wright's fiction, acquires a symbolic dimension. In the first place, the word itself is used with a frequency that goes far beyond the requirements of denotation. In several senses Bigger sees his world in black and white. Mrs. Dalton's whiteness haunts him. Upon first seeing her, he notices that "her face and hair were completely white; she seemed to him like a ghost." Three hours later Bigger goes to the kitchen for a drink of water: "What he saw made him suck his breath in; Mrs. Dalton in flowing white clothes was standing stone-still in the middle of the kitchen floor." He next sees her at the door of her daughter's bedroom: "A white blur was standing by the door, silent, ghostlike."[16] As this "awesome white blur" floats toward the bed, Bigger's fear increases and his fingers press down on the pillow over Mary's face. This same feeling of fear returns to Bigger at each subsequent meeting with Mrs. Dalton. Frequently accompanying Mrs. Dalton is her white cat, which becomes Wright's equivalent to Poe's black one as a symbol of guilt and fear. As Bigger struggles to force Mary's body into the furnace, "A noise made him whirl; two green burning pools—pools of accusation and guilt—stared at him from a white blur that sat perched upon the edge of the trunk. His mouth opened in a silent scream and his body became hotly paralyzed. It was the white cat and its round green eyes gazed past him at the white face hanging limply from the fiery furnace door."[17] Later when Bigger is in the basement with the reporters, the white cat leaps to his shoulder and perches there like a demon of doom.

Wright's use of Mrs. Dalton and her white cat is rather too self-consciously Gothic. More effective is his equation of white power with elemental forces of nature. As Max explains at the trial, blacks vis-à-vis whites in America do not feel " 'that they are facing other men, they feel that they are facing mountains, floods, seas: forces of nature whose size and strength focus the minds and emotions to a degree of tension unusual in the quiet routine of urban life.' " Bigger's image of the alien world is "that white looming mountain of hate."[18] The most persistent symbol of white hostility, however, is snow. Snow clouds are first seen, ominously, when Jan and Mary force the unwilling Bigger to ride in the front seat of the Dalton automobile with them. Later that night as Bigger leaves the Dalton basement, the first flakes are beginning to fall. In Book Two the snow becomes all-pervasive as the blizzard increases its intensity. For Bigger it falls with the relentlessness of his fate: "Around him were silence and night and snow falling, falling as though it had fallen from the beginning of time and would always fall till the end of the world." Book Two ends as Bigger sinks into the ubiquitous, enveloping, suffocating white snow, overwhelmed and mastered by the power of whiteness: "Two men stretched his arms out, as though about to crucify him; they placed a foot on each of his wrists, making them sink deep down in the snow. His eyes closed, slowly, and he was swallowed in darkness."[19]

The Crucifixion image is emphatic in this final passage of Book Two, and this is not the only place in the novel in which Bigger assumes that role familiar in American literature generally and even more common in Afro-American writing—the Christ figure. In his suffering, Bigger is a black Christ crucified by white America. At the trial Buckley manipulates the sexual phobias of the white judge by speculating that the burning of Mary's body must have been motivated by Bigger's need to destroy the evidence of his bestiality: " 'That treacherous beast must have known that if the marks of his teeth were ever seen on the innocent white flesh of her breasts, he would not have been accorded the high honor of sitting here in this court of law! O suffering Christ, there are no words to tell of a deed so black and awful!' " By appealing to the lynch spirit of the judge, Buckley is actually placing Bigger, "that treacherous beast," in the role of "suffering Christ," as the mob burning the fiery cross had done before. At one point, when his family and companions visit him in his cell, Bigger even feels that his suffering has redemptive power: "Bigger felt a wild and outlandish conviction surge in him: *They ought to be glad!* It was a strange but strong feeling, springing from the very depths of his life. Had he not taken fully upon himself the crime of being black? Had he not done the thing which they dreaded above all others? Then they ought not stand here and pity him, cry over him; but look at him and go home, contented, feeling that their shame was washed away."[20]

There is considerable irony in Wright's use of religious language and symbolism, however, for Bigger rejects totally the consolations of Christianity. When he sneaks into his flat to get his pistol to prepare for robbing Blum's delicatessen, his mother is singing a hymn: "*Lord, I want to be a Christian, / In my heart, in my heart.*" But his mother's religion is wholly ineffective in this world; it does nothing to forestall his violence. When Bigger is hiding in an empty apartment, he hears singing from a small church. The mood of security and resignation that it induces in the worshipers is not without appeal to Bigger, but he cannot accept the surrender, the acquiescence, that religion represents: "Would it not have been better for him had he lived in that world the music sang of? It would have been easy to have lived in it, for it was his mother's world, humble, contrite, believing. It had a center, a core, an axis, a heart which he needed but could never have unless he laid his head upon a pillow of humility and gave up his hope of living in the world. And he would never do that." [21] After his capture he ignores the humble Reverend Hammond and his wooden crucifix. A more militant kind of religion is represented by the Ku Klux Klan's fiery cross on top of the building near the Dalton home. The function of Christianity, Wright is implying, is to serve as an opiate of the black masses and to lynch those who will not be lulled into oblivion of their condition. After seeing the flaming cross, Bigger rejects violently, not merely passively, the wooden crucifix, Reverend Hammond, and later a Catholic priest.

Instead of religious acquiescence, Bigger chooses rebellion as his way of life. The theme of rebellion is the central meaning of *Native Son,* which the particulars of Wright's craft—structure, characterization, and symbolism—are designed to express. In his rebellion, alienation, anguish, and isolation, Bigger is as much an existential hero as Cross Damon, the protagonist of Wright's next novel, *The Outsider* (1953).[22] Bigger rebels against religion, against his family, against his companions and black life in general, and against the white society that oppresses him. The two most important specific forms that this rebellion takes are rape and murder, crimes of which Bigger both is and is not guilty.

The strongest of all racial taboos, of course, is the sexual. Bigger's feelings toward Mary Dalton are deeply ambivalent, his fear and hatred combining with an attraction to her. She in turn is fascinated by him, by the unknown and, she believes, passional race to which he belongs. Bigger is Othello to Mary's Desdemona, and Buckley is a treacherous Iago.[23] Though Bigger does not actually rape Mary, he is on the point of doing so when Mrs. Dalton appears. When Max questions him on this point, he analyzes his feelings with accuracy:

> "Yeah; I reckon it was because I knew I oughtn't've wanted to. I reckon it was because they say we black men do that anyhow. Mr. Max, you know what some white men say we black men do? They say we rape white women when we got the clap and they say we do that because we believe that if we rape white women then we'll get rid of the clap. That's what some white men *say*. They *believe* that. Jesus, Mr. Max, when folks says things like that about you, you whipped before you born. What's the use? Yeah; I reckon I was feeling that way when I was in the room with her. They say we do things like that and they say it to kill us. They draw a line and say for you to stay on your side of the line. They don't care if there's no bread over on your side. They don't care if you die. And then they say things like that about you and when you try to come from behind your line they kill you. They feel they ought to kill you then. Everybody wants to kill you then. Yeah; I reckon I was feeling that way and maybe the reason was because they say it. Maybe that was the reason."

The taboo stimulates the attraction, so that sexual contact with white women becomes a form of defiance, of rebellion against the white creators of the taboo. To enforce the taboo, white society must punish the violators. Buckley recognizes this duty when he shifts the emphasis in his final plea at the trial from murder to rape: " 'He planned to rape, to kill, to collect! He burned the body to get rid of evidence of *rape!* He took the trunk to the station to gain time in which to burn the body and prepare the kidnap note. He killed her because he *raped* her! Mind you, Your Honor, the central crime here is *rape!* Every action points toward that!' "[24] The almost intolerably ironic truth is that although he intends coitus with the unconscious white Mary, he does not perform it; but he does possess the unwilling black Bessie on the cold floor of the abandoned building. Further, his killing of Mary is an accident; his murder of Bessie is deliberate.[25]

Mary's death is an "accident," but at the same time it is not. Like George Hurstwood before the door of the safe and Clyde Griffiths in the rowboat, Bigger

Thomas by the bed is in a situation and frame of mind in which the notion of volition becomes highly ambiguous. As Max explains in court, Bigger's entire personality is rebellious to a murderous degree:

> "This Negro boy's entire attitude toward life is a *crime!* The hate and fear which we have inspired in him, woven by our civilization into the very structure of his consciousness, into his blood and bones, into the hourly functioning of his personality, have become the justification of his existence.
>
> "Every time he comes in contact with us, he kills! It is a physiological and psychological reaction, embedded in his being. Every thought he thinks is potential murder. Excluded from, and unassimilated in our society, yet longing to gratify impulses akin to our own but denied the objects and channels evolved through long centuries for their socialized expression, every sunrise and sunset make him guilty of subversive actions. Every movement of his body is an unconscious protest. Every desire, every dream, no matter how intimate or personal, is a plot or a conspiracy. Every hope is a plan for insurrection. Every glance of the eye is a threat. *His very existence is a crime against the state!*"

With the death and cremation of Mary, Bigger has achieved an ultimate level of rebellion. Because of this achievement he is caught up in exhilaration, a feeling of elation, freedom, and self-mastery such as he has never known before. For him the act of murder becomes a regenerative force; out of death for Mary comes life for Bigger: "He had murdered and had created a new life for himself." Again Max, speaking for Wright, offers the correct explanation: "It was the first full act of his life; it was the most meaningful, exciting and stirring thing that had ever happened to him. He accepted it because it made him free, gave him the possibility of choice, of action, the opportunity to act and to feel that his actions carried weight."[26]

The difficulty is that such a rebellion is futile, both because of the perversion of human values that it entails and because it brings sure retribution from white society. Bigger's sense of freedom after Mary's death is delusive, for his flight actually draws him closer to his fate. The ultimate truth about Bigger Thomas, a truth from which even Max recoils in horror, emerges at the very end of *Native Son:*

> "I didn't want to kill!" Bigger shouted. "But what I killed for, I *am!* It must've been pretty deep in me to make me kill! I must have felt it awful hard to murder...."
>
> Max lifted his hand to touch Bigger, but did not.
>
> "No; no; no.... Bigger, not that...." Max pleaded despairingly.
>
> "What I killed for must've been good!" Bigger's voice was full of frenzied anguish. "It must have been good! When a man kills, it's for something.... I didn't know I was really alive in this world until I felt things hard enough to kill for 'em.... It's the truth, Mr. Max. I can say it now, 'cause I'm going to die. I

know what I'm saying real good and I know how it sounds. But I'm all right. I feel all right when I look at it that way. . . ."[27]

Insofar as Bigger is representative of black people, this is the final social meaning of the novel: white American society has so oppressed the black man that except for the narcosis of religion, the only outlet for his tortured emotions is a futile, murderous, and self-destructive rebellion; Bigger can attain a sense of life only by inflicting death.

Max, however, offers Bigger the vision of a more constructive kind of rebellion—or revolution. He tries to supplant Bigger's racial consciousness with class consciousness. Here lies the novel's most serious conceptual and artistic weakness. The point is not that Communist or other propaganda is inadmissible or even necessarily detrimental in a serious work of fiction; nor is any question of party control of art involved. If the propaganda is fully assimilated into the imaginative life of the novel, it may indeed prove a positive advantage. But this is not the case in Native Son.

The difficulty seems to be that Wright superimposed a consciously held intellectual conviction on a story that otherwise engaged his imagination and experience on the deepest emotional levels. In How "Bigger" Was Born Wright makes much of his own recognition that the Bigger Thomas type could be white as well as black. Just as the southern racial system was "but an appendage of a far vaster and in many respects more ruthless and impersonal commodity-profit machine,"[28] so Bigger Thomas was merely a local species of the genus proletariat. Max makes the same point, but Bigger never fully recognizes it. " 'But they hate black folks more than they hate unions,' "[29] Bigger says to his Marxist tutor. Though Wright thinks that he agrees with Max's rebuttal, his heart is really with Bigger's statement. In How "Bigger" Was Born he speaks of the "concrete picture"—his sense of his racial experience—and the "abstract linkages"[30]—his Communist theory. The two never completely merge in the novel, just as the understanding between Bigger and Max is never total. Max's speech to the court is an eloquent discourse, but Bigger's bitter comment to Gus at the beginning of the novel is more trenchant, more authentic, and finally more convincing: " 'Goddammit, look! We live here and they live there. We black and they white. They got things and we ain't. They do things and we can't. It's just like living in jail.' "[31]

In addition to Wright's failure to resolve fully his intellectual (Max) and his emotional (Bigger) understanding of black life, there are other, less important weaknesses in Native Son—a certain unevenness in style, the inevitable but still somewhat damaging decrease of tension in Book Three—but these fade before the undeniable total impact of the book. This power—the word was used by virtually all reviewers—that one feels in the work is partly inherent in Wright's materials and theme, but it is also created by his careful attention to his craft in the matters of structure, action, characterization, and symbolism. Native Son is a major document of the American racial dilemma, but its art makes it also an important American novel.

NOTES

[1] *Native Son* (New York, 1940), pp. 9, 17, 19.

[2] Ibid., pp. 155, 29, 123. Italics mine. It should be recalled here that the weapon used to murder Mrs. Johnson in the Nixon case was a brick.

[3] Ibid., p. 41. Cf. pp. 60, 85, 115, 119, 138, 251, 281, 282.

[4] Ibid., p. 73. Cf. pp. 74, 77, 78, 94, 200, 315.

[5] *A Grammar of Motives* (New York, 1945), p. 339.

[6] *How "Bigger" Was Born* (New York, 1940), pp. 35–36.

[7] Leslie Fiedler thinks that Bigger Thomas "is identified by his very name as a reaction to Uncle Tom. . . ." *Waiting for the End* (New York, 1964), pp. 106–7. It should be noted, though, that Wright had known a person named Biggy Thomas in Jackson. See Wright, *Letters to Joe C. Brown* (Kent, Ohio, 1968), pp. 10, 11.

[8] *Native Son*, p. 24. My analysis at this point is indebted to Horace R. Cayton, "A Psychological Approach to Race Relations," *Présence Africaine*, no. 3 (March–April 1948), pp. 418–31; no. 4 (n.d.), pp. 549–63.

[9] *Native Son*, p. 9.

[10] Ibid., pp. 12, 306. "Looming" occurs over and over in *Native Son* and other works by Wright to describe the threatening white presence.

[11] " 'My folks in the old country feel about England like the colored folks feel about this country. So I know something about colored people.' " Ibid., p. 49. It is possible that this passage looks forward to Max's emphasis in Book Three on the solidarity of the oppressed, but it seems more likely that Wright, like James Baldwin in his famous meeting with Attorney General Robert Kennedy in 1963, is here grimly aware of the qualitative difference between black and Irish suffering.

[12] *How "Bigger" Was Born*, p. 36.

[13] *Native Son*, p. 153.

[14] Ibid., p. 19.

[15] Ibid., p. 14.

[16] Ibid., pp. 40, 52, 73.

[17] Ibid., pp. 74, 78–79.

[18] Ibid., pp. 327, 306. For the use of the same image in "Bright and Morning Star," see Theodore Ward, "Five Negro Novelists: Revolt and Retreat," *Mainstream*, I (Winter 1947), 108–9.

[19] *Native Son*, pp. 157, 229. Like the end of "Bright and Morning Star," the first of these two passages is reminiscent of the final paragraph of Joyce's "The Dead." By my count, snow is mentioned exactly 101 times in the novel, all but three of these in Book Two. See pp. 59, 80, 83, 85, 87, 91, 94, 96, 97, 98 (twice), 102, 103 (twice), 106, 111, 119, 125, 126, 127, 130 (three times), 131 (twice), 140, 146 (twice), 147 (twice), 148, 151, 154 (twice), 155, 156 (twice), 157 (twice), 165 (four times), 168 (twice), 178, 187 (seven times), 188 (four times), 189 (twice), 195, 196, 204, 205 (five times), 206 (twice), 208 (twice), 209, 210, 211, 216 (twice), 217, 218, 219, 221 (three times), 222 (twice), 223, 224 (three times), 225 (three times), 226 (twice), 227, 228 (three times), 229 (three times), and 236.

[20] Ibid., pp. 344, 252.

[21] Ibid., pp. 30, 215.

[22] For an interesting, if overstated, case for Bigger as existential hero, see Esther Merle Jackson, "The American Negro and the Image of the Absurd," *Phylon*, XXIII (Fourth Quarter 1962), 359–71.

[23] For further development of the Shakespearean resemblance, see Keneth Kinnamon, "Richard Wright's Use of *Othello* in *Native Son*," *CLA Journal*, XII (June 1969), 358–59.

[24] *Native Son*, pp. 297–98, 344–45.

[25] In an early version of the first sexual scene involving Bigger and Bessie, Wright made Bigger think of Mary as he is making love to Bessie: "He placed his hands on her breasts just as he had placed them on Mary's last night and he was thinking of that while he kissed her." The reference to Mary is eliminated in the final version of this passage: "He leaned over her, full of desire, and lowered his head to hers and kissed her." *Native Son*, p. 114. For details concerning the early version of the novel, see Keneth Kinnamon, "Richard Wright Items in the Fales Collection," *Bulletin of the Society for Libraries of New York University*, no. 66 (Winter 1965).

[26] *Native Son*, pp. 335–36, 90, 333.

[27] Ibid., p. 358.

[28] *How "Bigger" Was Born*, p. 12.

[29] *Native Son*, p. 295.

[30] *How "Bigger" Was Born*, p. 13.

[31] *Native Son*, p. 17. Edward Margolies develops a similar interpretation in *The Art of Richard Wright* (Carbondale, Ill., 1969), p. 113. For different views of the Bigger-Max relationship, see two important recent articles: Donald B. Gibson, "Wright's Invisible Native Son," *American Quarterly*, XXI (1969), 728–38, and Lloyd W. Brown, "Stereotypes in Black and White: The Nature of Perception in Wright's *Native Son*," *Black Academy Review*, I (Fall 1970), 35–44.

Dorothy S. Redden

RICHARD WRIGHT AND
NATIVE SON: NOT GUILTY

Published in 1940, *Native Son* is being read and misread again, after a relatively peaceful critical interlude of several decades. In many ways recent American criticism of this novel is more sophisticated than that of the '40s. But in at least one fundamental area it has not materially changed—and this area invites exploration, for it involves the assumption that the novel is an attack on white society. Some critics still maintain that Wright, overwhelmed by the bitterness of his feelings, and advancing Communist propaganda, "blames" white America for its racism, and threatens retaliation.

Sorting out the motley comments by critics both Black and white, one finds a cluster of opinions surrounding each of three related issues. First, *Native Son* is charged with being too emotional, the emotions most frequently cited being hatred, rage, and vengefulness. Second, the book is allegedly too didactic, particularly in the long summing-up by the lawyer for the defense, Mr. Max, who is supposedly a confirmed Marxist. And finally, though this is not always stated in the form of a charge, the novel is said to use emotionalism and didacticism to place a burden of guilt heavily on the shoulders of its intended white audience.

The claim that Richard Wright was the witless instrument of wild and overpowering feelings over which he had no control is applied mostly to Books I and II of *Native Son.* One of the first reviews of the book, for example, called it "a blinding and corrosive study in hate." The reviewer, David L. Cohn, did not mean merely that Bigger Thomas hated all whites, or even that twelve million Negroes did, but that Wright himself was "hate-consumed." According to Mr. Cohn, the book was an "incitement to violence," and "the preaching of Negro hatred of whites by Mr. Wright is on a par with the preaching of white hatred of Negroes by the Ku Klux Klan."[1]

Later we find James Baldwin discovering in much of Wright's work a "murderous bitterness" and violence:

From *Black American Literature Forum* 10, No. 4 (Winter 1976): 111–16.

This violence ... is gratuitous and compulsive. It is one of the severest criticisms that can be leveled against his work.... The root is rage. It is the rage, almost literally the howl, of a man who is being castrated.... Thus, when in Wright's pages a Negro male is found hacking a white woman to death, the very gusto with which this is done, and the great attention paid to the details of physical destruction reveal a terrible attempt to break out of the cage in which the American imagination has imprisoned him for so long.[2]

Irving Howe concurs that Wright's work is "choked" with such uncontrollable feelings. In telling white readers that they are hated, he says, Wright strikes them with "the full weight of his anger." (Unlike Baldwin, however, Howe finds this to be good, since if the Negro is to "assert his humanity," as both Baldwin and Wright discovered, "he must release his rage."[3])

As another of *Native Son*'s reviewers put it, the book "does not beg; it indicts.... It bends no knees, it asks no pity, it seeks to scourge."[4] Still another early critic asserted that "Richard Wright is playing with dynamite. He is holding a loaded pistol at the head of the white world while he mutters between clenched teeth: 'Either you grant us equal rights as human beings, or else this is what will happen.' "[5]

Supposedly the feeling in which these other feelings culminate is that of vengefulness, and indeed it is probable that if Wright were as swamped by hate and fury as he is said to be, he would also be swamped by a lust for revenge.

But he is not swamped at all, and the charge that *Native Son* is emotionally abandoned cannot be supported. Books I and II are certainly dramatic, if not melodramatic. From the hysterical killing of the huge fanged black rat in the crowded apartment to the shoot-out on top of the ice-covered water tank, the narrative whirls forward on a flood of surging feelings. Authentic passion there is, but the issue is not so much what Wright felt as how he disciplined, or failed to discipline, what he felt. How could a man who was "choked" with any emotions, let alone rage and hatred, produce a novel of this caliber? Wright may well have harbored powerful feelings, but he was not having some sort of lengthy tantrum when he constructed the coherent, meaningful, expressive story of Bigger Thomas.

Think what Wright might have done with uncontrolled emotions in this novel, and did not. He did not make his whites hateable. The worst one can say of the various Daltons is that they are literally or figuratively blind; they are not "evil." Even Buckley, the prosecutor, is more stupid than satanic. And it is a white man, Max, who is clearly intended to be the most intelligent and humane person in the book—the author's spokesman for the truth.

Wright did not fill up his stage with angelic, appealing Blacks, either—least of all his protagonist. He might have drawn a gentle, suffering martyr-Bigger or a grand Othello-Bigger of noble character and intellect, or even a modest, everyday sort of Bigger. Instead he created almost a stereotype of the skulking Black brute who violates and kills pale virgins in their beds. Wright does not stop with the stifling of Mary, which might be interpreted as a horrible accident; he makes Bigger murder

Bessie, his girl, in an even more gruesome way. Nor does Wright flinch from the sexual overtones in either case; here too he meets the myths head on. Surely a Black writer in the grip of violent passions would have invented a different sort of Black protagonist.

And why, if Wright were simply vengeful, did he not fully exploit Bigger's treatment at the hands of callous whites? There is some of that, to be sure, particularly in the fear-crazed mob in Book III. But on the whole Wright exercises restraint. He might have included some graphic police brutality, for instance, between the time of Bigger's capture and the beginning of his trial—beatings, tortures, perversions. Wright chooses to mention only one small detail: that somewhere, somehow, in the chaos, Bigger lost two fingernails, he does not know how.

Again, why did Wright consciously reject, as he has stated explicitly,[6] his original ending for the book, which showed Bigger strapped and waiting in the electric chair? Wright was not carried away by his emotions, and he did not want his readers to be so, either; we are not intended to dissolve in pity or fear, but to see clearly.[7] The stress was not to be on the pathos or cruelty of Bigger's death, but on its meaning, on what Wright called "the moral . . . horror of Negro life in the United States."[8]

Native Son is not choked with rage, hatred, or vengefulness. It is taut with emotion, but that emotion is contained and transcended. Certainly Richard Wright was a man of scalding feelings which inevitably found their way into his work. But he knew what he was about in *Native Son,* and one accepts his flat, exasperated, explicit refutation of Mr. Cohn's reading: "No *advocacy* of hate is in that book. *None!"*[9] The italics are his own.

The second major critical charge against *Native Son* focuses on its third section and especially on Max's long speech to the Court. Frequently this criticism is indirect, alleging that Richard Wright has failed as an artist. "The whole of Book III," Edward Margolies is typical in declaring, "seems out of key with the first two-thirds of the novel." Among other deficiencies, the section is unrealistic and "transparently propagandistic."[10] One of the earlier Signet afterwords (which, as the Cold War thawed out, seemed to become progressively less shrill) calls Book III "a tract" and an "absurd switch to didacticism."[11] Robert Bone uses the word "agitprop,"[12] and Brignano repeats the accusation that in Book III Wright simply follows the Party line: the section is not that which "will tend to stand in the way of favorable aesthetic judgments," of course, but it evidences Wright's "heavy-handed manipulation of his Marxist materials."[13]

It is true that in some ways Book III is different from Books I and II. Wright shifts from dramatization to exposition, from exciting, suspenseful, even sensational action to talk, from the concrete and specific to the more general and abstract, from a psychological to a sociological emphasis, and so on. But in fact the shift is not so radical as easy phrases make it seem; there are "ideas" in the first part of the novel, and "feelings" in the latter, for instance. And the realistic framework remains. Book III is constructed around a trial, credibly enough, and what is more logical in a trial than for lawyers to argue at length? In any case, literal realism is not the overriding consideration here, as Wright saw it. (In "How 'Bigger' Was Born," he notes that if a scene seemed improbable to him he would not just tear it up, but ask himself, "Does it reveal enough of what I feel to stand in spite of its unreality?"[14])

Furthermore, Wright has reasons for handling Book III as he does. In the first two books much is perceived through the barely awakened consciousness of Bigger, and although this matures somewhat, it is never the instrument that Wright needs to tell the whole story. To place Bigger's life in perspective, he requires another angle of vision, a perception more intellectual and informed. Max's speech may or may not be too long for some readers, but surely there is nothing inherently wrong with the idea of letting an educated, articulate, and ranging mind supplement Bigger's limited responses.

In short, there is no good reason why a writer should not shift gears in the course of a novel, if he has cause and can bring it off. It is interesting that so far no one has troubled to construct a tight case for or against the artistry of Native Son. Perhaps some of the hostility to Max's speech on ostensibly "literary" grounds is really a jab at Max's—or Wright's—supposedly radical ideas.

As far as that goes, it is doubtful that Max would be recognized as a Communist if he were not so labeled. He is not a very convincing one. He does not employ the orthodox phraseology, nor does he dwell on anything which might not also be noticed by any reasonably sensitive observer of the inequities in our society. (Native Son did in fact irritate the Party, as Wright had suspected it might.[15]) Bigger is not a proletarian hero; he is something of an anti-hero who, among other heresies, murders a poor working girl, admires Hitler and Mussolini, and perhaps worst of all, takes full responsibility for his acts. Yet the fact that Wright was for a period actually a Communist—though not a very convincing one, either, despite his sincerity—may still make some people nervous.

At any rate, although Max's speech does contain a few Marxist clichés, there seems little justification for calling it "agitprop." It is to some extent propaganda, of course; in a large sense, all literature is that, since every writer wants to convince someone of something, if only that his subject is worth reading about. For the sake of argument one can concede that Max's speech is forthrightly partisan, partly in the sense that it represents a lawyer defending his client in court, partly in that it serves as a vehicle for Wright's deeply felt ideas about racism, but it is not primarily, or even significantly, a statement of Communist ideology. The charge of "absurd . . . didacticism" simply will not stick.

Possibly the most wrong-headed (and provocative) reading of Native Son, published by Black critics as well as white, holds that the book allocates blame to and threatens punishment of white society; i.e., that it is a study in the "guilt" of its intended readership.

James Baldwin, for example, has discussed the novel in terms of "rightful vengeance" against the "wickedness" of a society "consumed with guilt."[16] Ralph Ellison believes that Wright's most important achievement is that he has been able to "throw his findings unashamedly into the guilty conscience of America."[17] Bone asserts that *Native Son* presents a "guilt-of-the-nation thesis,"[18] while Nathan A. Scott is sure that it must be "Hell" for white readers.[19] Irving Howe says that Wright is "speaking from the black wrath of retribution" in telling white readers that "history can be a punishment."[20]

Obviously, one must confront the existence of racism and its consequences in American society. But while one can agree that the book is addressed primarily to white readers, and clearly establishes a relationship between (white) racism and (Black) crime, it does not follow that Richard Wright is talking about guilt as it is ordinarily conceived.[21] It would be a mistake to leap to the conclusion that he must be vindictively fixing blame on white America and promising an eye for an eye. Reading Max's speech carefully, one sees that it does nothing of the sort. It says very plainly that the traditional guilt theory, as applied to race relations, is simplistic and pernicious, and that we had best discard it. It says so not only in regard to black Bigger,[22] but—one can't have it both ways—in regard to white society.

The guilt theory, deep in our culture, inculcated in us from childhood, is so familiar that it hardly bears describing, except to emphasize that it really is a theory and not a fact. It comprises a group of moralistic assumptions never proved, often doubted, yet tenaciously held in Western thought: that such terms as "good" and "evil" refer to absolutes, that we know what they mean and how to apply them, that we make "right" and "wrong" choices with something called a "free will," that we are thereupon "rewarded" or "punished" according to our "innocence" or "guilt." The very word "guilt" evokes this whole construct, which, however refined, remains polar and righteous in nature. The guilt theory stresses our "sins" or "crimes" of whatever degree, and the retribution appropriate thereto. Such critics as are quoted above (and some are among our best) seem to attribute to Richard Wright the characteristics of an old-style evangelistic preacher—emotionalism and didacticism in the service of a fundamentalist view of life.

Actually, in *Native Son,* Wright does not really talk about guilt itself (he implies by his social and psychological explanations that there is no such thing), but about guilt *feelings* or the *sense* of guilt, which are incontrovertible realities. Through Max, he tries to diminish, if not eliminate, such feelings. To play on them, he shows, is usually to elicit one of two responses. If the accused person accepts the verdict of guilty, he tends to grovel in self-contempt. To prevent this response to his book Wright had determined in advance that *Native Son* was not going to be something which people could "read and weep over and feel good about."[23] He did not intend that his readers escape genuine responsibility by wallowing in remorse and self-abasement. Rather, the accused is invited to reject the charge and hit back. It is for this reason that Max repeatedly asks his listeners not to feel sorry for Bigger:

"... if one insists upon looking at this boy in the light of sympathy, he will be swamped by a feeling of guilt so strong as to be indistinguishable from hate.

"Of all things, men do not like to feel that they are guilty of wrong, and if you try to make them feel guilt, they will try desperately to justify it on any grounds; but, failing that, ... they will kill that which evoked in them the condemning sense of guilt."[24]

The sense of guilt, then, wastes valuable energies in destructive reactions. It is this feeling of guilt, Max says, " 'which has caused all of the mob-fear and mob-hysteria' " (p. 328). Accomplishing nothing good, it brings about horrors of its own. We can, he continues, " 'salve our feelings of guilt and rage with more murder' " by executing Bigger. " 'Kill him! Burn the life out of him!' " But what will be the result?

"... There will be murder again. How can law contradict the lives of millions of people and hope to be administered successfully? Do we believe in magic? ... The surest way to make certain that there will be more such murders is to kill this boy. In your rage and guilt, make thousands of other black men and women feel that the barriers are tighter and higher! Kill him and swell the tide of pent-up lava that will some day break loose, not in a single, blundering, accidental, individual crime, but in a wild cataract of emotion that will brook no control." (P. 330)

Far from promoting the traditional guilt theory in this novel, Wright actively opposes it. In contrast to James Baldwin, who embodies much of his fundamentalist training in his work, Wright puts his Seventh Day Adventism behind him. To Wright, improved race relations are not a question of assigning or admitting guilt, but of rejecting the idea of guilt entirely, and getting on with the business of living together.

But how is this to be accomplished? What can replace the guilt theory, which so often fails to assure moral behavior? Are there viable alternatives to the old patterns of thinking? Max suggests a different concept, for which—since there is no less ambiguous term—the word "accountability" will have to serve. Accountability, in this sense, means only that, despite our very limited control over our behavior, we have to answer for its results. Recognizing that we are formed by all the conditions of our lives, and that this is not a matter of fault, Wright suggests that we simply accept the reality (including the desirability or undesirability) of these conditions and of their relationship to us. Events are viewed as causally linked, without moralistic reference. In fact, it is important to read Max's remarks without imposing on them any flavor of righteousness. An explanation is not an excuse, but neither is it an indictment. Max is, as he explicitly says, neither morally condemning the white man nor striving to arouse pity for, let alone fear of, the Black; he simply states the facts as he sees them.

And he sees them as links in the long chain of causation. Historically speaking, the " 'first wrong' " was committed by the whites when they obtained and exploited slaves. This act was " 'understandable and inevitable' " (p. 327).

"Our forefathers came to these shores and faced a harsh and wild country. . . . They had either to subdue this wild land or be subdued by it. . . . But in conquering they *used* others, used their lives. . . . Lives to them were tools and weapons to be wielded against a hostile land and climate.

"... Let us not be naïve: men do what they must. . . . Exalted by the will to rule, they could not have built nations on so vast a scale had they not shut their eyes to the humanity of other men, men whose lives were necessary for their building." (Pp. 328–29)

The result, however, is equally a fact: " 'a separate nation, stunted, stripped, and held captive *within* this nation, devoid of political, social, economic, and property rights' " (p. 333). Twelve million people (in 1940), " 'longing to gratify impulses akin to our own' " are " 'denied the channels evolved through long centuries for their socialized expression' " (pp. 335–36). To Black men who are " 'looking for a land whose tasks can call forth their deepest and best,' " we say, " ' "This is a white man's country!" ' "(p. 332).

Naturally, such repression has had violent consequences. We must deal, says Max, with " 'hot blasts of hate engendered in others by that first wrong, and then the monstrous and horrible crimes flowing from that hate' " (p. 327). For men do what they must in reaction as well as in action. All life seeks fulfillment, and " 'the more you kill, the more you deny and separate, the more will they seek another form and way of life, however blindly and unconsciously' " (p. 334). " '. . .We should not pretend horror or surprise when thwarted life expresses itself in fear and hate and crime' " (p. 328).

Such acts as Bigger's, he continues, will inevitably occur under these conditions. " '. . . Remember that men can starve from a lack of self-realization as much as they can from a lack of bread! And they can *murder* for it, too!' " (p. 335). Given who and where he was, Bigger had to kill. It is the sharpest irony of the book that he feels that " 'his act of *creation*' " could come about only through the death of others; their dying meant " 'his way of *living*' " (pp. 335–36).

And Bigger is not an isolated freak.

"The consciousness of Bigger Thomas, and millions of others more or less like him, white and black, according to the weight of the pressures we have put upon them, forms the quicksands upon which the foundations of our civilization rest. Who knows when some slight shock, disturbing the delicate balance between social order and thirsty aspiration, shall send the skyscrapers in our cities toppling?" (P. 337)

The fire next time. Max's vision is as apocalyptic as Baldwin could wish. " 'Your Honor, another civil war in these states is not impossible . . .' " (p. 338).

Out of context, this last may sound like a threat. But Wright is talking factually, about causes and consequences, and not judgmentally, about faults and punishment. That is, he is describing accountability rather than guilt. Although unfortunately our language often fails to distinguish between these two words, and uses them inter-changeably, Wright is clearly separating two very different concepts. In fact, he is separating three concepts, for the idea of accountability stands between the tra-ditional extremes of free will and necessity, agreeing with each to some extent, while refusing to accept either entirely.

For example, Wright shares with the determinists a belief in causation, and he is consistent in applying this as much to Bigger Thomas as to Bigger's oppressors. Bigger is the product of complex forces, and Wright never implies that he "should" or "ought to" have done other than he did. (He even suggests that, had Bigger been white, "then he *too* would hate, if *he* were *they*" [p. 306].) But Wright refuses to relieve Bigger of all responsibility. The principle which distinguishes the idea of accountability from that of free will holds that a person cannot avoid the conse-quences of his behavior in spite of the fact that he had to act as he did.

The position that Wright takes in *Native Son* is subtle and easily misunder-stood if one insists on either/or terms. "There is a philosophical confusion at the heart of *Native Son*," says Robert Bone. On the one hand, Wright takes the "environmentalist" view, and "Bigger's actions are presented as inevitable, compul-sive, beyond conscious control, or, in a word, unfree." On the other hand, Wright says that Bigger has, through murder, "created a new life for himself," which presumes "the elements of decision, purpose, choice, and moral agency. The em-phasis is on the creative act, which by definition cannot be unfree."[25]

This criticism, while accurate in its facts, assumes that there are only two (contradictory) possibilities open to Wright, determinism and what Bone terms "existential freedom." Actually, Wright believes in both necessity and a measure of personal freedom; one can exercise choice in immediate, limited ways despite the fact that the "I" which is making these decisions has been shaped by forces outside of itself. For all practical purposes, there need be no contradiction. To set up two mutually exclusive extremes, and then to demand that Wright choose one or be accused of "philosophical confusion," is to oversimplify Wright, if not life itself. Bigger, like the rest of us, need not have a totally free will in order to feel and act as if he does. In any event, he is "accountable."

It is often argued that such a view is impractical, that eliminating the concept of guilt and its resultant feelings will lead to a breakdown of morality. This is true in respect to certain aspects of traditional moralism (as distinguished from morality); a great deal of dead wood, accumulated over millennia, would indeed be carted off with the guilt theory. Both the guilt theory and determinism, however, have tended to encourage irresponsibility and to undermine the power to act constructively. The former emphasizes self-abasement or retaliation rather than reconstruction, and the latter, pleading powerlessness, neglects reform because it does not allow that an individual can alter the workings of grim necessity. Reexamining moral terms can only make us look harder at what is really better or worse for our common future. Human beings will always need to evaluate—but they can do so for con-structive, rather than punitive, purposes. They will still recognize hurtful acts or errors, but not necessarily "sins" or "crimes." One can acknowledge consequences without dealing in "punishments."[26]

Such changes in terminology are not semantic quibbles; there is a demonstrable difference between believing that despite the mitigating circumstances, a murderer like Bigger must be held accountable for his acts, as Max believes, and believing that he must "pay his debt to society," as Buckley would put it. However, since it is almost impossible to use a word like "accountability" without invoking a heavy crust of connotations, we need a new vocabulary, which Wright neither found at hand nor invented.

Richard Wright (and of course he is not unique in this) is suggesting, not a moral vacuum, but a more rational, workable morality, one which takes a fresh look at what is best, in the long run, for human beings. He knew that the questions he was raising about race relations were moral questions. In 1945 he wrote:

> If, within the confines of its present culture, the nation ever seeks to purge itself of its color hate, it will find itself at war with itself, convulsed by a spasm of emotional and moral confusion. If the nation ever finds itself examining its real relation to the Negro, it will find itself doing infinitely more than that; for the anti-Negro attitude of whites represents but a tiny part—though a symbolically significant one—of the moral attitude of the nation. Our too-young and too-new America, lusty because it is lonely, aggressive because it is afraid, insists upon seeing the world in terms of good and bad, the holy and the evil, the high and the low, the white and the black; our America is frightened by fact, by history, by processes, by necessity. It hugs the easy way of damning those whom it cannot understand, of excluding those who look different; and it salves its conscience with a self-draped cloak of righteousness.[27]

The passage continues: "Am I damning my native land? No," he answers, "for I, too, share these faults of character!" Whatever faults of character Richard Wright may have had, however he reflected America at times, in *Native Son* he was reaching toward a repudiation of conventional thinking about our accountability to ourselves and to each other.

NOTES

[1] "The Negro Novel: Richard Wright," *Atlantic Monthly*, 165 (May 1940), 661.
[2] "Alas, Poor Richard, I," in *Nobody Knows My Name* (New York: The Dial Press, 1961), p. 188.
[3] "Black Boys and Native Sons," *Dissent*, Autumn 1963, pp. 353, 355, 367.
[4] Milton Rugoff, *New York Herald Tribune Books*, March 3, 1940, p. 48.
[5] Charles E. Glicksburg, "Negro Fiction in America," *The South Atlantic Quarterly*, 45 (October 1946), 106.
[6] "How 'Bigger' was Born," *The Saturday Review of Literature*, June 1, 1940, p. 19.
[7] Concerning his previous work of fiction, *Uncle Tom's Children*, Wright says that he realized that "I had made an awfully naïve mistake. I found that I had written a book which even bankers' daughters could read and weep over and feel good about. I swore to myself that if I ever wrote another book, no one would weep over it; that it would be so hard and deep that they would have to face it without the consolation of tears" (ibid.).

[8] Ibid., p. 20.

[9] Richard Wright, "I Bite the Hand That Feeds Me," *Atlantic Monthly*, 165 (June 1940), 828. He goes on: "What Mr. Cohn mistook for my advocacy of hate in that novel was something entirely different. In every word of that book are *confidence, resolution,* and the *knowledge* that the Negro problem can and will be solved."

[10] Edward Margolies, *Native Sons* (Philadelphia and New York: Lippincott, 1968), pp. 72, 80.

[11] Richard Sullivan, "Afterword," in Richard Wright, *Native Son* (New York: Signet, 1961), p. 396.

[12] *Richard Wright* (Minneapolis: University of Minnesota Press, 1969), p. 23.

[13] Russell Carl Brignano, *Richard Wright: An Introduction to the Man and His Works* (Pittsburgh: University of Pittsburgh Press, 1970), p. 82.

[14] "How 'Bigger' Was Born," p. 19.

[15] See "How 'Bigger' Was Born," p. 18.

[16] "Many Thousands Gone," in *Notes of a Native Son* (Boston: Beacon Press, 1955), passim.

[17] "Richard Wright's Blues," in *Shadow and Act* (New York: Random House, 1964), p. 94. See also "The World and the Jug" in this volume.

[18] *The Negro Novel in America* (New Haven: Yale University Press, 1968), pp. 143, 151.

[19] "The Dark and Haunted Tower of Richard Wright," in *Five Black Writers*, ed. Donald B. Gibson (New York: New York University Press, 1970), p. 18.

[20] "Black Boys and Native Sons," p. 355.

[21] He does remark that a "guilt theme" runs straight through *Native Son* ("How 'Bigger' Was Born," p. 20). But that is all that he says under this head; he does not define the term or apply it either to Bigger or to whites inside or outside of the book.

[22] Wright does not apply the concept of guilt to Bigger, whom he portrays as one of the inevitable creatures of racism. Therefore, he has no need to excuse his protagonist, as he says: In *Native Son* I did not defend Bigger's actions; I explained them through depiction" ("I Bite the Hand that Feeds Me," p. 83).

[23] See note 7, above.

[24] *Native Son* (New York and London: Harper, 1940), p. 329. All subsequent citations refer to this edition and will occur parenthetically in the text.

[25] *Richard Wright,* pp. 23–24. See also Edward Margolies, pp. 73–74 and 79–80. "Since moral responsibility involves choice, can Wright's deterministic Marxism be reconciled with the freedom of action that choice implies? The contradiction is never resolved ... " (Margolies, p. 74).

[26] Our legal and judicial system is today moving ponderously away from the guilt theory. Alleged criminals are more and more often sent first to a psychiatrist to determine if the individual can be held to standards of "right" and "wrong," and thus to "innocence" or "guilt." We are also witnessing the growth of the no-fault concept in certain applications, such as auto insurance and divorce.

[27] "The Man Who Went to Chicago," in *Eight Men* (New York: Avon Books, 1961), p. 169. (This essay was originally part of the last third of Wright's autobiography, *Black Boy;* the first two-thirds were published in 1945 as a complete volume.)

Charles De Arman

BIGGER THOMAS: THE SYMBOLIC NEGRO AND THE DISCRETE HUMAN ENTITY

From the response to *Uncle Tom's Children,* Wright came to understand that there was something missing in the version he presented of Blacks in America. He knew that Big Boy must leave home, that Mann must die trying to escape, that Silas must fight, that the Reverend Taylor must feel the imminence of death, not because their lives were determined by social, political, or any other external forces, but because the racist circumstances in which Blacks live give rise to these acts and because they were representative figures—alienated from themselves by their experiences of themselves as objects in the sight of the existential Other. They all embody the agonizing experiences of Black people in the United States. Bigger, Black Boy, Cross, *freddaniels,* Saul—they, too, are representative figures. But each of these characters holds within himself the feeling of being a dis-crete entity, of being something other than that which others see him as being. In other words, each of them feels or comes to feel he is an individual in his own right, by reason of his own experiences and choices. Each reveals, implicitly, an attempt to live "authentically," to recognize the existence and demands of moral freedom.

Until the final pages of *Native Son,* Bigger holds within himself the tension between the "symbolic Negro," and the embodiment of the *effects* of racism, and the desire to be recognized as a discrete human entity, as a fully *human* being living "authentically," transcending the absurdity of the world. At no point in the novel do others truly "see" Bigger as a product of his acts; instead, they create an image which depends completely on the color of his skin. This stereotype not only gives rise to his isolation, but it also helps conceal his individuality from himself. For more than two-thirds of the novel, Bigger, like Max in Book Three, does not think of Bigger Thomas as a discrete entity who creates a self through moral choices and the assumption of responsibility for his acts. Instead, he acts as if he is not responsible for what he has been and as if he is not free to choose what he will be; in other

From *Black American Literature Forum* 12, No. 2 (Summer 1978): 61–64.

words, Bigger's sense of himself, in most of the novel, exemplifies what Hazel E. Barnes calls "bad faith."[1]

Book Three opens with Bigger having given up on his life. He is a vapid, doll-like figure who offers no resistance to the buffeting he receives at the hands of the authorities: "He looked without hope or resentment, his eyes like two still pools of black ink in his face."[2] But he comes to live "in a thin, hard core of consciousness" (p. 305).

At first Bigger does not sense the meaning that the "white force" (p. 97) attaches to his acts or the example it wants to make of him, but as he looks at the faces in the crowd during his first courtroom appearance, he senses their "patient certainty," their "calm conviction":

> They were determined to make his death mean more than a mere punishment; they regarded him as a figment of that black world which they feared and were anxious to keep under control. The atmosphere of the crowd told him that they were going to use his death as a symbol of fear to wave before the eyes of the black world. (P. 235)

But he is determined he will not succumb. Unlike the first two books, the third focuses on Bigger's attempt to extricate himself from that other symbol—the representative of the "Negro Problem"—Max would have him be. In this section, Wright moves into Bigger's "core of being." The tension between the Other's projection of Bigger and his conviction that, in John Reilly's words, he "should have the opportunity to realize himself"[3] is tacitly implied, hinted at. It is not a well-informed emotional, psychological, or intellectual "fact" in Wright's prose. The exfoliation of Bigger's emotions causes him to come face to face with unequivocal knowledge, " 'I got to die' " (p. 358). For Bigger this revelation comes just in time, especially when seen from the perspective of his not wanting to die without having plumbed his soul for the way to an authentic life.

Although there are periods, earlier in the novel, when he has fleeting intuitions of his death—namely, being struck down without time for reflection on the past or for thought or meditation on his life—they differ from his knowing within that death is imminent. The opening scenes of the third book indicate the problem Bigger faces as an isolated individual, his preoccupation with the problem of identity:

> Under and above it all, there was the fear of death before which he was naked and without defense; he had to go forward and meet his end like any other living thing upon the earth. . . . There would have to hover about him, like the stars in a full sky, a vast configuration of images and symbols whose magic and power could lift him up and make him live so intensely that the dread of being black and unequal would be forgotten; that even death would not matter, that it would be a victory. This would have to happen before he could look them in the face: a new pride and a new humility would have to be born in him springing from a new identification with some part of the world in which he

lived, and this identification forming the basis for a new hope that would function in him as pride and dignity. (Pp. 234–35)

But Bigger vacillates. He wants this "new identification" spoken of in the passage; however, he still has little or no faith in himself. He has always depended on the rejection, the humiliation, the dehumanization of the "white force" (p. 97) for his identity in the "part of the world in which he lived" (p. 235). He hungered for "another orbit between two poles that would let him live again; for a mode of life that would catch him up with the tension of hate and love" (p. 234). Though he despised being a dispossessed and disinherited man living in a dehumanizing society where "being black" meant being "unequal," at least in that situation he knew who he was, what to expect, where he was going. Despite the fact that his life has developed in a racist world whose fundamental assumptions he took for granted, now he must "form a new identification with some part of the world in which he lived" if he is not to die "in a fog of fear" (pp. 234–35, 305).

After one of his long talks with Max, Bigger comes to this conclusion about his present state: "If he were as confused as this when his time came, they really *would* have to drag him to the chair. He had to make a decision; in order to walk to that chair he had to weave his feelings into a hard shield of either hope or hate. To fall between them would mean living and dying in a fog of fear" (p. 305). Before, his decisions were made in response to fear; now he dreads he will be caught in a paralysis of feeling, that he will die in a state of confusion. But despite the dread which haunts him through the last book, he does not respond to this dread—basically existential dread—as he responds to fear. Now, for the first time in his life, he realizes that he will have to decide what constitutes a *freely* chosen course of action. He can no longer wait for some thing or some one to ignite in him some response. His fear of the "white force"—the one power in the novel that helps maintain Bigger's invisibility, since he hides behind the "white force" quite well —gives way to the inexorable belief that there is no one, aside from himself, who can "make" his decisions for him. He has to *make* himself: "He was balanced on a hairline, but there was no one to push him forward or backwards, no one to make him feel that he had any value or worth— no one but himself" (p. 305). Furthermore, Bigger, in his conversation with Max, comes to see the extent of his moral confusion. He "glared about the small room, searching for an answer. He knew that his actions did not seem logical and he gave up trying to explain them logically. He reverted to his feelings as a guide in answering Max" (p. 297). As illogical as his answers seem to Max, their illogicality reflects the reality and illogic of the absurd world in which Bigger feels he lives.

While Bigger feels that he should direct his life toward "a new identification with some part of the world in which he lived" (pp. 234–35), he also thinks of white people as being " 'like God' " (p. 299). He tells Max that whites " 'don't even let you feel what you want to feel. They after you so hot and hard you can only feel what they do to you. They kill you before you die' " (p. 299). And in another exchange, during the same conversation, Max speaks first:

> "I don't understand, Bigger. You say you hated her [Mary] and you say you felt like having her when you were in the room and she was drunk and you were drunk...."
>
> "Yeah, that's funny, ain't it? ... Yeah; I reckon it was because I know I oughtn't've wanted to. Mr. Max, you know what some white men say we black men do? They say we rape white women when we got the clap and they say we do that because we believe that if we rape white women then we'll get rid of the clap. That's what some white men *say*. Jesus, Mr. Max, when folks say things like that about you, you whipped before you born. What's the use?" (P. 297)

Indeed: what's the use? If Bigger is condemned from the very beginning, does it make any difference what he does? Can he make his life, not to mention his death, mean something? "He would not mind dying now if he could find out what this [life] meant, what he was in relation to all the others that lived, and the earth upon which he stood" (p. 307). He wonders "if Max had been able to see the man in him beneath those wild and cruel acts of his" (p. 306). "Was there some battle every-body was fighting, and he had missed it?" (p. 307). Max never really sees the man "beneath those ... acts" (p. 306). On the other hand, Bigger's latter query requires a twofold answer, yes and no. On the affirmative side, others are fighting "some battle" (p. 306)—like that against the "white force"—through which they hope to give meaning to their lives, but like Bigger throughout most of the novel they are trying to derive this meaning within a closed system, from a world that had or-dained white-approved modes of life as meaningful and all others as meaningless. And no, he has not "missed it" (p. 307); he has extended his fight for meaning beyond the parameters set for him by the "white force." He is carrying on the fight in the very core of his being. "He felt that he could not fight the battle for his life without first winning the one raging within him" (p. 309). His "fight" to "find out what this new tingling, this new elation, this new excitement meant" (pp. 308, 309) overshadows any feelings of hate or fear he has.

Despite the fact that he had moments when "he wished bitterly that he had not felt those possibilities [of hope, of freedom], when he wished he could go again behind his curtain" (p. 308; see n. 4), Bigger recognizes now, more than ever before, that there is nothing standing between him and his "new identification with some part of the world in which he lived" (p. 235) but himself. He no longer cares about the social ramifications of his trial or his acts, as Max obviously does. Max says to him, as they stand waiting in the antechamber, " 'Well, this thing's bigger than you son.' " Bigger, thinking only of his impending doom and what this trial means to him, a way of creating his very identity, responds, " 'They going to kill me anyhow' " (p. 312). He allows nothing to be bigger than Bigger.

Unfortunately he does not learn, until the last two pages, that as Sartre put it in another context, "man is nothing else but that which he makes of himself,"[5] and he does not affirm his belief in his ability to "make" himself until the third book of the novel. But when he does, he says to Max, " 'Ah, I reckon I believe in myself . . . I ain't got nothing else. . . . I got to die . . .' "(p. 358; Wright's ellipses). Unfortunately this affirmation of his separate, isolated being does not resound through the trial episode, for the Bigger of the last two pages is not the one Max pictures in his defense. Bigger, for most of the novel, confuses, as he does Max, Bigger's particular, individual, discrete self—that self which he must "make"—with that of his social, composite, representative, symbolic self—that of the Oppressed Black Man.

In the last two pages of the novel, this confusion no longer exists; at least it does not exist in Bigger's mind. But it still exists in Max's. Bigger *has* begun to define himself:

> "Mr. Max, you go home. I'm all right. . . . Sounds funny, Mr. Max, but when I think about what you say I kind of feel what I wanted. It makes me feel I was kind of right. . . ." Max opened his mouth to say something and Bigger drowned out his voice. "I ain't trying to forgive nobody and I ain't asking for nobody to forgive me. I ain't going to cry. They wouldn't let me live and I killed. Maybe it ain't fair to kill, and I reckon I really didn't want to kill. But when I think of why all the killing was, I begin to feel what I wanted, and what I am. . . ."
>
> Bigger saw Max back away from him with compressed lips. But he felt he had to make Max understand how he saw things now.
>
> "I didn't want to kill!" Bigger shouted. "But what I killed for, I *am!* It must've been pretty deep in me to make me kill! I must have felt it awful hard to murder. . . ." (P. 358; Wright's ellipses)

His new sense of his self does not depend on Max's perception of him; it has been drawn from within, from introspection and inspection of his relation with others, the world, and, most importantly, with himself (see pp. 306, 350–51). Searching for meaning, wholeness and unity—man's desire for happiness—in a meaningless universe, Bigger seeks to understand and transcend his despair. But Max, the observer, prefers to see Bigger, the observed, as a symbol: "Max groped for his hat like a blind man; he found it and jammed it on his head. He felt for the door, keeping his face averted. He poked his arm through and signaled for the guard. When he was let out he stood for a moment, his back to the steel door. Bigger grasped the bars with both hands" (pp. 358–59)

Clearly Max's sense of Bigger does not agree with Bigger's new sense of his self. As Bigger says, " 'I didn't know I was really alive in this world until I felt things hard enough to kill for 'em . . .' " (p. 358). Max refuses to try to *see* Bigger, the discrete individual; he keeps "his face averted"; he turns away. Max's sense of Bigger, the symbolic Oppressed Negro, stands between Max and Bigger, the discrete entity. Though Bigger, the individual, stands just behind Max's image, grasping "the bars with both hands," his face pressed up against them, peering out, Max cannot see him for he stands with his "back to the steel door." He will not even look at Bigger; his hat "jammed . . . on his head," he closes his mind to Bigger's assertion, " 'what I killed for, I am' " (pp. 358, 359)!

For most of the novel we see Bigger from the perspective of the white world, acting the object in the mind of the white Other. Then, finally, in the closing pages of the novel, there is a change. Bigger does not fully define himself but he "surges up in the world" and takes the "leap"—to "define himself"—that existentialism speaks of: "that leap towards existence."[6] It is a process which has been going on intermittently throughout the novel, but not so intensely as in the last book. By presenting Bigger as being saved from "dying in a fog of fear" (p. 305) through his own efforts, Wright begins to resolve the tension which arises in a discrete individual warring to free himself from the symbolic figure others believe him to be—and which, for a time, he believed himself to be. Wright implies that the individual can achieve meaning through his own willed efforts, through taking responsibility for making his self. Still, the image with which Wright leaves the reader is that of the observer not looking at the observed. Though the observed can speak and look through the bars of his imprisoning image, through his "object-ness," he is still caged by an objectifying world terrified of Black "subjects," terrified of freedom and authenticity and, to use a phrase from Sartre's Anti-Semite and Jew, terrified "of the human condition."[7]

Though Bigger continues to speak, his words are heard but not understood. " 'What I killed for must've been good!' Bigger's voice was full of frenzied anguish. 'It must have been good! When a man kills, it's for something . . .' " (p. 358; Wright's ellipses). He is not fixed in the acts of murder. Instead, he is free to be himself; " 'it's for something.' " His acts, when judged by traditional criteria, are immoral. He is guilty, but he acknowledges his guilt. Thus he transcends his acts by living and making a new choice of his self. He exists in relation to his acts; he chooses what his specific relation will be to these acts, and, for Sartre, this is a life of "good faith," authenticity, freedom.[8]

NOTES

[1] The Literature of Possibility (Lincoln, 1959), p. 50.

[2] Richard Wright, Native Son (New York and London, 1940), p. 233. All future citations from the novel refer to this edition.

[3] "Afterword," in Native Son by Richard Wright (New York, 1966), pp. xxiv–xxv.

[4] Here it would be useful to quote from Kierkegaard's "The Concept of Dread": "He who is educated by dread is educated by possibility, and only the man who is educated by possibility is educated in accordance with his infinity. Possibility is therefore the heaviest of all categories. . . . When such a person, therefore, goes out from the school of possibility and knows more thoroughly than a child knows the alphabet that he can demand of life absolutely nothing, and that terror, perdition, annihilation dwell next door to every man, and has learned the profitable lesson that even dread which alarms may the next instant become a fact, he will then interpret reality differently, he will extol reality, and even when it rests upon him heavily he will remember that after all it is far, far lighter than the possibility was" (The Worlds of Existentialism: A Critical Reader, ed. Maurice Friedman [New York, 1964], pp. 370–71). Without doubt Bigger has been "educated by possibility," and he finds little comfort in it, for it provides too many uncertainties with which to contend. But the very fact that he is about to die provides a reality with which he can contend, distasteful though it may be.

[5] *Existentialism from Dostoevsky to Sartre,* ed. Walter Kaufmann (Cleveland and New York, 1956), p. 291.
[6] Ibid., pp. 290, 291.
[7] *Anti-Semite and Jew,* trans. George J. Becker (New York, 1965), p. 54.
[8] *Existentialism from Dostoevsky to Sartre,* p. 269.

Ross Pudaloff

NATIVE SON AND MASS CULTURE

In his 1965 introduction to Malcolm Lowry's *Under the Volcano,* Stephen Spender suggested that "someone should write a thesis perhaps on the influence of the cinema on the novel—I mean the serious novel."[1] Since then there has been no lack of scholarly research and criticism on the relationship of literature and film. Still, most of the criticism devoted to the influence of film on literature has taken as its major texts the work of high modernist art with particular emphasis on such authors as James Joyce, Marcel Proust, and Virginia Woolf.[2] Such criticism tends to evaluate the cinematic in literature, the fundamental premise of which is the complexity of individual consciousness in an age of mass culture. As a result, both criticism and literature tend to celebrate consciousness at the expense of the external world. These critical approaches repudiate the function of both novel and film as the expression of mass culture and thus a challenge to other art forms. The work of Richard Wright is particularly significant in this regard, especially his most famous novel, *Native Son.* Bigger Thomas' story is the presentation of the fate of a young man who takes his values from a society dominated by movies, magazines, newspapers, and detective stories. Every critical episode in *Native Son,* from the initial scene in which Bigger confronts the rat to his capture and execution, is framed, perceived, and mirrored in and through the images provided by mass culture. Bigger knows only the self and the world mass culture presents to him. As such, Bigger lacks the depth of character that traditionally marks the protagonist of the modern novel and whose presence in a literary character has often been used as a standard for the success or failure of a literary work. Instead, Bigger lives in a world of images and external gestures and is himself seen in this stereotyped way by the other characters. *Native Son* may be said to succeed insofar as that absence of inherent character disturbs the reader by deranging his traditional conception of novelistic character.

Remarkably few critics have attempted to gauge the influence of mass culture

From *Studies in American Fiction* 11, No. 1 (Spring 1983): 3–18.

on Richard Wright. Of these, most observe the conventional distinction between high and mass art, seeking the moment when Wright passed from the *Argosy All-Story Magazine* and *Flynn's Detective Weekly* of his youth to the Theodore Dreiser, Gertrude Stein, and Marcel Proust of his adult life.[3] For Michael Fabre, whose biography of Wright is the most authoritative and exhaustive available, this crucial transition occurred while Wright was living in Memphis. There "Wright did not suddenly discover his literary talents so much as he discovered good literature, represented by the great novelists of the nineteenth and twentieth centuries, in opposition to the detective stories, dime novels, and popular fiction that had been his usual fare."[4] A glance at Wright's autobiographical writings not only confirms his stated preference for literature over popular culture but also reveals the political basis for such a preference. When he first came to Chicago in the late 1920s, Wright was astounded by more than the absence of legal segregation. In "Early Days in Chicago" he reflected upon the waitresses with whom he had worked; in his words, they would "fix their eyes upon the trash of life," an act which "made it impossible for them to learn a language that could have taught them to speak of what was in theirs and others' hearts."[5] In the same essay, he went on to speak of "the Negro" as sharing that "lust for trash," a lust which for Wright "condemns him" to the same fate as his white counterpart.[6]

Wright's condemnation of mass culture, however, does not mean that he felt free to disregard its effects on the individual while he went on with the business of writing literature. In his daily life he remained fascinated as well as entertained by the movies, and the interviews he gave after the publication of *Native Son* reveal his interest in photography and cinema to the extent that "he sometimes went to as many as three movies a day."[7] That his interest in these media went well beyond recreation is apparent in the conversations he had with Harry Birdoff, whom Wright met during rehearsals for the dramatization of *Native Son* in 1941. According to Birdoff, Wright "confessed that he had not seen a single play on Broadway and said that he didn't particularly care. The movies were his 'dish.' When I questioned him, he said, 'Because I think peoples' lives are like the movies.' "[8] Apparently Wright did not explain the meaning of this statement to Birdoff. Nevertheless, its implications can be seen in his use of mass culture as a general theme and the movies as a particular demonstration of that theme in much of his early writing. Certainly he was interested enough in the movies to bring *Native Son* to the screen as a movie, even to the point of filming it in Argentina and playing the role of Bigger himself when he was over forty years old. According to Wright, the movie "was a dream which I had long hugged to my heart and it was quite powerful until it happened."[9]

That Wright acknowledged the impact of the literary authors of his age is not in question. What must be challenged is the assumption that the influence of popular art was negative and had to be discarded before Wright could attain any significant artistic achievement, an assumption pervasive in the criticism of his work.[10] To call attention to the presence of references, allusions, and images of mass culture in his writings is to suggest not only a new emphasis in its content but also the presence of a different esthetic than that normally associated with this author. It is to challenge the major assumption implicit in the literary criticism of *Native Son:* "It was that rarest of coups—a work familiar in form but unfamiliar in content."[11]

The conventional distinction between high art and popular art is missing from the writing of Richard Wright. His fiction, especially, describes worlds in which mass culture serves as the locus of personal identity. Consciousness reflects rather than opposes the world. When Wright read Stein's "Melanctha" to stockyard workers, he did more than simply rebut the Stalinist literary cliché that she "spent her days reclining upon a silken couch in Paris, smoking hashish. . . ."[12] Both his admiration of and their response to her writing had, he believed, a single source. Stein's art, in Wright's view, succeeded because it had accepted the world. Mass culture, then, is that content which alters form.

Wright's adaption of mass culture for literature is clear in two early works of fiction, *Lawd Today,* his first novel, and "Long Black Song," one of the stories included in *Uncle Tom's Children.* Since *Lawd Today* remained unpublished until after Wright's death, the critics must be forgiven for overlooking the importance mass culture obviously had for Wright during the 1930s. "Long Black Song" has also remained relatively undisturbed by anthologies and criticism since its first appearance. More attention has been expended upon "Big Boy Leaves Home" and "Fire and Cloud." These stories, the first and last in the original edition of *Uncle Tom's Children,* direct attention to the confrontation between black male and white female, as well as the necessity, as Wright then perceived it, for collective interracial resistance to those he called the "Lords of the Land" in *Twelve Million Black Voices.* "Long Black Song" has consistently been judged "of only secondary interest"[13] because it pairs the white male with the black female and, in this respect, serves as only a way station on the path to the heroic resistance and unity of "Fire and Cloud."

The fragility of folk culture when it comes in contact with mass culture is the implicit topic of "Long Black Song." In it the heroine, Sarah, is seduced by a white salesman of clock-phonographs while her husband, a man who owns land and has middle-class aspirations, is away selling his cotton at market. The husband, Silas, is enraged when he discovers his wife's infidelity; Silas beats her and then kills the salesman when he returns the next day. Eventually Silas engages in a shootout with a white lynch mob, a conflict that ends with his death in the flaming farmhouse while Sarah looks on from a distance. Ironically enough, Sarah's susceptibility to the white salesman stems not only from her essentially passive nature but from the factors that made her choose Silas as a husband. In both cases, her desires are shaped more by the rational calculation of the modern world than the emotional responses of the folk culture. In other words, Wright created a heroine who was ready to be seduced by a representative of modern civilization with his clock-phonographs. The salesman himself is from Chicago, an otherwise irrelevant detail which suggests that city served Wright as the epitome of modern society.

The power of mass culture to absorb and manipulate folk culture is evident in the salesman's decision to play a spiritual and by Sarah's deeply emotional response to hearing that song. The parallelism between the fates of cultures and the fates of individuals is obvious. As the power of Sarah's subjectivity has proven no match for Silas' power to possess her, so too are even the most authentic aspects of folk culture transformed into a destructive force by their incorporation within mass culture. In this respect, Sarah clearly prefigures Bigger. Both are seduced by an urban society in which joy, sex, and pleasure originate in mechanized external sources and gain much of their appeal because they represent a world beyond the ordinary experience of the protagonists.[14]

While Sarah is also associated with the rhythms of music and nature, Bigger, in contrast, lacks any folk culture to which to return. Closer in this respect to Bigger than Sarah is Jake Jackson, the protagonist of *Lawd Today,* a man who fills his life outside of work with the "trash of life." This novel covers one day in his life, February 12, 1932, and begins with the sound of a radio program celebrating the birthday of Abraham Lincoln, a program which often reappears in the text. The historical irony is obvious as the reader listens to the story of the Great Emancipator while he follows the life of Jake Jackson, slave to a dehumanizing job he hates, to an ill wife he resents and abuses, and to culturally induced desires he follows in the vain hope of fulfillment. He finds a spurious substitute for freedom in the mass media. Early in the novel there is a pointed series of lessons about Jake's enslavement to the media as he responds to the newspaper at the breakfast table. In a manner not unlike that of Bigger, he endorses Hitler's anti-Semitism, stating that "foreigners" should be sent "back where they came from. That's what I say."[15] Jake also finds communists to be "the craziest guys going," a judgment by which Wright further marks how far his hero is from understanding his true interests. The same form of self-deception characterizes Bigger through much of *Native Son.*

Jake and Bigger share a love for the movies. Bigger actually goes into the theater, however, and sees there a distorted presentation of class conflict, the rich, and blacks, while Jake merely stops to gaze at a series of posters advertising *The Death Hawk.* A movie about the loves and adventures of an aviator, its plot is the most conventional kind of melodrama. The movie's appeal to Jake not only stereotypes hero, heroine, and villain but also sexually titillates the audience. The villain, complete with waxed mustache, attempts to seduce the golden-haired, blue-eyed heroine before the final triumph of good which finds the hero and heroine in his plane, "their lips . . . meeting in a blissful kiss. . . ."[16] For Jake, all this is more than enough reason to want to see the movie; the poster elicits a judgment that shows he is unable to distinguish mass-produced fantasy from personal desire. As he explains," 'being an aviator sure must be fun, 'specially when you on top of another plane and can send it spinning down like that.'. . . As he turned away, his eyes lingered on the poster where the girl was tied so that her thigh was exposed."[17] As Jake gazes at the thigh, he also reveals his identification with the villain of the movie, a "darkly handsome stranger" whose "delicate snowwhite hands . . . had never worked hard and honestly for a living" and whose "slitty black eyes fastened hard upon the girl's exposed thigh...."[18] Such identification with the aggressor goes beyond the formula that only villains are allowed to express sexual desire overtly. Not only does it imply Jake's acceptance of the values presented by the movie, it also suggests that the movie accurately represents what he actually wants, albeit that which is forbidden him. Ultimately it offers Jake the role of villain as his identity, which he accepts, as, one could argue, does Bigger in the end.

The connection between sex and power is obvious, but at least it is still limited to the world of fantasy in *Lawd Today*, even if the character does not realize that fact. Both Jake and Bigger do not just believe in the values of the movies; they also locate their objects of desire solely within those mass-produced fantasies. The last step of living one's life as if it were a movie is taken both by Bigger and by Saul, the protagonist of Wright's "The Man Who Killed a Shadow." In his detachment from his behavior, Saul is a more complete version of Bigger. Both kill a white woman, both are forced to hide the body, both take up their lives "as though nothing had happened,"[19] both are accused of rape, and both, most significantly, perceive their own actions as if these exist through and in the language of mass culture. The distinction between cultural fiction and personal reality dissolves when Saul awakes the day after the murder. He remembers the incident as if it were a movie: "When at last the conviction of what he had done was real in him, it came only in terms of flat memory, devoid of all emotion, as though he were looking when very tired and sleepy at a scene being flashed upon the screen of a movie house."[20]

To live one's life as if it were taking place upon a movie screen is to participate in the dehumanization of self, as well as of others. Saunders Redding has already pointed out that Wright's heroes seek the "better life" which they have learned about "from the movies, the picture magazines, and the screaming headlines in the daily press."[21] But they do more than learn about the world in this melodramatic fashion. They live and fulfill themselves only as their lives approach that of the hero or the villain, thus their lives are fit for reproduction as melodrama to be consumed by a public seeking its fulfillment from those media. Bigger, as the most fully developed of these heroes, most desires to achieve that kind of identity made available to him through mass culture. Even those acts that defy sociological or psychological theory and only partially fulfill the demands of the plot follow the pattern of the melodramatic hero. Bigger's fate is the triumph of the image over the individual.[22]

The most obvious instance of the media's influence is Bigger's decision to accept a job with the Daltons after seeing the movie *The Gay Woman*. He gains a "great mind to take that job" and is "filled with a sense of excitement about his new job," even though he was unsure about accepting it until that moment despite the threat to cut off his family's relief if he refused.[23] The irony is, as readers of *Native Son* have long recognized, that Bigger's movie-inspired fantasies about the Daltons correspond very well to the situation he encounters:

Yes, his going to work for the Daltons was something big. Maybe Mr. Dalton was a millionaire. Maybe he had a daughter who was a hot kind of girl; maybe she spent lots of money; maybe she'd like to come to the South Side and see the sights sometimes. Or maybe she had a secret sweetheart and only he would know about it because he would have to drive her around; maybe she would give him money not to tell (p. 36).

What Bigger cannot realize is that he is going to be taken into the lives of the Daltons. Although the specifics of their life will match those in the fantasy engendered by the movie, the Daltons and not Bigger will direct the turns of the plot. This awareness comes to him, if only dimly, when he carries a drunken Mary upstairs; he feels "as if he were acting upon a stage in front of a crowd of people" (p. 83).

An even more significant aspect of mass culture's influence upon Bigger occurs after Mary's death, at a time when he appears so fearful that he cannot shake down the ashes of the furnace where he disposed of her body. Bigger repeatedly desires to read the newspaper stories about the presumed disappearance of his victim. He has previously taken no interest in newspapers, with the possible exception that he may have used them to research the details of the ransom note which "he had read . . . somewhere" (p. 167). With the intrusion of the reporters into the Daltons' basement, however, Bigger's interest in the publicity generated by his exploits assumes overwhelming importance in his life. When he sees the newspaper on the floor of the basement, his only wish is to read, even though Mary's body is still in the furnace. As he reads it, the reality of the story, which lists her as missing or kidnapped, is persuasive, even though he knows better: "It seemed impossible that she was there in the fire, burning" if indeed the paper states otherwise (pp. 194–95).

Bigger continues to seek his identity in the newspapers even as his destiny grows progressively bleaker throughout the rest of the book. He wants to read "the story, his story" (p. 208) in the papers, and with this pun Wright collapses history into the contents of the front page to suggest that Bigger can understand himself only as a product of mass culture at its most destructive. Bigger searches for that "fullness" which he finds not in reality so much as in the representations of reality he encounters "when he read the newspapers or magazines, went to the movies, or walked along the streets with crowds . . ." (p. 226). Accordingly, he seeks "to lose himself in it so he could find himself" (p. 226), but the self he finds can only be found in those images of himself that the culture presents to him.

So important is this search for an identity that Bigger devises elaborate strategies to steal a paper in order to read about himself (pp. 226–27). Yet more revealing is his decision to risk exposure by leaving his hiding place to spend his last two cents on a newspaper (p. 228). Even after his capture, Bigger desires to read what the papers are saying about him. So, after he has fainted at the coroner's inquest, he awakes in his cell physically and psychologically hungry. He appeases his appetites by first eating a meal with great relish, the first since his capture, and then asking the guard for a newspaper. It can be no accident that these two forms of consumption are linked in the text. What gives Bigger the ability to live and assert himself in the world is the act of consuming what the world gives him.[24]

Bigger's hunger after the coroner's inquest emphasizes the importance of consumption in a novel where many of the critical episodes occur during, or because of, eating and drinking. What is more, Bigger's initial response to his arrest had been to refuse to eat; his refusal can be understood as an attempt to establish a separate identity outside the power of mass culture. The scene in his prison cell also provides a perspective on Wright's use of documentary material in his fiction, what is sometimes called his "naturalism." The source for this scene is almost certainly the *Chicago Tribune's* stories about Robert Nixon, whose murder case Wright followed from its beginning to Nixon's execution. According to the *Tribune,* Nixon showed animation only "when he spoke of food" and "when he told of having been in the movies."[25] When Wright seized upon these seemingly dehumanizing and gratuitous details to compose his protagonist, he was not simply correcting the *Tribune's* racism. He used them to explore the unsettling relationship between consumption and identity which they suggested to him. In 1948, Wright openly discussed the profoundly disturbing implications of consumption in mass society. Believing that it obliterated the basis for conventional political distinctions, he wrote, "The Right and Left, in different ways, have decided that man is a kind of animal whose needs can be met by making more and more articles for him to consume."[26]

Even though Bigger ultimately rejects the newspapers on grounds that they print "the same thing over and over again" (p. 340), his rejection of the overt aspects of mass culture does not mean he can reject that self that has derived from the media. Much of Bigger's character is best understood as having its origin in that popular figure of thirties melodrama, the tough guy. After Mary's body is discovered in the furnace, for example, Bigger reaches for his gun, thinking to himself "he would shoot before he would let them take him; it meant death either way, and he would die shooting every slug he had" (p. 208). Since this fantasy does not materialize, it prompts the reader to ask where the gratuitous lines come from and what function they serve in the novel. They obviously come from gangster movies and detective stories to shape Bigger's character; he has become what he has consumed. His attitudes about Bessie similarly mimic those of the hard-boiled school when he thinks to himself, "a woman was a dangerous burden when a man was running away." Furthermore, Wright locates the source of this notion of sex in what Bigger "had read of how men had been caught because of women" (p. 135). Most disastrously for Bessie, his decision to kill her comes as much from such American myths of sex, crime, and punishment as it does from any real danger she poses to him. Bigger knows that "some cold logic not his own, over which he had no control" demands her death (p. 215). This explanation of his decision speaks to an otherwise controversial aspect of the text, for Bigger is under no other immediate necessity to kill Bessie, whom, paradoxically, he has forced to accompany him.[27]

Wright was aware that this "logic" might elude readers even as he was writing the novel. At the time, he lived with Herbert and Jane Newton and read portions of the book to Jane as he completed them. Jane objected strenuously to Bessie's murder as "both unnecessary for the development of the plot and insufficiently motivated."[28] Michel Fabre offers an explanation of Bigger's motive as proto-existentialist. The murder, claims Fabre, exemplifies the "right to 'create,'... by rejecting the accidental nature of the first murder with further proof of his power to destroy."[29] This argument, however, equates Bigger with Cross Damon, the hero of Wright's *The Outsider,* who makes such claims himself. Bigger never quite comes to that point, however. As Wright states, the issue for him is whether he can "trust bare, naked feeling this way?" (p. 335). Cross Damon, in contrast, listens to the radio announcement of his death in a subway accident and realizes that his life has become a form of mass entertainment: "They're acting like it's a baseball game, he thought with astonishment."[30] Damon understands early on what Bigger never quite realizes about the power of a mass culture to determine his identity.

By 1935, when he finished "Big Boy Leaves Home," Wright had already critiqued the desire for an identity acquired from mass culture by contrasting it with an identity chosen by the individual. While Big Boy is hiding in the kiln to escape the lynch mob, he fantasizes a heroic death in which he kills many of his attackers before the mob kills him. The desire for revenge is unremarkable in itself. Indeed, if that were all to Big Boy's fantasy, the reader might be tempted to place Big Boy in a more militant Afro-American tradition than the one represented by his terrorized parents. Big Boy makes this impossible when he chooses the mass media as the form of this identity: "N the newspapersd say: NIGGER KILLS DOZEN OF MOB BEFORE LYNCHED! Er mabbe theyd say: TRAPPED NIGGER SLAYS TWENTY BEFO KILLED! He smiled a little. Tha wouldnt be so bad would it?"[31] For a moment, Big Boy believes as Bigger often does that celebrity creates identity. In the story, however, the destructive effects of the fantasy are counteracted by a community that helps Big Boy to escape. Lacking such a community, Bigger is fatally attracted to the identity one achieves through publicity.

Bigger's last appearance in the novel may have more in common with the roles provided by the popular media than with the claim he makes that "what I killed for, I *am*" (p. 392). The sincerity of this sentiment, notwithstanding, it fails to distinguish an authentic personal identity from an identity formed by mass culture. The very last words of the novel, a portrait of Bigger awaiting execution after Max's departure, show Bigger adopting the tough guy as his final identity: "He still held on to the bars. Then he smiled a faint, wry, bitter smile. He heard the ring of steel against steel as the far door clanged shut" (p. 392). In smiling, Bigger calls to mind the dying gangster Jake Jackson describes in *Lawd Today:* "He just looked at 'em and smiled! By Gawd, it takes guts to die like that."[32] Furthermore, Jake's admiring reaction may have more to do with the origin of Bigger's last presentation of self than with the creation of an authentic self through violence. The separation of the reader from the hero, the emphasis on maintaining external appearances, and the gestures of irony and alienation are all too familiar from the tough guy of movies and fiction. If the reader leaves Bigger's consciousness to stand totally outside him, this is so, at least in part, because Bigger has nothing but an outside to know.

Although Bigger is the most complete victim of mass culture in *Native Son,* Wright will not allow the reader to forget that he is emblematic rather than unique. The Daltons pay homage to the influence of mass culture despite their wealth and color. When they pose for newspaper photos, their behavior goes beyond any desire to communicate with their daughter's kidnapper and procure her safe return (p. 201). When the reporters all but break into their house, they send coffee to them, at the very least showing their enormous respect for the power of the press, if not granting that institution the right to invade one's house and private life.

Max, Bigger's lawyer, is the most important of these other characters who present the world in the language of mass culture, mainly because his role in the text has remained so controversial. His speech to the judge provides the subject of an ongoing critical debate over the extent to which this character speaks for Wright's position as a communist. The issue is whether Max's speech fulfills or undercuts the ideology of the text as a whole. By examining Max's language with an eye toward its dependence on mass culture, this central issue can be redefined. His speech necessarily places Max in a world in which the effects of mass culture dominate the lives of every character. Without any specific request from Bigger, Max sends him a newspaper, an acknowledgment of Bigger's curiosity and, as it turns out, an act revealing Max's participation in his society. In the speech to the judge, he decries the invidious influence of the media. He notes "how constantly and overwhelmingly the advertisements, radios, newspapers and movies play upon us!" as he seeks to explain Bigger to the judge as well as to the reader (p. 363).

Ultimately, Max is not so detached from the influence of the media as his statement would seem to indicate. He conceives his task as Bigger's lawyer in terms of constructing a sort of counter-movie to the one created by the press. As he says, "how can I, I asked myself, make the picture of what has happened to this boy show plain and powerful upon a screen of sober reason, when a thousand newspaper and magazine artists have already drawn it in lurid ink upon a million sheets of public print?" (p. 355).[33] Like Bigger, and like those who seek to destroy Bigger, Max sees the world as being composed as a series of images rather than as a place filled with individual and autonomous characters. Accordingly, Max defends Bigger as the "hapless actor in this fateful drama" (p. 357). He has no quarrel with acting as the definition of being nor, as a Marxist, with determinism in general.

The implications of the power Wright grants to mass culture are extraordinarily significant in both psychological and esthetic terms. Wright's transformation of character from an autonomous being into an image created by a mass culture did perplex an early Marxist critic of *Native Son,* Samuel Sillen, who wrote for the *New Masses.* Sillen found two serious faults in other reviews of *Native Son.* The first was a conventional Marxist critique noting the failure of other critics to stress the relationship of the individual to society depicted in the novel. But the second point, in reality a sophisticated development of the first, focused on the development of Bigger's personality: "It is only partly true to say that capitalism makes him what he is; it is even more important to insist that capitalism *unmakes* what he is, a sensitive, imaginative, and creative personality."[34] To grant capitalism the power to unmake as well as to make the individual is to question the possibility of a future according to Marxist theory. Instead, Sillen's insight predicts a world in which human psychology is forever manipulated by the ruling elite to maintain its profits and hegemony. It does so through that ever increasing consumption that Wright found so threatening.

In esthetic terms, *Native Son*'s subversion of the authenticity of character may bring it closer to a cinematic manipulation of the image than to a novelistic valorization of character. Germane to this issue is George Bluestone's argument that cinema and fiction are antithetical because they depend upon quite opposite concepts of character, a difference between the internalized characters of the novel and the externalized characters of film.[35] In "How 'Bigger' Was Born," Wright stated that "the burden of all serious fiction consists almost wholly of character-destiny" (p. xxxi). This statement may seem to be the only non-controversial one in the entire essay, devoted as it is to defending criminality to the law abiding, communism to the noncommunists, and literary effort to the communists. But Bigger lacks those ingrained patterns of belief and habit that denominate character in the realist tradition and in the legacy of nineteenth-century thought. As the destiny of his character is quite different, the novel in which he works out that destiny changes accordingly. Though Bluestone's distinction may hold true for the characters of the traditional novel, it clearly breaks down to the extent that Bigger is a cinematic rather than a novelistic character.

Wright himself specifically called for literature to go "beyond the realism of the novel" in order to create a novel "bigger, different, freer, more open."[36] Such a novel, one might argue, is Thomas Pynchon's *Gravity's Rainbow,* especially in its characterization of Tyrone Slothrop. As Slothrop seeks his origins, he learns, as does the reader, that he possesses no stable and inherent self but is a product of the Pavlovian conditioning he underwent as an infant. His discovery of that fact does not, however, allow him to express his true feelings and develop the authentic self that Marxism, Freudianism, the traditional novel, and nineteenth-century culture as a whole promised. Rather Slothrop disappears; he scatters. He has no self and no identity beyond that which was imposed upon him. In this respect, both Bigger and Slothrop exemplify what John Bayley has called the replacement of character by consciousness in the novel, whose function "is to explore" rather than "to conserve and habituate."[37] Consciousness, however, discovers that its own stability is destroyed in the exploration of the world. Bayley locates the shift to consciousness in the transition from literary figures who are in society to those who are outsiders.[38] To this, it must be added that this transformation is brought about by the pervasive extension of mass culture throughout contemporary society. In theory at least, that extension makes everyone an outsider in the most fundamental sense for it means that the origin of personal identity is imposed from the outside.

Perhaps ironically, given his literary intentions and political beliefs at the time of the composition of *Native Son,* Richard Wright returned the novel to its original function as the popular expression of ordinary life, an expression which both ignores and defies the dictums of higher consciousness, whether be it political or literary.[39] In doing so, he gave *Native Son* a disturbingly prophetic status. Its participation in the world of Superman and tough guys, of popular fantasies of omnipotence, prefigures the writings of Thomas Pynchon and Ishmael Reed more than it extends the literary and philosophical traditions of realism or modernism.

NOTES

[1] Introduction to Malcolm Lowry, *Under the Volcano* (New York: Signet, 1966), p. xiv.

[2] Spender did overlook Claude Edmonde Magny's *The Age of the American Novel* (New York: Ungar, 1972), possibly because it was not translated into English until 1972. Recent examples of scholarship and criticism concerned with film and literature and emphasizing high modernist art are Alan Spiegel, *Fiction and the Camera Eye* (Charlottesville: Univ. Press of Virginia, 1976) and Keith Cohen, *Film and Fiction: The Dynamics of Exchange* (New Haven: Yale Univ. Press, 1979).

[3] Wright refers to the influence of such pulp literature in *Black Boy: A Record of Childhood and Youth* (New York: Harper and Row, 1966), pp. 147, 186.

[4] *The Unfinished Quest of Richard Wright*, trans. Isabel Barzun (New York: William Morrow, 1973), p. 66. In *The Emergence of Richard Wright* (Urbana: Univ. of Illinois Press, 1972), Keneth Kinnamon noted the limited reading material available to a young black in Jackson, Mississippi, at this time: "Such pulp fiction as Zane Grey, *Flynn's Detective Weekly*, the *Argosy All-Story Magazine*, Horatio Alger, and the Get-Rich-Quick Wallingford Series" (p. 27). In "Wright, Ellison, Baldwin—Exorcising the Demon" (*Phylon*, 37, No. 2 [1976]), Jerry H. Bryant connected the melodramatic qualities of *Native Son* to the "action and crime stories . . . that Wright says he grew up on" (p. 181).

[5] Originally 1945. Reprinted as "The Man Who Went to Chicago," *Eight Men* (New York: Pyramid, 1969), pp. 180–81.

[6] "The Man Who Went to Chicago," p. 200.

[7] Fabre, *The Unfinished Quest*, p. 200.

[8] "Personal Impression," in *Richard Wright: Impressions and Perspectives*, eds. David Ray and Robert M. Farnsworth (Ann Arbor: Univ. of Michigan Press, 1973), p. 81.

[9] Jeanine Delpech, "An Interview with Native Son," *The Crisis*, 57 (November, 1950), 625.

[10] The long promised but as yet unpublished edition of Wright's letters may well provide yet more evidence about Wright's relationship to mass culture and his debt to it at the expense of attribution of influence to more conventionally literary sources. Edward Margolies, one of the editors of the edition, informs us that the "The Man Who Lived Underground," conventionally seen as reflecting the example of Dostoyevsky, is in fact more influenced "by a news story" Wright had read. Margolies also notes that "The Man Who Killed a Shadow" and *Savage Holiday* "derive from journalistic sources" (Edward Margolies, "The Letters of Richard Wright," in *The Black Writer in Africa and the Americas*, ed. Lloyd W. Brown [Los Angeles: Hennessey and Ingalls, 1973], p. 107). While there is a great difference between the popular source and the literary result, one should not quickly assume that Wright ignored the esthetic and psychological effects of the sources of his work.

[11] Warren French, "The Lost Potential of Richard Wright," in *The Black American Writer, Volume I: Fiction*, ed. C. W. E. Bigsby (Baltimore: Penguin, 1971), p. 126.

[12] Originally *PM*, March 11, 1945, p. 5. Reported in Fabre, *The Unfinished Quest*, p. 544.

[13] Dan McCall, *The Example of Richard Wright* (New York: Harcourt, Brace & World, 1969), p. 26.

[14] Kinnamon discusses "Long Black Song" in some detail and pays special attention to the clock as the symbol of the machine age (pp. 96–100). He does not discuss the implications of the phonograph.

[15] *Lawd Today* (New York: Avon, 1963), p. 36.

[16] *Lawd Today*, p. 58

[17] *Lawd Today*, p. 58

[18] *Lawd Today*, p. 57.

[19] "The Man Who Killed a Shadow," *Eight Men*, p. 167.

[20] "The Man Who Killed a Shadow," p. 167.

[21] Saunders Redding, "The Alien Land of Richard Wright," in *Soon, One Morning: New Writing by American Negroes, 1940–1962*, ed. Herbert Hill (New York: Alfred A. Knopf, 1969), p. 54.

[22] Fiction is in advance of non-fiction here. It was not until 1951 that Wright, in the process of commenting upon and publicizing the film version of *Native Son*, articulated the proposition inherent in Bigger's character and fate: "It gradually dawns upon the writer that there is a mystery about the image; that it is not only not reality, but it is a reality of its own, different in kind from what he sees on the street" ("*Native Son* Filmed in Argentina," *Ebony* [November, 1951], 83).

[23] Richard Wright, *Native Son* (New York: Harper and Row, 1966), p. 35. Subsequent page references to *Native Son* will be given parenthetically in the text. In "Images of Vision in *Native Son*," *University Review*, 36, No. 2 (1969), James Nagel notes that "Bigger's view of the white world is, essentially, a simplistic re-creation of the images in the popular media" (p. 111).

[24] In fact, hunger and eating are almost always given metaphoric and thematic significance by Wright. His original title for the autobiography was *American Hunger*, in many ways a more apt and revealing title than *Black Boy*. An interesting example of Wright's use of consumption is found in *Lawd Today*. Jake finds himself "hungering for more" as he dances with Blanche, a prostitute. The music promises him "an unattainable satisfaction." But what it provides is a particularly pernicious example of mass culture; the band plays "Is It True What They Say about Dixie," a lie Jake consumes and which consumes him. To further underline the damage done by mass culture, Jake and Blanche's verbal response to the music reveals a meaning of which they remain unaware: " 'That's murder, Papa.' 'I want to be electrocuted,' he said" (*Lawd Today*, p. 207).

[25] *Chicago Daily Tribune* (June 5, 1938), p. 6. There can be no doubt that Wright saw this story as he quoted other parts of it almost word for word, especially in the description of Bigger in *Native Son* (pp. 260–61). There was, of course, a more reasonable explanation of Nixon's interest in food provided by the *Chicago Defender* (June 18, 1938), p. 2. According to Robert Nixon, "they gave us that after they had whipped and kicked us and made us confess."

[26] Quoted in Fabre, *The Unfinished Quest*, p. 325.

[27] For example, Addison Gayle finds Bessie's murder "the weakest incident in the novel" because it violates the black nationalism he sees as the basic thrust of the novel (*The Way of the New World: The Black Novel in America* [Garden City: Doubleday, 1975], p. 171). Perhaps the strongest defense of Bessie's murder is made by Donald B. Gibson, "Richard Wright and the Tyranny of Convention," *CLA Journal*, 12 (June, 1969), 349. He argues that Bigger kills Bessie so as to be "emotionally convinced that he has murdered Mary, for he projects the consciousness of the later act back into the former." But even such an explanation does not fully answer the question of the origin of Bigger's motives, for Gibson does not argue that Bigger is aware of these reasons. One significant change in the dramatized version of *Native Son* was the manner and cause of Bessie's (renamed Clara in the play) death. After she has accidentally led the police to Bigger's hideout, he grows angry with her, threatens to kill her, and does hit her. But when the police start to shoot, Bigger is "holding Clara protectively in front of him" and she is killed by a police bullet (Paul Green and Richard Wright, *Native Son* (*The Biography of a Young American*): *A Play in Ten Scenes* [New York: Harper and Brothers, 1941], pp. 119–20). Such a change gains sympathy for Bigger by making him the victim rather than the villain of melodrama.

[28] Quoted in Fabre, p. 171.

[29] Fabre, p. 171.

[30] *The Outsider* (New York: Harper & Row, 1953), p. 80.

[31] *Uncle Tom's Children*, p. 44.

[32] *Lawd Today*, pp. 34–35.

[33] In *Richard Wright* (New York: Frederick Ungar, 1973) David Bakish calls attention to the difficulty Bigger has in communicating with Max not only because of racial, political, and educational differences, but also because "the twilight, unclear world in which he was forced to live was dangerously ambiguous, filled with shadows, play-acting, motion pictures, newspaper headlines, all elements of second-hand living, and that he could not grasp either himself or the world until he had killed" (p. 39).

[34] Samuel Sillen, "The Meaning of Bigger Thomas," *New Masses*, 35 (April 30, 1940), 26 (Sillen's emphasis). Both the importance and problematic nature of *Native Son* to American communists are reflected in the fact that *New Masses* published four articles on it written or compiled by Sillen. The last, "*Native Son*: Pros and Cons," *New Masses*, 35 (May 21, 1940), quoted a letter from a Joseph Cole, who argued that Wright's use of melodrama "is completely at loggerheads with what must have been the author's intentions" (p. 24).

[35] George Bluestone, *Novels into Film* (Berkeley: Univ. of California Press, 1966), p. 23. In *Theory*

of Film, Siegfried Kracauer distinguishes between two essential but contradictory tendencies in photography, the "formative" and "realistic" (*Theory of Film: The Redemption of Physical Reality* [New York: Oxford Univ. Press, 1960], p. 16). Insofar as the formative gains ascendency, the traditional character loses the supremacy it once had in the novel and on the stage. Both Kracauer (p. 44) and Bluestone (p. 26) discuss the displacement of the animate by the inanimate in film. Stanley Aronowitz has even asserted that film's basis of characterization and character marks the transformation of "human persons from a thinking, emotionally laden individual into an object which moves among other objects" ("Critic as Star," *Minnesota Review,* n.s. 9 [Fall, 1977], 88).

[36] Richard Wright, "E. M. Forster Anatomizes the Novel," *PM* (March 16, 1947), p. 3. How appropriate that Forster's *Aspects of the Novel,* the source of so many of the ways in which we think of the novel and its characters, should have provoked Wright to this conclusion.

[37] John Bayley, "Character and Consciousness," *New Literary History,* 5 (Winter, 1974), 225.

[38] Bayley, 227.

[39] What Walter Benjamin claimed is true for the work of art as a result of the introduction of mechanical reproduction is true as well for the literary character and perhaps for the self of modern man: "When the age of mechanical reproduction separated art from its basis in cult, the semblance of its autonomy disappeared forever" ("The Work of Art in the Age of Mechanical Reproduction," *Illuminations,* ed. Hannah Arendt [New York: Schocken Books, 1969], p. 226). The very concept of authenticity is lost to art in the mechanical age according to Benjamin (p. 224), a loss that leads to the politicization of art and the estheticization of politics, either Communism or Fascism. Benjamin's comments remind us that Wright saw Bigger as ready for a Fascist leader and movement. I would argue that he is ready because he can only live as a melodramatic reproduction of the world and its definition of him. So *Native Son* is a political novel, though one which achieves that status by giving character and novel over to those conceptions of mass culture against which so much modern literature and criticism have protested.

Robert James Butler

THE FUNCTION OF
VIOLENCE IN *NATIVE SON*

Since the appearance of *Native Son* in 1940, critics have raised questions about its heavy preoccupation with violence. In an early review of the book, Malcolm Cowley, then a strong defender of Wright, nevertheless worried that "the author's deep sense of the inequities heaped upon his race" would result in his "revenging himself by a whole series of symbolic murders" in his fiction (67). David Daiches complained in a subsequent review that the novel's thesis was seriously undercut because the killing of Mary Dalton was so "violent and unusual," a melodramatic action which was too bizarre to verify the book's claims about the general condition of blacks in America (95). Twenty-one years later, James Baldwin put the case most pointedly in *Nobody Knows My Name*, arguing that "one of the severest criticisms that can be leveled" against *Native Son* is Wright's "gratuitous and compulsive" interest in violence in the book: "The violence is gratuitous and compulsive because the root of the violence is never examined. The root is rage. It is the rage, almost literally the howl, of a man who is being castrated" (151).[1] Baldwin claimed that because of this fixation with sensationalistic outer action Wright failed to provide an adequate portrayal of character and theme, reducing both to simplistic formulae. Echoing Baldwin's view, Nathan Scott complained in 1970 that Wright's obsession with "the raging abysses of violent criminality" forced him "to practice a terrible brutalization upon his characters" (19). And Cecil Brown objected in 1968 to Wright's "gratuitous" use of violence, especially in his depiction of relationships between black men and white women (174). Even as late as the mid-seventies when Wright's bold treatment of violence was still cited by many as evidence of his credentials as a revolutionary writer, Addison Gayle was aesthetically uncomfortable with the murder of Bessie Mears because he felt it detracted from the basic thrust of the novel: an indictment of the white society intent on destroying Bigger (170–71).

My purpose is to demonstrate that Wright was always in full artistic control of

From *Black American Literature Forum* 20, Nos. 1–2 (Spring–Summer 1986): 9–25.

the violence in his best fiction. *Native Son,* his masterwork, uses violence extensively but as a necessary and powerful reflector of the deepest recesses of its
central character's radically divided nature. Wright emphasizes throughout the
novel the fact that "there were two Biggers" (214), one trapped by environmental
determinants and the other aspiring to a better life and a more fully realized self.
The early scenes with Gus vividly dramatize this polarity. Although one part of
Bigger resents Gus and almost kills him in a poolroom brawl, another part of Bigger
responds to Gus in a very personal, even affectionate, way. Indeed, he shares with
his friend his most deeply felt longing, a desire not only to be a pilot but also to
" 'fly' " beyond the harsh determinants which rule his life (14). When Gus reminds
him of the way in which white society will frustrate these hopes, Bigger does not
lash out with reflexive hatred but instead jokes about the situation, in effect trans-
forming his pain into an ironic awareness which the two of them enjoy.

In other words, Bigger is neither the "depraved and inhuman beast" (16)
described by Scott nor the "monster created by the American republic" (26)
imagined by Baldwin in *Notes of a Native Son.*[2] He is instead a richly imagined
character who surely does have a "soft," humane side to his personality which
naturally responds to what he perceives as the opportunities of American life.
Leaning against a "red-brick wall" (13) which is an obvious symbol of an environment intent upon reducing his life to stasis, he nevertheless has a deeply felt urge
to transcend this narrow existence and become part of a fluid world of movement
and possibility:

> Bigger took out his pack and gave Gus a cigarette; he lit his and held the
> match for Gus. They leaned their backs against the red-brick wall of a building,
> smoking, their cigarettes slanting white across their black chins. To the east
> Bigger saw the sun burning a dazzling yellow. In the sky above him a few big
> white clouds drifted. He puffed silently, relaxed, his mind pleasantly vacant of
> purpose. Every slight movement in the street evoked a casual curiosity in him.
> Automatically, his eyes followed each car as it whirred over the smooth black
> asphalt. A woman came by and he watched the gentle sway of her body until
> she disappeared into a doorway. He sighed, scratched his chin and mumbled,
> "Kinda warm today." (13)

This is the Bigger Thomas that most critics fail to see because his actions violate
their conventional view of him as simply a "bad nigger" or a victim of society.
Despite the fact that Bigger will later kill two women after his normal drives toward
love have been twisted, here he takes an altogether normal pleasure in watching
the "gentle sway" of a woman's body as she enters a building. And whereas most
of the novel's key scenes of violence are acted out at night during powerful
snowstorms which reflect the turbulent, uncontrolled emotions of the characters,
Bigger here enjoys the "sun burning a dazzling yellow" and the white clouds floating
in a bright sky. Rigidly trapped in confining rooms throughout the book, Bigger at
this point is given a rare opportunity to become momentarily a part of a natural,

fluid world. The fast-moving cars, the drifting clouds, the gracefully walking woman, and the high-flying plane touch Bigger at the core of his being, revealing a person who has all the usual American instincts for a life of change and possibility.

This duality in Bigger is even more powerfully revealed in his relationships with Bessie and Mary, who represent the extreme poles of his divided self. Whereas Mary represents a side of Bigger which may be called "romantic" because it is centered in an idealized set of longings for a radically new life based upon expanded possibilities, Bessie epitomizes an aspect of his personality which may be called "naturalistic" since it is severely conditioned by the economic, political, and social pressures of his actual environment. It is one of the novel's most deeply significant ironies that Bigger is never permitted to relate positively to either woman but is instead driven to destroy them because of his deep-seated fears of what he realizes they represent in him. For one of the more terrifying aspects of his world is that genuine consciousness of self is almost always equated with death: "He knew that the moment he allowed what his life meant to enter fully into his consciousness, he would either kill himself or someone else" (9). In destroying Mary and Bessie, Bigger ironically accomplishes both tasks. For Wright portrays these women not only as separate characters who frustrate Bigger but, more importantly, as externalizations of the extreme limits of his divided self, two poles which he feels compelled to destroy because his world never gives him an opportunity to know, accept, and love them. The net result is not only Bigger's literal death in the electric chair but his own acts of self-destruction, which result in a kind of moral suicide.

Throughout Books One and Two Bigger and Mary are subtly linked, even though they appear to come from separate universes. Both characters are alienated from their environments and are perceived as aberrant by many of the people who are closest to them. In the novel's opening scene, Bigger's mother becomes so exasperated by his behavior that she calls him " 'crazy' " and warns him about the direction his life is taking: " 'You'll regret how you living some day. . . . If you don't stop running with that gang of yours and do right you'll end up where you never thought you would' " (8). In the same way, Peggy, the Daltons' maid, characterizes Mary as " 'kind of wild,' " a well-intentioned but naive girl who worries her folks " 'to death' " by running around with " 'a wild and crazy bunch of reds' " (49). Just as Mrs. Thomas views her son's erratic behavior as a threat to the well-being of their family, Peggy claims that Mary's activities run counter to order and stability in the family: " 'If it wasn't for Mary and her wild ways, this household would run like a clock' " (104). To further reinforce these similarities between the two characters, Mr. Dalton describes Mary as " 'that crazy daughter of mine' " directly after he has characterized Bigger as a sort of " 'problem boy' " (139).

What Wright suggests here by these important parallels is that Bigger and Mary share a common humanity, despite the obvious dissimilarities arising from their radically different social and economic backgrounds. Although this humanity is frustrated in different ways by environment, the same results are produced: alienation and rebellion. Mary's physically comfortable life has given her privileges and opportunities denied to Bigger, but it has also stunted her growth by making her "blind" (91) to reality. Just as Bigger has been walled off from many aspects of life by his stark poverty and his status as a black man in a white world, Mary has been separated from real experience by overly protective parents and her privileged status as a rich white girl. Both respond to their situations in very similar ways— Bigger in forming a gang which engages in acts of rebellion by robbing stores, and Mary by developing friendships with Communists who are committed to over- turning society by redistributing wealth. Both characters rebel strongly against the families into which they are born because they sense that these families block their own human development. Because Bigger is "sick of his life at home" (11) he becomes part of a peer group that represents everything of which his mother does not approve. Mary too feels stifled by the limits imposed upon her by her family and deliberately opposes their wishes by running away to New York, taking off with Jan to Florida, and entering his circle of radicals.

On a more basic level, the common humanity shared by Bigger and Mary is dramatized by their strong sexual attraction to each other. Mary, who wants to know more about the rougher aspects of life from which she has been protected, is romantically attracted to Bigger, just as he is drawn to her apparently glamorous life because it represents a world of pleasure and possibility from which he has been excluded and which he has seen only in movies. From the beginning, Bigger connects Mary with the film he has seen which gives a romantic view of rich white women who will " 'do anything' " (26). Such films fill him with a sense of excitement because they evoke a sense of possibility which is a natural part of his character that has been frustrated by environment. Linking his perception of the movie with a remembered story of a white woman who has actually married her chauffeur, he goes to work for the Daltons with a sense that the job might contain " 'something *big*' " (21) for him. Although he is not consciously aware of it, he has made a number of assumptions about Mary even before he has met her: She symbolizes a world for which a substantial part of himself has been longing, and he feels that this world may be reachable through sex.

Because Mary represents the fluid, open world which stands in such vivid contrast to his own static, closed environment, Bigger very often perceives her in terms of romantic images of softness. Helping her out of her automobile, he becomes excited by the "softness" (70) of her body, just as he will later be fully aroused by the "tips of his fingers feeling the soft swelling of her breasts" (71). When she "swayed limply" against him, thus permitting him to feel the "soft curves of her body," he experiences a strong sense of "physical elation" (72). Exposed to such a luxuriant world, Bigger's hard exterior melts—his skin "glowed warm" as he looks at her face in the dim light. Tiptoeing lightly to her room and closing the door "softly," he sharply contrasts Mary with Bessie: "She was much smaller than Bessie, his girl, but much softer" (73).

One of the novel's bitterest ironies is the fact that this "soft" and "warm" erotic world is profoundly destructive for both Bigger and Mary. This is so for two reasons: (1) He is never comfortable with the side of his character which Mary evokes, and (2) the social world in which they are placed exacts enormous penalties for human warmth and love, encouraging instead behavior which is essentially "hard" and "cold." Indeed, Bigger has been so damaged by the environment which tries to freeze him into a brutally naturalistic role that he deeply resents Mary because she responds to him as if he were " 'human' " (60).[3] When she asserts her belief that blacks are people, he feels an immediate need to "blot . . . out" (60) not only her but himself and Jan as well. Although one part of him is attracted to her because she touches aspects of him which his environment has tried to destroy, another part of him recoils from such human contact. His reactions to her, therefore, are painfully ambivalent—"a mingled feeling of helplessness, admiration, and hate" (71). Even when sexually aroused by Mary, Bigger feels a combination of "excitement and fear" (72). His romantic self is understandably excited by her, but his naturalistic self is fearful of her because he is acutely aware of the harsh penalties his environment exacts for black/white sexual relationships.

What Wright suggests here is that Bigger's tangled duality has damaged him at the very center of his being. Because the opposed aspects of his divided self are at such odds, his drives toward love have been ensnarled with his impulses toward hate. For this reason, his attempts to touch people through romantic love almost always get displaced by his desire to destroy people with violence triggered by environmental pressures. To dramatize this, Wright repeatedly uses ironic images of sexual inversion throughout the novel.[4] Lovemaking is consistently described in terms of violence, and violence is often described with images of sexual satisfaction. The death of Mary Dalton, perhaps the most revealing sequence Wright ever wrote, is a brilliant illustration of this inversion.

Although the scene begins romantically with Mary's encouraging Bigger's sexual attentions and his reciprocating, Mrs. Dalton's entry into the room abruptly turns their lovemaking into death making. But Wright artfully persists in using erotic images to describe the scene, turning them inside out for shockingly ironic effect. As Mrs. Dalton approaches the two, all of Bigger's violent tendencies become "erected": ". . . he grew tight and full, as though about to explode" (74). When Mary's fingernails tear at him, he covers her entire face with a pillow and her suffocation is described in terms of copulation: "Mary's body surged upward and he pushed downward upon the pillow with all of his weight, determined that she must not move or make any sound that would betray him. Again Mary's body heaved and he held the pillow in a grip that took all of his strength. For a long time he felt the sharp pain of her fingernails biting into his wrists" (74). After her "surging and heaving" (74) body finally relaxes and Mrs. Dalton leaves the room, Bigger orgasmically utters "a long gasp" (75). In the afterglow of this strange experience, he is depicted as "weak and wet with sweat" (75), listening for some time to his heavy breathing filling the darkness.

Although the scene begins with Bigger's tough self dissolving as he gives in to his warmer, more humane feelings, it reverses suddenly when he feels a deep environmentally induced fear that Mrs. Dalton will "touch" him (73). The romantic Bigger who desires to touch Mary intimately is now replaced by the naturalistic Bigger intent on protecting himself with violence. His first imagined response to Mrs. Dalton is "to knock her out of the way and bolt from the room" (73). Overcome by a panic which crystallizes all of the fears he has been taught as a black male, he literally hardens into a defensive violence: "His muscles flexed taut as steel and he pressed the pillow . . ." (74).

In its most basic terms, *Native Son* dramatizes a bleak environment in which people touch each other only in violence, almost never in love or friendship. When Bigger remembers the moment when Jan shook his hand at their first meeting, he reflects that it was "an awful moment of hate and shame" (84). He feels even worse later, in the car, when Mary's leg accidentally nudges him and he recoils in fear and confusion. Likewise, he is revulsed by Bessie's entire life when he places his hand on her shoulder: "It brought to him a full sense of her life, what he had been thinking and feeling when he had placed his hand upon her shoulder. The same deep realization he had that morning at home at the breakfast table while watching Vera and Buddy and his mother came back to him; only it was Bessie he was looking at now and seeing how blind she was. He felt the narrow orbit of her life . . ." (118). Indeed, most of the times when Bigger physically makes contact with other people result in acts of automatic violence—poking Gus with his knife, suffocating Mary, crushing Bessie's skull, and knocking out a policeman with his revolver. Even when his own family gets too close to him, he has an urge "to wave his hand and blot them out. They were always too close to him . . ." (85).

This problem is not restricted to Bigger but affects nearly everyone in the novel. The Daltons, for all their superficial calm and apparent love, never really touch each other deeply. Mr. and Mrs. Dalton are usually portrayed as coldly detached from each other, and Mary has grown so distant from them that they are unable either to understand or to communicate with her. Mr. Dalton's business dealings touch people in a crudely exploitative way, contributing to much of the violence portrayed in the novel. Max, for all his good intentions, is never able to contact Bigger on a fundamentally human level and in the final scene is described as perfunctorily shaking Bigger's hand while he gropes for his hat "like a blind man" (358). And our final image of Bigger shows him grasping the bars of his cell with "both hands" (359) as Max walks away from him, his head "averted" (358) in fear.

If Bigger is compelled by environment to kill not only Mary but also the romantic self she represents, he is also driven by the same environment to destroy the other part of his personality, the naturalistic self which alternates between violence and apathy.[5] It is this latter personality which emerges in his contacts with Bessie, who in Bigger's mind is diametrically opposed to everything he associates with Mary. Mary is seen in terms of the open possibilities that money and social position give her, while Bessie is viewed in terms of the impotence that her poverty forces upon her.

To stress the function of the two women as aspects of Bigger's radically divided self, Wright has him acting in two distinctly different ways when responding to each woman. With Mary, Bigger usually acts in an outwardly quiet and deferential way, but with Bessie he almost always acts in a thoroughly aggressive manner. When he meets her in Ernie's Chicken Shack he speaks to her "gruffly" (63) and later in her apartment tries to dominate her by grabbing her arm and roughly kissing her. Directly after making love to her he begins coldly to plan his extortion scheme, deciding to "use" (117) Bessie in it. In a later episode in which he actually forces her to write the extortion note, he treats her even more harshly, acting out the role of the gangster he has probably observed in detective magazines. He shoves her, yells at her, and at one point smacks her solidly in the face. And in the scene in which he kills her, he brutally imposes his sexual desires upon her and then crushes her skull in a grimly deliberate way.

Bigger's expressed motives for involving Bessie in the extortion plot and later murdering her do not make real sense when seen in terms of the novel's outward action. Although he consciously thinks that he can "use her" (117) in carrying out his scheme, she obviously is a burden to him from the very beginning. And although he later thinks that he must kill her because "it was his life against hers" (200), such is not literally the case. By the time he kills Bessie, the police already know that he killed Mary, and Bigger would, moreover, be better off simply fleeing after Mary's body is found. The lengthy episode with Bessie slows him down, and his killing her surely leaves more tracks for the police to follow.

Bigger's consciously formulated thoughts therefore have little to do with his actual treatment of Bessie. Their entire relationship, especially his murder of her, is instead a revelation of his deepest subconscious drives. Part of the explanation for involving her in the crime is his unarticulated need for human contact, something which will relieve his extreme isolation. But he also subconsciously links Bessie with a way of alleviating his deepest fears. It is no coincidence that each of his three visits with her takes place after his dealings with the white world have aroused his anxieties to such a point that he instinctively recoils from everything whites represent and retreats into the world he shares with Bessie. For example, when he becomes disturbed by the emotions which Jan and Mary stir in him, he contemplates Bessie as relief: "He wanted to run. Or listen to some swing music. Or laugh or joke. Or read a *Real Detective Story Magazine*. Or go to a movie. Or visit Bessie" (24). Bessie clearly represents that side of Bigger's character which avoids life through either the violence he can vicariously experience in a detective story or the passivity he can lapse into while listening to swing music. His three visits to Bessie are triggered by this simple desire for release, first from the horror at having killed Mary, then by the anxiety brought on by conversations with Jan and Mr. Dalton, and finally by the terror resulting from Mary's bones' being discovered in the furnace. Bessie, therefore, serves the function earlier supplied by Gus—both represent a world which allows Bigger to act out safely the compensatory role of tough guy, all the while he is threatened by a naturalistic environment.

Bigger kills Bessie in Book Two for precisely the same reasons he almost killed

Gus in Book One. Although part of Bigger is attracted to the naturalistic world which Bessie and Gus symbolize, another part of him despises this world because its impotence and despair have infected his character. His desire to "blot out" (119) Bessie, therefore, is finally stronger than his impulse to love or even rape her. In the final analysis, Bigger sees Bessie as a mirror into which he can no longer bear to look.

Just as Bigger in Mary's bedroom reflected some of Mary's "softness," he strongly resembles Bessie in the scene in which he murders her. Drinking heavily in the initial portions of the scene, he becomes strangely lethargic. He complains of feeling " 'tired and awful sleepy' " (192). Although he should be intent on keeping his mind alert and his body active for escape, he drinks from the whiskey bottle she keeps in her purse. Because "the whiskey lulled him, numbed his senses" (197), it reduces him for the time being to Bessie's level of passivity. The net effect is to nullify his impulse to escape: "It seemed that his body had turned into a piece of lead..." (192). To underscore further this transformation of Bigger into Bessie, Wright tells us: "Bessie cried again. He caught her face in his hands. He was concerned; he wanted to see this thing through her eyes at that moment" (193). Touching Bessie, he momentarily assumes her perspective, fully assimilating the despair she articulates soon afterwards: " 'I wish to God I never seen you. I wish one of us had died before we was born. All you ever caused me was trouble, just plain black trouble.... I see it now. I ain't drunk now. I see everything you ever did to me. I didn't want to see it before. I was too busy thinking about how good I felt when I was with you. I thought I was happy, but deep down in me I knew I wasn't. But you got me into this murder and I see it all now. I been a fool, just a blind dumb black drunk fool' " (195). Bessie, who at this point simply repeats the negative things Bigger's mother has said about him in the novel's opening scene, becomes an externalization not only of Bigger's environment but also of the self-hatred induced by that environment. In this sense, Bigger *is* driven to kill her and what she represents in an effort "to save himself" (195). Although his conscious mind falsely justifies her murder on the basis that she will physically hinder his escape, his subconscious thinking provides the real motive: Killing her is an attempt to destroy that part of him which is trapped in self-loathing and despair. In this sense he is correct when he claims that "it was his life against hers" (200). What she symbolically represents must be destroyed if he is to become a full person.

Whichever way Bigger turns, therefore, he is driven to moral suicide. If he gives in to the romantic part of himself he will go mad with frustration because his society tempts him with false images of success which will forever remain out of his grasp. Despite the glamorous images of whites which Bigger sees in films and despite occasional folk stories he hears about chauffeurs marrying rich white women, people like Mary will always remain phantoms to him. But if he opts to live according to the tough, naturalistic self that he exposes to Bessie, he must pay an equally terrible price. As much as American society glamorizes outlaws in movies, it simply annihilates them in real life. As Mrs. Thomas makes clear in the novel's first scene, there is only one path which Bigger the "hard guy" can travel: the inevitable road leading to the electric chair. For society views *his very existence [a]s a crime against the state"* (336).

In a subtly ironic way, Book Three allows Bigger to experience temporarily another mode of existence, one which permits him briefly to develop a fuller, more substantial self which transcends the polarities and divisions which Bessie and Mary suggest. Bigger eventually achieves a rich existential awareness of himself which allows him to move well beyond the shallow romanticism associated with Mary and the confining naturalism represented by Bessie. But just as he is on the verge of actualizing this self, society does to him precisely what he did to Mary and Bessie—it kills him, partly out of fear and partly out of hatred. Thus Bigger is finally revealed as a true "native son" and what Wright once termed in *White Man, Listen!* "the metaphor of America" (72): His own violent actions are gruesomely reflected in the murderous society in which he is placed.

From the very outset of Book Three, Bigger is presented as hungering for "a new mode of life" (234), one which will release him from the emotional traps he has been confined to in the earlier parts of the novel. We are told, for example, in the first paragraph of Book Three: "Toward no one in the world did he feel any fear now, for he knew that fear was useless; and toward no one in the world did he feel any hate now, for he knew that hate would not help him" (233). For the first time in his life Bigger is released in a meaningful way from the fear which resulted in his killing of Mary and the hate which erupted in his murder of Bessie. He will temporarily give in to these emotions in Book Three when, for example, he lashes out in hatred at Reverend Hammond or when he is reduced by fear to speech-lessness in court. But, for the most part, Bigger is partially able in the final stages of his life to transcend these emotions and develop a liberating view of himself.

A revealing key to this development is his desire and ability to touch others. Although Book Two ends with his hands metaphorically and literally frozen, the final book contains several important scenes in which Bigger makes meaningful contact with himself and others. Encouraged by Jan and Max "to believe in himself," he begins "holding his life in his hands" (264). Observing a fellow black prisoner being manhandled by guards, he feels genuine "sympathy" (291) and a desire to reach out to another human being: "For the first time since his capture, Bigger felt that he wanted someone near him, something physical to cling to" (292). On a broader level, Bigger is able to experience a vision of human solidarity in which all people "touch" one another:

> Slowly he lifted his hands in darkness and held them in mid-air, the fingers spread weakly open. If he reached out with his hands, and if his hands were electric wires, and if his heart were a battery giving life and fire to those hands, and if he reached out with his hands and touched other people, reached out through these stone walls and felt other hands connected with other hearts—

if he did that, would there be a reply, a shock? . . . And in that touch, response of recognition, there would be union, identity; there would be a supporting oneness, a wholeness which had been denied him all his life. (307)

Here Bigger is no longer divided into two mutually exclusive selves. As a result of his momentary wholeness, he can tentatively reach out to the world in love rather than violence. Although his efforts to touch people will finally be canceled out by the "shock" of his being executed in the electric chair, Wright nevertheless stresses that Bigger in Book Three achieves a range of human responses not possible for him previously.

Clear evidence of this development is his changed view of most of the people he earlier wanted to "blot out." He finally overcomes the feelings of shame and resentment he had previously felt toward his mother and at the end of the novel asks Max to tell her " 'not to worry none' " because he is " 'all right' " (358). Listening to Jan reveal his deepest feelings about Mary, he grasps Jan's humanity and feels genuine remorse for hurting him: "For the first time in his life a white man became a human being to him; and the reality of Jan's humanity came [to him] in a stab of remorse . . ." (246). He likewise identifies with Jan as he is baited on the witness stand by Buckley, sensing a basic kinship with Jan as an outsider to American society. And part of him comes to realize that his killing of Bessie and Mary is no cause for pride. Rather, he begins to understand that his acts stemmed from his own "blindness," which resulted in his harming other people and himself:

> Another impulse rose in him, born of desperate need, and his mind clothed it in an image of a strong blinding sun sending hot rays down and he was standing in the midst of a vast crowd of men, white men and black men and all men, and the sun's rays melted away the differences, the colors, the clothes, and drew what was common and good upward toward the sun. . . .
> Had he killed Mary and Bessie and brought sorrow to his mother and sister and put himself in the shadow of the electric chair only to find out this? Had he been blind all along? (307)

Bigger's human awareness is never adequate to resolve fully all of his problems because he is never given sufficient time to sustain and develop such an awareness. But Wright does portray him as moving away from the dehumanized violence and impoverished consciousness which characterized him in Books One and Two. Through the depth of his own suffering and genuine contact with other people, Bigger is able to "see" much of what he was earlier blind to. He comes to understand that his mother, Jan, Bessie, and Mary are victims of the same society which has brutalized him, and he responds to them with compassion rather than defensive hatred. He also realizes that he killed two people not out of any heroic motives but simply because he was " 'scared and mad' " (300). Moreover, he consciously tries to reconcile his blind feelings with an existential consciousness that can assimilate, transform, and direct those feelings: "He felt he could not move again unless he swung out from the base of his own feelings; he felt he would have to have light in order to act now" (264). Because he makes such a conscious attempt to move from "blind impulses" to "understanding" (306), he begins to live in "a thin, hard core of consciousness" (305).

Unfortunately, Bigger's emerging consciousness is too thin and hard, permitting only a partial and very fragile understanding of his world. It finally congeals into the narrow, ironic perspective suggested by his "wry, bitter smile" (359) at the conclusion of the novel. He can clearly see, through Max's lack of nerve and reliance on cold abstraction, two factors which explain the reason that Max fails to respond adequately to Bigger in the novel's final episode. But when Bigger claims " 'what I killed for, I *am!*' " (358), he is mistaken. Although he *was* that person, one completely governed by the violent compulsions induced by a pathological environment, he has for a time in Book Three moved beyond this toward a deeper, fuller humanity. His existential self, although awakened by shocking acts of violence, can be nurtured only by a consciousness which can understand and transcend the limits of both environmental conditioning and romantic yearning.

Bigger's incomplete development is vividly illustrated in the novel's final episode. Although usually read as Max's failure to respond adequately to Bigger as a person, it is in fact a more complicated scene, because both characters fail to understand and meet each other's needs. Although Bigger wants to communicate to Max "a sure and firm knowledge" (350) of his entire life before dying, he succeeds in conveying a mixture of knowledge and misconceptions about himself. He is surely correct when he claims he is not " 'hard' " (355), despite the appearances he has created for much of his life. And he reaches an important insight when he says that the men who sentenced him to die are " 'like' " him because they too used violence to " 'get something' " (355), a sense of control over experience. But when Bigger asserts that his violence has illuminated all of the larger truths of his life he is mistaken. His statement " 'What I killed for must've been good!' " (358) is at best a half-truth. Although such violence has awakened in him a vision of how his world in fact operates, it is not seen by Wright as finally "good" because it is a dead end, canceling out love, rather than a true mode of human development. Bigger's statements, although deeply felt, are not clearly thought out and therefore result in clouding his vision of himself and breaking off the contact he wishes to establish with Max. Although the scene begins with the two establishing eye contact and embracing each other, it ends with their speaking "across a gulf of silence" (356), their heads averted and their minds at odds with each other.

Likewise, Max tries sincerely to communicate with Bigger but manages only to create more distance between them. The political consolations he offers that certain beliefs will " 'make the world live again' " (357) leave Bigger unaffected because they are too remote and abstract. When he tries to reach Bigger on a more personal level, he fails even more disastrously because he can give him little more than clichés from Hollywood melodrama such as " 'Men die alone' " (354) and " '. . . you've got to . . . believe in yourself ' " (358).

In short, neither person is sufficiently equipped to understand the full density and complexity of the other's life. Max's fear of Bigger's true feelings and his separation from concrete reality caused by his excessive devotion to ideology make him a "blind man" (358) who is ultimately forced to turn his back on Bigger and most of the disturbing realities which he represents. And Bigger's eyes are described as "wide and unseeing" (355) because they have been opened too quickly and violently. Although they now see the hard, clear light of a reality no longer blurred by racist preconceptions, they are essentially unfocused and therefore miss the precise outlines, sharp details, and real depths of his own experience.

Rollo May observes in Love and Will that:

> There is a dialectical relationship between apathy and violence. To live in apathy provokes violence and . . . violence provokes apathy. . . . Violence is the ultimate destructive substitute which surges in to fill the vacuum where there is no relatedness. . . . When the inward life dries up, when feeling decreases and apathy increases, when one can not affect or even genuinely touch another person, violence flares up as a daimonic necessity for contact, a mad drive forcing touch in the most direct way possible. . . . to inflict pain and torture at least proves that one can affect somebody. (30)

Although Bigger Thomas's acts of violence may appear as monstrous, Bigger is always presented by Wright in complexly human terms, as a person caught up in a world which forces upon him the two equally dehumanizing options which May describes: a numbing apathy and a destructive violence. Given the grim demands of such a world, it is no small triumph for Bigger to establish a human vision of himself, however fragile that vision may be. Wright's extensive portrayal of violence in Native Son, therefore, is neither gratuitous nor sensationalistic. Rather, it is a powerful reflector of both the central character's drive for selfhood and the social environment which is intent on wasting that drive by forcing Bigger into a "vacuum where there is no relatedness."

Despite all his efforts to endow his life with meaning, Bigger is finally confronted by society with a vacuum—death in the electric chair. And, ironically, Bigger's violent death is remarkably similar to those experienced both by Mary Dalton and Bessie Mears: All three deaths take place when intimate human activity is initiated but is then suddenly aborted by environmentally induced fear and hatred. Just as Bigger's and Mary's lovemaking is inverted into killing when Mrs. Dalton strikes terror into Bigger's heart, Bessie is murdered when Bigger's attempts to "love" her are overcome by his deep hatred of the impotent self which she reflects. In a comparable way, the serious conversation begun by Max and Bigger at the end of the novel is cut short by Max's terror, Bigger's incomplete understanding, and society's fear that real human and political bonds might eventually develop between two such hated people. Native Son, therefore, concludes with the same brutal irony which vibrates throughout the novel: Death comes precisely at the threshold of our most deeply human experiences. This finally becomes Wright's most terrible revelation of a world that encourages and even necessitates fear and hatred but violently blocks love and understanding at every stage.

NOTES

[1] More recently, Jerry Bryant has argued that Wright's use of violence in *Native Son* is quite functional because it forcefully demonstrates the pathological nature of the outer world which shapes Bigger's conduct (303). While agreeing with Bryant that the violence in the novel does function in this way, I would like to stress that it is even more importantly an index to Bigger's inner nature—his consciousness and emotional life.

[2] The charge that Wright constructed a "monster" in Bigger Thomas continues to be made. Maria K. Mootry has recently argued that Bigger is a fundamentally dehumanized "macho" figure who, because he is incapable of love, is intent upon destroying all women who touch his life. Like Baldwin and Scott, she sees Wright's characters as brutally stereotyped ones designed to serve the novel's thesis. Thus, Bigger is reduced to a male monster, Mary to "the bitch goddess success" (123), and Bessie to "mindless whoredom" (126). Although Wright does use stereotypes to capture his characters' outer appearances and the social role imposed upon them, he is careful to depict each of his major characters in such a way as to transcend these stereotypes.

[3] Recently Ross Pudaloff has argued that much of Bigger's character is formed by the gangster movies he sees. Pudaloff claims that Bigger is so overtaken by the "tough guy" role he observes in films that he has lost an interior life and has "nothing but an outside to know" (12). Although this argument has some merit, it ultimately oversimplifies Bigger's character by denying his "soft," romantic impulses. His naturalistic self resents Mary, but his romantic self is attracted to her and wants to love her.

[4] For a fuller discussion, see my article on Zola's influence on Wright. Zola's *La Bête Humaine* and *Thérèse Racquin*, which are exhaustive studies of the psychology of violence and sexuality, were extremely useful to Wright as he imagined the relationship between Bigger and Mary.

[5] Fabre points out that Wright's friend Jane Newton, while reading an early draft of the novel, objected to Bessie's murder because she thought it was "both unnecessary for the development of the plot and insufficiently motivated" (171). Although Wright respected Jane Newton as a critic and actually incorporated several of her suggestions into the final draft of the novel, he insisted that Bessie's murder remain in the book. It is a crucial scene because Bigger's subconscious motives for killing Bessie reveal an important part of his character.

WORKS CITED

Baldwin, James. "Alas, Poor Richard." *Nobody Knows My Name*. 1961. New York: Dell, . 1963. 146–70.

———. "Many Thousands Gone." *Partisan Review* 18 (Nov.–Dec. 1951): 665–80. Rpt. *Notes of a Native Son*. 1955. New York: Bantam, 1968. 18–36.

Brown, Cecil. "Richard Wright: Complexes and Black Writing Today." *Negro Digest* 18 (Dec. 1968): 78–82. Rpt. *Richard Wright's* Native Son: *A Critical Handbook*. Ed. Richard Abcarian. Belmont: Wadsworth, 1970. 167–77.

Bryant, Jerry. "The Violence of *Native Son*." *Southern Review* 17 (1981): 303–19.

Butler, Robert James. "Richard Wright's *Native Son* and Two Novels by Zola: A Comparative Study." *Black American Literature Forum* 18 (1984): 100–05.

Cowley, Malcolm. *New Republic,* 102 (18 Mar. 1940): 382–83. Rpt. *Richard Wright: The Critical Reception*. Ed. John M. Reilly. New York: Burt Franklin, 1978. 67–68.

Daiches, David. *Partisan Review,* 7 (May–June 1940): 245. Rpt. *Richard Wright: The Critical Reception*. Ed. John M. Reilly. New York: Burt Franklin, 1978. 94–95.

Fabre, Michel. *The Unfinished Quest of Richard Wright.* Trans. Isabel Barzun. New York: Morrow, 1973.

Gayle, Addison. *The Way of the New World: The Black Novel in America.* Garden City: Doubleday, 1975.

May, Rollo. *Love and Will.* New York: Dell, 1969.

Mootry, Maria K. "Bitches, Whores, and Woman Haters." *Richard Wright: A Collection of Critical Essays.* Ed. Richard Macksey and Frank Moorer. Englewood Cliffs: Prentice-Hall, 1984. 117–27.

Pudaloff, Ross. "Celebrity as Identity: Richard Wright, *Native Son,* and Mass Culture." *Studies in American Fiction* 11 (1983): 3–18.

Scott, Nathan. "The Dark Haunted Tower of Richard Wright." *Five Black Writers.* Ed. Donald B. Gibson. New York: New York UP, 1970. 12–25.

Wright, Richard. *Native Son.* New York: Harper & Row, 1940.

———. *White Man, Listen!* Garden City: Doubleday, 1957.

Tony Magistrale

WRIGHT'S *CRIME AND PUNISHMENT*

Michel Fabre and Constance Webb, in their separate biographies of Richard Wright, document their subject's attraction to the fiction of Fyodor Dostoevski. When Wright gave advice to aspiring young writers or discussed his own literary inspirations, Dostoevski's novels were frequently mentioned.[1] Wright read *Crime and Punishment* for the first time in 1928, when he was twenty years old. The novel impressed him tremendously and he returned to it often, but not until the writing of *Native Son,* nearly two decades later, is there evidence of its influence exerting a definite shape over Wright's fiction. This topic has been suggested by Kenneth Reed,[2] but his sketchy treatment is much too brief and requires supplementary material and distinctions.

Crime and Punishment and Native Son share obvious similarities: both revolve around the theme of an impoverished youth who commits a double homicide and is subsequently captured and imprisoned. The victims in both novels are women; each of the youths is the product of a maternally based family; and to some degree both are influenced by morally conservative sisters while neither knows his father. The comparison between the two novels, however, extends beyond plot and character parallels. Dostoevski heightened Wright's awareness of the psychological dimensions of physical space, the sense of the city or a bedroom in possession of certain traits which influence human behavior. But even more important than this, was Dostoevski's model of the criminal mind—the motivations and consequences of antisocial behavior—and the antithetical struggle toward moral advancement and spiritual growth. Wright's personal experiences would have sufficed to enable the construction of a story about Bigger Thomas without knowledge of *Crime and Punishment,* but *Native Son* would have been a far less complex and engaging book had its author never been aware of Dostoevski. As Edward Margolies suggests, Wright's work is a psychological as well as sociological novel, which not only shocks the reader's conscience, but also raises "questions regarding the ultimate nature of man."[3]

From *Comparative Literature Studies* 23, No. 1 (Spring 1986): 59–70.

I

One of the most important aspects shared by *Crime and Punishment* and *Native Son* is an examination into the ways in which environmental conditions and society shape the individual personality. Dostoevski was strongly influenced by both the romantic and naturalistic schools of the eighteenth and nineteenth centuries. His vivid descriptions of room and city dwellings owe much to Poe, Balzac, Vidocq, and Dickens.[4] Unlike the fiction of his contemporaries in Russian literature—Tolstoy, Turgenev, Chekhov—*Crime and Punishment* does not take place behind the expansive backdrop of nature or the countryside. *Crime and Punishment,* like the urban *Native Son,* has a distinctive sense of confinement throughout and the major events invariably take place in the crowded city, among the heat and press of buildings and people. As Raskolnikov haunts the suffocating streets of St. Petersburg before and after his crime, so too does the hunted Bigger Thomas move within the condemned and stinking buildings of the Chicago ghetto. James A. Emanuel argues persuasively that Bigger's entire perception of the city—and, by extension, reality—is presented through images of restriction: urban closure, walls, curtains, and blurred vision.[5] In both *Crime and Punishment* and *Native Son,* the individual characters are confined by small apartments, narrow streets, and each other's presence. Compare, for example, these two environmental descriptions, the first from *Native Son:*

> He stretched his arms above his head and yawned; his eyes moistened. The sharp precision of the world of steel and stone dissolved into blurred waves. He blinked and the world grew hard again, mechanical, distinct.[6]

Raskolnikov, likewise, inhabits a similar cityscape:

> A terrible heat had settled upon the street; and then there was the closeness, the bustle of the crowd, plaster all around, scaffolding, bricks, dust, and that stench which is so peculiar to summer. The unbearable stench that was emitted from taverns, which were particularly numerous in that part of town, and the drunks, whom one encountered at every step, served to complete the picture's revolting and miserable tonality.[7]

Both Dostoevski and Wright lavish minute descriptions on the interiors of the living quarters occupied by their respective antiheroes. Raskolnikov's room in St. Petersburg is described as a "coffin," a "cupboard," a "tomb," where he sits "like a spider" in constant meditation. Similarly, Bigger's one room apartment must accommodate four people; their lack of privacy is a continual source of conflict and humiliation; and the family must cohabit this space with vermin the size of cats. The setting suffocates the characters by its tightness, noise, and filth; everything here, like Raskolnikov's garret, indicates a separation from nature. Both writers use the sordid cityscapes of *Crime and Punishment* and *Native Son* to create a world of chimera and illusion, where their antiheroes dissipate hours fluctuating between intense personal frustration and dreams of fantasy. Raskolnikov's gloomy room contributes to his depressed state and at one point he attributes to hunger his plan for murder. As the critic Konstantin Mochulsky points out, it would almost seem that the poisonous vapors that rise from the city's contaminated and feverish breath have penetrated the impoverished student's brain and there have helped give birth to his thoughts of murder.[8] Raskolnikov passes his life in thought; the exterior world, people, reality—these have ceased to exist.

Bigger Thomas's Chicago is as confining as Raskolnikov's St. Petersburg. Chicago's physical aspects—noisy, crowded, filled with a sense of power and fulfillment—make Bigger continually aware of the advantages available to whites, while simultaneously underscoring the impossibility of achievement for blacks. As Bigger acknowledges to his friend Gus early in the novel, " 'They don't let us do nothing. . . . Everytime I think about it, I feel like somebody's poking a red-hot iron down my throat' " (p. 20). Consequently, Bigger seeks escape from the frustrations that accompany a black man living in a white milieu, by losing himself in the fantasies of motion pictures. As Raskolnikov escapes from his St. Petersburg reality through dreams of wealth and power, so Bigger escapes to the narrow confines of his ghetto realm in a world where wealth and power are commonplace and where desires are magically fulfilled: "He wanted to see a movie; his senses hungered for it. In a movie he could dream without effort; all he had to do was lean back in a seat and keep his eyes open" (p. 17).

Bigger's interest in movie fantasies and Raskolnikov's turgid daydreams find further extension in their similar thoughts regarding world historic figures. On one level of being, *Crime and Punishment* and *Native Son* are novels which illustrate, for uniquely different reasons, the lure of power, and both Raskolnikov and Bigger are attracted to leaders who translate this desire into worldly conquests. Related to Raskolnikov's belief that the death of one human is justified when it alleviates the suffering of others and brings humanity a "new word," is Bigger's dream of a powerful individual who will come to rescue the oppressed black populace. Bigger is acutely aware of the fear and shame experienced by black people stemming from their treatment by the white world. He anticipates his own version of Raskolnikov's "extraordinary man" who will free blacks from the white force that has kept them separate and despairing: "He liked to hear how Japan was conquering China; of how Mussolini was invading Spain. He was not concerned with whether these acts were right or wrong; they simply appealed to him as possible avenues of escape. He felt that someday there would be a black man who would whip the black people into a tight band and together they would act to end fear and shame" (p. 110). Raskolnikov's initial justification for the pawnbroker's death emerges from a similar logic; it is the quest to end the life of a pernicious and cruel usurer in order to bring happiness to those who otherwise might perish. Early in the novel he says to Sonya, " 'By my very nature I cannot simply stand by and allow a miscreant to bring some poor defenseless being to ruin. I will interfere. Kill her, take her money and with the help of it devote oneself to the service of humanity and the good of all' " (p. 60).

Hegel's historic leaders—Alexander, Caesar, and Napoleon—become the basis for Raskolnikov's theory of the "extraordinary man" as an individual who possesses the right to circumvent conventional social ethics in order to become humanity's benefactor. While Bigger looks to contemporary political figures as illustrative of men who also exercised power to rise above the masses, it is important to note that he remains oblivious to Raskolnikov's larger issue of "the service of humanity and the good of all." This is less an indication of Bigger's insensitivity to the world or lack of a sophisticated intellect, than a reflection of the level of personal despair he must confront. Bigger simply does not share the comparative "leisure" of Raskolnikov's life; his awareness of power therefore exists only on the level of providing "possible avenues of escape."

While Bigger and Raskolnikov share similar environmental conditions and dreams of frustrated power, there exists an enormous difference between Raskolnikov's theoretical calculations and Bigger's existential bewilderment. In *Crime and Punishment* a good part of Raskolnikov's alienation proceeds from the interior sin of pride and deliberately cultivated speculation. In contrast, Bigger feels himself smothered by forces beyond his control. While environmental factors do play a major role in influencing Raskolnikov's personality, he, unlike Bigger, is able to exert his will upon circumstance. Raskolnikov *decides* to kill, he is not driven to do it.[9] Pinned between the grave of tomorrow and the racist barriers of yesterday, Bigger does not choose his choice; he lacks the initial freedom that allows Raskolnikov to construct his alternative superman theory: "He [Bigger] had been so conditioned in a cramped environment that hard words alone or kicks knocked him upright and made him capable of action—action that was futile because the world was too much for him" (p. 225).

The distinction between the two characters can also be extended to include their relationship to the crimes they commit. Raskolnikov's motives for the murders of the two women are as complex as the character himself. Dostoevski's notebooks are filled with various reasons, and at one point he has Raskolnikov murder in order to obtain money to aid his family. Bigger's crimes, by contrast, are nothing more than a desperate means of winning, through acts of spontaneous violence, the initial freedom denied him by the environment. Wright continually underscores the fact that Bigger is an impotent prisoner in a hostile land.[10] Since Mary Dalton is representative of all that the white world has traditionally held most sacred—aristocratic white womanhood—her murder brings Bigger his first real sense of power and identity. Consequently, a portion of the horror he experiences in committing the crime is alleviated by the knowledge that he, who is considered insignificant by whites, has actually killed a member of their race and outwitted them in their attempt to discover his identity. Essentially, Raskolnikov kills to test a self-will theory: the right of *l'homme superieur* to transgress the laws of morality.[11] Although *Native Son* does not attempt to condone the crime of murder, it does insist that only through that crime did Bigger manage to assert himself against those who had treated him as though he were merely a rat in a maze: "And, yet, out of it all, over and above all that had happened, impalpable but real, there remained to him a queer sense of power. He had done this. He had brought all this about. In all of his life these two murders were the most meaningful things that had ever happened to him" (pp. 224–25). Both Raskolnikov and Bigger kill out of the desire to attain freedom. However, the first understands freedom to mean the will to power; the second sees freedom as the legitimate claim of a human being.

In one sense, Bigger Thomas is a victim of his environment as Raskolnikov is a prisoner of his own self-willed theories. The crimes in both novels, then, stem directly from Raskolnikov's theory of a superior self and Bigger's contrasting inability to gain a satisfying concept of self. Neither Wright nor Dostoevski, however, draws a one-dimensional protagonist. Raskolnikov is more complex than merely another prefiguration of a Nietzschean *Übermensch,* while Bigger finally becomes a more complete character than most representatives of naturalist fiction. Although it may be argued that Raskolnikov and Bigger kill out of very different reasons, their crimes pave the way for similar moral awakenings. While Bigger and Raskolnikov experience a certain degree of "elation" in the commission of their respective murders, both men cannot escape the sense of guilt in reflecting upon their actions.

Despite Bigger's violent impulses and brutal reactions, there is in him none of the visceral delight in cruelty or perverse sexuality attributed by the Chicago newspapers and Buckley, the State's attorney. When he kills Bessie by hitting her with the brick, it is late at night, when she is asleep and the room is dark. Furthermore, the horror inherent in his disposal of Mary's corpse affects him so strongly that he has to force himself to go through each step of its dismemberment, fighting an omnipresent nausea and hallucinatory images. Indeed, Bigger is constantly beset by guilt and fear, from the haunting reappearance of the Dalton's white cat to the image of Mary's severed head, the dark curls wet with blood. He attempts to rationalize his actions by judging the white girl's behavior as foolish and conducive to a violent response, but eventually, as his dream subsequent to Mary's death effectively dramatizes, Bigger becomes aware that in performing the crime of murder he has also destroyed himself. In Bigger's dream, the streetlamp's light is the color of blood, and this "red glare of light" is associated with the fire from the furnace he has used to burn Mary's corpse. The dream forces a connection between the street (Bigger's life) and the Dalton furnace (Mary) and continues this affiliation until Bigger finally exchanges places with his female victim:

> . . . in a red glare of light like that which came from the furnace and he had a big package in his arms so wet and slippery and heavy that he could scarcely hold onto it and he wanted to know what was in the package and he stopped near an alley corner and unwrapped it and the paper fell away and he saw—it was his own head—his own head lying with black face and closed eyes and lips parted with white teeth showing and hair wet with blood. . . . (p. 156)

It is possible that Wright borrowed from Dostoevski the use of dream symbolism as a method for revealing the criminal's repressed guilt and unconscious identification with his victim's suffering.[12] It is through the language of dreams that Wright and Dostoevski represent their protagonists' early stages of remorse. Similar to Bigger's nightmare, wherein he exchanges identities with the murdered Mary, Raskolnikov's dreams of Mikolka and the mare (I, iv) and the pawnbroker (III, vi) are warnings to the student that the old woman's death cannot be separated from his own life. In the dream of the beaten mare, Raskolnikov identifies with the little boy witnessing the brutal act, Mikolka performing it, and the mare itself who receives it. The dream of the pawnbroker comes after he has re-examined his "extraordinary man" theory and the crime itself. In this dream Raskolnikov not only relinquishes his power in failing to kill the woman, but becomes the one tormented by her derisive gestures and "noiseless laughter":

> He stealthily took the axe from the noose and struck her one blow, then another on the skull. But strange to say she did not stir, as though she were made of wood. He was frightened, bent down nearer and tried to look at her; but she too bent her head lower. He bent right down to the ground and peeped up into her face from below, he peeped and turned cold with horror: the old woman was sitting and laughing, and shaking with noiseless laughter, doing her utmost that he should not hear it. (p. 250)

Both of these dreams reveal that Raskolnikov, like Bigger in his own dreamscape, is inextricably tied to the dual roles of the helpless victim and aggressive victimizer.

II

In relying on an axe as the instrument of murder in Raskolnikov's double homicide and Bigger's decapitation of Mary, the two men symbolically sever whatever bonds remain of their link to humanity as they split open the heads of their victims. The repulsive dreamscapes of *Crime and Punishment* and *Native Son* serve to introduce Bigger and Raskolnikov to the prison of self, incarcerating them both in spiritual isolation and torment. By themselves, neither man is capable of advancing beyond the acute awareness of his condition. Raskolnikov essentially acknowledges this after the death of the pawnbroker: "Did I murder the old woman? I murdered myself not her" (p. 297). In *Crime and Punishment* it is Sonya Marmeladov and Porfiry Petrovitch who lend relief to Raskolnikov by providing his suffering with moral direction. In *Native Son* the strength and concern of Jan Erlone and Boris Max convince Bigger that his life is important because it is linked to the fate of other people. Raskolnikov needs Sonya to forgive and love him and Porfiry to challenge his intellectual positions. Bigger's hostility is transformed into trust and love by the forgiveness of Jan and the sense of self-belief that Max helps him articulate at the end of the novel.

In Raskolnikov's acceptance of suffering as a way to salvation, Sonya becomes the only person capable of comforting him. She is the sainted whore whose abilities to express empathy give her the strength to accept Raskolnikov's cross. As is foreshadowed by the symbolic scene in which Raskolnikov and Sonya are united over the Biblical story of Lazarus (IV, iv), Raskolnikov, through the love of Sonya, comes to see and trust in the possibility of a "full resurrection to a new life, to a new and hitherto unknown future" (p. 492). Near the end of the book, when he leaves the police station unable to confess, it is Sonya's silent figure of suffering that makes Raskolnikov return and admit to the murders.

Just as Sonya comprehends and communicates her love to Raskolnikov, Jan Erlone forgives Bigger for killing the girl he loves and conveys to the black youth his first sense of a white man's humanity. When Jan first enters the room where Bigger is held after his capture, Bigger's initial thought is that Jan has come for revenge. Instead, Jan recounts his realization that if he were to kill Bigger, the dreadful cycle of violence would never stop, and asserts that his own suffering has led him to see deeper into Bigger's. By dissociating himself from hatred and revenge, Jan becomes the impetus to Bigger's change in perception:

> . . . a particle of white rock had detached itself from that looming mountain of white hate and had rolled down the slope, stopping still at his feet. The word had become flesh. For the first time in his life a white man became a human being to him; and the reality of Jan's humanity came in a stab of remorse: he had killed what this man loved and had hurt him. He saw Jan as though someone had performed an operation upon his eyes, or as though someone had snatched a deforming mask from Jan's face. (p. 268)

Sonya and Jan serve as the embodiments of the deeply human qualities Bigger and Raskolnikov desperately need—acceptance of other people's differences, compassion, and selfless love. Sonya and Jan struggle not through ideas and sermons, but by deeds and example. They do not intellectualize and do not moralize, but trust and love. " 'One can be great even in humility,' " says Sonya, and Jan's image in *Native Son* corresponds with few modifications.

In *Crime and Punishment* reasonings about life and about the meaning of spiritual suffering pass from Sonya to Porfiry Petrovitch. A corresponding movement can be traced in *Native Son* with the introduction of Boris Max. Max, in his capacity as Bigger's lawyer, is able to elicit from his client a comprehension of his hopes and dreams, his frustrations and rages. In his courtroom arguments, Max shows a clear understanding of how Bigger's crimes were both destructive and liberating, in the sense that they furnished Bigger with his first real identity. Although it is too late for Bigger to join the others who, like Max, support principles of human worth and dignity, the lawyer continues to embellish Bigger's evolving commitment to other human beings: "He had lived outside the lives of men. Their modes of communication, their symbols and images, had been denied him. Yet Max had given him the faith that at bottom all men lived and felt as he felt. And of all the men he had met, surely Max knew what he was trying to say" (p. 386).

Like the version of Boris Max we find in *Native Son*, Porfiry Petrovitch in

Crime and Punishment understands both the situation and context for Raskolnikov's crimes. Unlike Poe's Dupin or Hugo's Javert, the literary models Dostoevski
initially may have had in mind in the development of his own magistrate, Porfiry is
a new type of "super-cultured" administrator, straight-forward and sympathetic; he
is aware of the struggle for man's soul—for the inspector assumes he has one—the
contest for the individual psyche as it is pulled between two abysses, good and evil.
It is for this reason that he does not simply arrest Raskolnikov. Porfiry seeks more
than merely the apprehension and punishment of a law breaker; he is interested in
Raskolnikov's moral regeneration. Porfiry understands that the student's soul requires "fresh air, fresh air" (p. 412). Siberia is literally that fresh air, which Raskolnikov breathes after he is transplanted from the polluted depths of St. Petersburg.
Thus, Porfiry's role is similar to Boris Max's: they exist to inspire Raskolnikov and
Bigger to continue the process of self evaluation, and from this struggle to attain
insight into moral development.

The influence of Sonya and Porfiry as well as the personal struggles of good
and evil that tear at his soul, give Raskolnikov at least the possibility of a resurrection
and a future life with Sonya. Dostoevski leaves his young student invested with the
ability to distinguish good from evil and the capacity for exerting his moral will.
Through the assistance of Porfiry and Sonya, Raskolnikov comes to acknowledge
the principle of equipoise: that the evil in one's nature must be balanced through
love, understanding, and suffering.[13]

In *Native Son* Bigger Thomas is not provided the chance for a new life in
Siberia, and American society, as represented by a Chicago courtroom, once again
forfeits the opportunity to liberate itself. But Bigger, like Raskolnikov, achieves his
own freedom before his execution takes place. Although he is condemned to die
as a violator of society's laws, his death is really a final triumph over forces that have
controlled his life since birth. While society fails to change in its attitude toward
Bigger, ironically his attitude toward society is transformed. His blind resentment
toward the limitations of his family develops into a comprehension of the cause and
compassion for their suffering; his violent outbursts against Gus, G.H., and Jack
evolve into an awareness that they, too, are victims of prejudice and rejection; and
his universal fear and distrust of white people are replaced by respect and love for
Jan and Max.

Richard Wright's use of parallel characters, atmospheric effects, and a similar
belief in the power of the human spirit to transform itself bear a marked resemblance to *Crime and Punishment*. The confluence between the two works, however, is never literal: it is not a matter of direct quotations or plagiarism,[14] but of
a relationship in situations, motives, effects, and procedures. *Crime and Punishment*
represented a reservoir from which Wright drew deeply—recasting characters and
reshaping themes—in order to produce material relevant to his own purposes. It
may be argued, for example, that Dostoevski's identification with a Christian vision
of life finds a parallel in Wright's secular humanism. While Sonya guides Raskolnikov
toward the philosophy of atonement as a method for counterbalancing evil, Bigger's

life is given new priorities through contact with men who embody Marxist principles. Wright's interest is not in religion itself (although there are certainly a number
of references to Bigger as a Christ-figure), but in its social excrescences: racism,
ignorance, hypocrisy. Even as the central themes of *Crime and Punishment* and
Native Son are filtered through each writer's personal affiliation with Christianity or
radical politics, their protagonists are left invested with a similar commitment to
other people and the capacity for moral growth. Unlike the naturalist tradition
which influenced both novelists, *Native Son* and *Crime and Punishment* are not
pessimistic evaluations of human destiny. In fact, quite the opposite is true, since
both Bigger and Raskolnikov are finally victorious over the brutal facts of their
personal histories. The differences between the two characters reveal much about
cultural opportunities; their similarities address those elements universal to human-
kind: a deathless faith in the potential for self-improvement and the dream of a final
reconciliation among all men.

NOTES

[1] See especially Constance Webb, *Richard Wright: A Biography* (New York: Putnam, 1968), pp. 93,
145–6.
[2] Kenneth Reed, "*Native Son*: An American *Crime and Punishment*," *Studies in Black Literature*, 1
(Summer 1970), 33–4.
[3] Edward Margolies, *Native Sons: A Critical Study of Twentieth Century Negro American Authors*
(Philadelphia: Lippincott, 1968), p. 82.
[4] For a more complete discussion of Dostoevski's relationship to these earlier writers, the reader should
consult the following sources: for Dostoevski's relationship to Poe, Alfred Kazin, *An American Proces-
sion* (Vintage, 1985); for Dostoevski's relationship to Balzac, Leonid Grossman, *Balzac and Dostoevski*
(Ardis, 1973); and for Dostoevski's connection to Dickens, Albert Guérard, *The Triumph of the Novel:
Dickens, Dostoevski, Faulkner* (Oxford, 1976).
[5] James A. Emanuel, "Fever and Feeling: Notes on the Imagery in *Native Son*," *Negro Digest*, 18 (Dec.
1968), 16–24.
[6] Richard Wright, *Native Son* (New York: Harper and Row, 1966), p. 19. Further textual references will
be cited parenthetically.
[7] Fyodor Dostoevski, *Crime and Punishment*, trans. Constance Garnett (New York: Random House,
1950), p. 169. Further textual references will be cited parenthetically.
[8] Konstantin Mochulsky, *Dostoevsky* (Princeton, New Jersey: Princeton University Press, 1967), pp.
290–91.
[9] Dostoevski purposely creates the character of Razumihin so that the latter might provide a mirror to
Raskolnikov and the subject of determinism: Razumihin faces almost the same problems as Raskolnikov;
nevertheless, he solves them differently. He gives lessons and translates articles to remain self-sufficient.
Even Raskolnikov recognizes that he too could earn a living in the same manner. He says so to Sonya
after the murder: " 'Razumihin works! But I turned sulky and wouldn't' " (p. 375).
[10] Wright further establishes his attitude toward the influence of environment on the individual in the
essay "How 'Bigger' Was Born": "I do say that I felt and still feel that environment supplies the instrumentalities through which the organism expresses itself, and if that environment is warped or tranquil,
the mode and manner of behavior will be affected toward deadlocking tensions or orderly fulfillment
and satisfaction" (p. xvi).
[11] Raskolnikov provides illumination into the actual motive behind his decision to murder in a conversation with Sonya (V, iv): " 'It wasn't to help my mother I did the murder—that's nonsense—I didn't do
the murder to gain wealth and power and to become a benefactor of mankind. Nonsense! I did the
murder for myself ... I wanted to find out then and quickly whether I was a louse like everybody else
or a man. Whether I can step over barriers or not...' " (p. 377).

[12] As André Gide points out in his study *Dostoevsky* (New Directions, 1961), there is a fascinating narrative blend in Dostoevski's prose, combining both realistic and dream elements into a weave in which it is often impossible to distinguish one from the other: "Strange how Dostoevsky, when leading us through the strangest by-paths of psychology, ever must needs add the most precise and infinitesimal of realistic details, in order to make more secure an edifice which otherwise would appear the extreme expression of phantasy and imagination" (p. 122).

[13] The duality of Raskolnikov's personality, which presents a moral conflict throughout the novel, ultimately provides the reader with a final aesthetic question at the conclusion of *Crime and Punishment*: namely, how credible is Raskolnikov's spiritual and religious awakening? Many critics, especially Edward Wasiolek in his book *Dostoevsky* (M.I.T. Press, 1964), have felt that the Epilogue is superimposed on the novel's overall structure and that Raskolnikov's rebirth is unjustified when examined in light of his prior behavior and strategies. Any conclusion about the novel must deal with the fact that there are always two Raskolnikovs: the lover of life and humanity, and the murderer, who is "further than ever from seeing that what [he] did was a crime" (*CP*, p. 466). As Ernest J. Simmons argues in *Dostoevsky* (Vintage, 1940), it is impossible for Raskolnikov to accept either route as an absolute salvation: the path of blood and crime to power or the road of submission and suffering to a Christ-like salvation (p. 151). On the other hand, it must also be argued that in a final analysis the influence of the other characters mixed with the personal torment that Raskolnikov undergoes, provides at least the promise of resurrection and credibility toward a personal renascence.

[14] Even in parallel passages such as the symbolic "soft and gentle eyes" of Raskolnikov's victim, Lizaveta (p. 249), reappearing in the piercing accusations of Bigger's victim, Bessie: "Suppose when he turned on the flashlight, he would see her lying there staring at him with those round large black eyes . . ." (p. 223).

Laura E. Tanner

THE NARRATIVE PRESENCE
IN *NATIVE SON*

"**P**erhaps the most insidious and least understood form of segregation," writes Ralph Ellison, "is that of the word. And by this I mean the word in all its complex formulations, from the proverb to the novel and stage play, the word with all its subtle power to suggest and foreshadow overt action while magically disguising the moral consequence of that action and providing it with symbolic and psychological justification. For if the word has the potency to revive and make us free, it has also the power to blind, imprison and destroy."[1] Recent Afro-American scholars, in the attempt to uncover the "magical disguise" of the word in all its implications, have adopted new paradigms for criticism that focus on what Ellison here defines as the inherently political nature of language.[2] In "Beyond Realism: Recent Black Fiction and the Language of 'The Real Thing,'" Graham Clarke proposes a critical framework that defines Richard Wright's *Native Son* as a model of narrative conservatism beyond which contemporary authors must move in order to "unmask the very nature of white America's language, its limitations and lies."[3] Reiterating what has come to be the standard criticism of Wright's novel, Clarke laments the stylistic weakness of *Native Son;* Wright's political message, he submits, surfaces in a narrative voice that "locks the fiction into a viewpoint intent on making the message 'stick' and hit home."[4] While that viewpoint is indeed articulated by the narrator of *Native Son*, Clarke's unwillingness to probe into the hermeneutical complexities generated by the act of narration results in his acceptance of a "symbolic and psychological justification" that the novel itself ultimately deauthorizes. By tracing the supposed stylistic and structural inadequacies of *Native Son* to their origin in the problematic narrative presence of the work, I hope to provide an alternative reading that uncovers the novel's surprisingly radical critique of the type of narrative conservatism attributed to it by Clarke and other recent critics.[5]

In the narrative, Bigger's voice and actions are supplemented by a description of his thoughts and emotions. The elaborate linguistic fabric with which the narrator

From *Texas Studies in Literature and Language* 29, No. 4 (Winter 1987): 412–31.

weaves that description, however, disguises and transforms Bigger's consciousness in the very act of representing it. While Bigger may be a black worker to Mary, a victim of circumstance to his attorney, or a "hairy ape" to the press, he is no less a symbol to the narrator who portrays his very thoughts and feelings. The effect of the narrative reading is not to increase our understanding of and sympathy for Bigger but to distort our perception of his existence by framing it within a highly metaphorical context. Throughout the novel, the narrative voice makes deliberate links between Bigger's acts of violence and his desire to communicate. "The impulsion to try to tell," we are told at one point, "was as deep as had been the urge to kill."[6] If we accept that narrator as Bigger's spokesperson, we come to see Mary's murder as an assault against an enslaving system of value rather than a fearful reflex response to a potentially dangerous situation:

> He had killed within himself the preacher's haunting picture of life even before he had killed Mary; that had been his first murder. And now the preacher made it walk before his eyes like a ghost in the night, creating within him a sense of exclusion that was as cold as a block of ice. Why should this thing rise now to plague him after he had pressed a pillow of fear and hate over its face to smother it to death? To those who wanted to kill him he was not human, not included in that picture of Creation; and that was why he had killed it. To live, he had created a new world for himself, and for that he was to die. (264)

The move in this passage from the literal to the symbolic, from the domain of instinctive response to the arena of sophisticated conceptual manipulation, establishes a paradigm within which the narrative comments on Bigger's existence. The narrator "reads" Mary's murder as an act of creation; by shattering this symbol of white womanhood, we are led to believe, Bigger also shatters the assumptions underlying the master language game and opens up the possibility of rewriting his own existence within a new language game and a new paradigm of reality. Clearly, this is the move that Bigger accomplishes symbolically: "The shame and fear and hate . . . had now cooled and softened. Had he not done what they thought he never could? His being black and at the bottom of the world was something which he could take with a new-born strength" (141). In the new world Bigger creates for himself, we are told, he becomes the measure of his own worth and assumes the role of creator of a new language: "There was another silence. They wanted him to draw the picture and he would draw it like he wanted it. He was trembling with excitement. In the past had they not always drawn the picture for him?" (149). Through the narrator's words and images, Bigger's act is raised to the level of symbol, and murder becomes a doorway to a new existence: "Why should not this cold white world rise up as a beautiful dream in which he could walk and be at home, in which it would be easy to tell what to do and what not to do? . . . He had committed murder twice and had created a new world for himself" (226).

Through the narrator's comments, we are forced to read both the text of Bigger's actions and the interpretive gloss that leads us away from the material substance of those actions into a symbolic universe in which they are reinscribed within the narrator's own language game. The narrator equates Bigger's act of murder with the creation of a universe in which Bigger's existence is governed not by the alien world view forced upon him by whites but by a reality of his own making. Ironically, however, it is the narrator's depiction of Bigger's murder as an attempt to achieve stable linguistic referentiality that exposes most clearly the radical instability of language. The clash between the literal and symbolic portrayal of Bigger's existence emphasizes for the reader the very problem that the narrator exposes: the capacity for distortion inherent in the mode of representation. Even as the narrator uses Bigger's character to comment on the necessity of demystifying language, the narrative itself participates in the kind of unauthorized "symbolic and psychological justification" against which Ellison warns.

Although the narrator's observations are clothed in layers of abstract, meta-phorical language, recent critics have had no difficulty in accepting those observations as the straightforward articulation of Bigger's thoughts.[7] In the passages where Bigger's thoughts are actually transcribed rather than translated, however, the distortion inherent in the narrator's rendering of those thoughts is fully apparent. The introduction of Bigger's language is usually signaled by a sudden shift to the short, choppy sentences that characterize his awkward relationship with the master language. Where the narrator's voice is defined by a smooth-flowing prose style that relies upon the complex use of balance and antithesis, compound construc-tions, and periodic sentences, Bigger's voice is marked by a form of halting ex-pression that frequently deteriorates into stuttering repetition. Bigger's uncultivated speech is often framed by the imagistic, lyrical voice of the narrator:

> He stared at the furnace. He trembled with another idea. He—he could, he—he could put her, he could put her *in* the furnace. He would *burn* her! That was the safest thing of all to do. He went to the furnace and opened the door. A huge red bed of coals blazed and quivered with molten fury. (89)

It is only in juxtaposition with the final sentence of this passage that the awkward diction and hesitant articulation of the lines preceding that sentence are revealed to the reader in all their clumsiness. Unlike the earlier sentences, the final sentence— with its internal rhyme, alliteration, and controlled imagery—has an ease and facility with language that expresses its author's relaxed association with words.

Bigger's awkward relationship to written language is expressed most clearly in his composition of the kidnap note. In the passage describing Bigger's act of cre-ation, the narrative assumes his voice; the crude diction and phrasing of the note[8] is uncomfortably emphasized by the linguistic deterioration of the narrative itself:

> He swallowed with dry throat. Now, what would be the best kind of note? He thought, I want you to put ten thousand . . . Naw; that would not do. Not "I." It would be better to say "we." *We got your daughter,* he printed slowly in big round letters. That was better. . . . Now, tell him not to go to the

police. . . . *Don't go to the police if you want your daughter back safe.* Naw;
that ain't good. (166)

Bigger's painful relationship with the master language assaults the reader's ear as
s/he hears the broken English of Bigger's kidnap note reflected in the dissonant
tones of the narrative itself. The sudden intrusion of the narrator's voice that
follows may be an attempt to "translate" Bigger's feelings into the sophisticated
prose to which he has no access; in fact, however, the narrator's intrusion wrests
the pen from Bigger's hand and undercuts any authority he might have had: "His
scalp tingled with excitement; it seemed that he could feel each strand of hair upon
his head. . . . There was in his stomach a slow, cold, vast rising movement, as though
he held within the embrace of his bowels the swing of planets through space"
(166–67). The magnitude of the narrator's metaphorical vehicle and his skillful
control of language contrast painfully with the limited scope of Bigger's action and
the unsophisticated way in which he uses words; thus, the passage actually subverts
Bigger's authority while appearing to validate it.[9]

The tension between narrative voice and subject exposed here erupts in a
condescending tone that verges on racist objectification at several points in the
novel. The narrator's command of language allows him an excuse for the generalizations he makes about Bigger; in lending a voice to those less articulate than
himself, he exposes the prejudices of the language game through which he speaks:
"To Bigger and his kind white people were not really people; they were a sort of
great natural force, like a stormy sky looming overhead, or like a deep swirling river
stretching suddenly at one's feet in the dark . . . whether they feared it or not, each
and every day of their lives they lived with it; even when words did not sound its
name, they acknowledged its reality" (109). Whomever "Bigger and his kind" may
be, it is clear that they do not partake of the narrator's superior vision or capacity
for self-expression; their wordlessness creates a vacuum in which he can construct
a reality which their silence is said to affirm. Neither his poetic alliteration nor his
imagistic description of that reality, however, can disguise the fact that the narrator's
vision relies upon a generalized notion of Bigger that is dangerously limited. In his
eagerness to speak for "Bigger and his kind," the narrator inadvertently discloses his
own narrow understanding of Bigger's identity: "But maybe it would never come;
maybe there was no such thing for him; maybe he would have to go to his end just
as he was, dumb, driven, with the shadow of emptiness in his eyes" (256). Is it really
Bigger who alternates between considering himself the sophisticated reader of his
own actions and the brute defined by existential emptiness? Both assessments
would seem to indicate conversely exaggerated and objectified "readings" of Bigger's existence; the character who holds "in the embrace of his bowels the swing
of planets through space" and his counterpart, the "dumb" and "driven" murderer,
are both narrative creations born of symbolic language and abstract analysis.

The inadequacy of the narrator's assessment of Bigger is further emphasized
by the fact that the language through which Bigger's consciousness is filtered is one

which he himself cannot adequately understand. " 'White folks and black folks is strangers,' " Bigger says at one point in the novel. " 'We don't know what each other is thinking' " (324–25). Like the "white folks" speech of the Daltons, the narrator's prose is linguistically sophisticated; Bigger's only response to such language, when articulated by the Daltons, is one of total bewilderment: "The long strange words they used made no sense to him; it was another language. He felt from the tone of their voices that they were having a difference of opinion about him, but he could not determine what it was about" (48). Although the Daltons, like Bigger, speak English, the ease with which they utilize the master language makes their words totally foreign to Bigger. The narrator's adoption of such language, therefore, implicitly undercuts the validity of Bigger's right to self-expression in the same way that the Dalton's speech excludes Bigger from participation in their dialogue.

If the linguistic sophistication of the narrative voice echoes the speech of the Daltons, the narrator's powerful grasp of rhetoric also allies his voice with that of Bigger's lawyer. The pure rhetorical structuring of Max's speech, calculated to impress and persuade, totally eludes Bigger's comprehension. Although Bigger listens earnestly to the long diatribe, we are told at its conclusion that he "had not understood the speech" (370). If, like the speech of the Daltons and Max, the narrative constitutes "another language" to Bigger, is it possible for that language to articulate Bigger's own thoughts successfully?

On a certain level, it may be argued, the shift from thought to utterance always involves a "translation," in the process of which meaning is distorted and sometimes lost. When that "translation" involves the recontextualization of thought within a new language, however, that distortion assumes overwhelming proportions. In the words of Benjamin Lee Whorf, thought "follows a network of tracks laid down in the given language, an organization which may concentrate systematically upon certain phases of reality, certain aspects of intelligence, and may systematically discard others featured by other languages. The individual is utterly unaware of this organization and is constrained completely within its unbreakable bonds."[10] While any fictional narrative involves a filtering of the character's consciousness through a narrator's or author's language game, the impact of such a process is most dangerous when the character has a relationship to language that is defined by alienation and distrust. To rewrite Bigger's thoughts within a secure and sophisticated linguistic framework is in some sense to distort the very nature of his thoughts, founded as they are in the consciousness of a man whose problematic relationship to the master language defines his very identity.

The tension that results from the translation of Bigger's thoughts into a sophisticated narrative voice is made all the more apparent by the narrator's attempts to disguise it. Recognizing that the abstract conceptual notions that he attributes to Bigger might be generated only with great difficulty in an individual with limited access to the master language and the concepts it embodies, the narrator attempts to gloss over any discrepancy by defining the complex conclusions he cites as manifestations of Bigger's feelings rather than conscious thoughts. While complex conceptual thought and metaphorical understanding seem to imply at least some familiarity with the languages of abstraction, logic, and analogy, emotions, it might appear, transcend the limitations of any one language game.

In the attempt to achieve plausibility, then, the narrator frequently seeks to rewrite Bigger's thoughts as emotions. At one point in the novel, the narrator records Bigger's fascination with political leaders like Hitler and Mussolini, who serve as models for a black leader who might one day act together with black people to "end fear and shame." After a detailed discussion of the role which that black leader comes to assume in Bigger's consciousness, the narrator claims that Bigger, after all, never "thought of this in precise mental images; he felt it; he would feel it for a while and then forget" (110). When not recasting thoughts as emotions, the narrator attempts to achieve plausibility by manipulating adjectives of intensity and degree that characterize those thoughts. While the reader might find difficulty in accepting Bigger's definitive authorship of a sophisticated, abstract idea, the narrator seems to feel that he can authenticate the source of such insights by claiming that they originate as hazy or undeveloped notions in Bigger's mind: "Dimly, he felt that there should be one direction in which he and all other black people could go whole-heartedly; that there should be a way in which gnawing hunger and restless aspiration could be fused; that there should be a manner of acting that caught the mind and body in certainty and faith" (109). Whether Bigger thinks such thoughts or merely feels them, whether he sees such images clearly or dimly, there still exists a discrepancy between the Bigger that we know through action and speech and the Bigger that the narrator creates before our eyes. The narrator's elaborate attempts to stitch together this textual rupture fail miserably, leaving scars which succeed only in calling attention to the division that the narrator seeks to erase.

The damage inflicted by such narrative surgery is more than merely cosmetic, however. At times, the narrator's attempt to achieve plausibility by rewriting Bigger's thoughts as feelings contradicts the substance of those very thoughts. Bigger, we are told,

> felt in the quiet presence of his mother, brother, and sister a force, inarticulate and unconscious, making for living without thinking, making for peace and habit, making for a hope that blinded. He felt that they wanted and yearned to see life in a certain way; they needed a certain picture of the world; there was one way of living they preferred above all others; and they were blind to what did not fit. . . . The whole thing came to him in the form of a powerful and simple feeling. (102)

At the same time that Bigger ponders the force that relegates his family to the status of "living without thinking," he himself is relegated to the same status by the narrator, who is quick to redefine Bigger's thought as a mere feeling. Can a recognition of the inadequacy of mere feeling be achieved through feeling alone? If Bigger himself is never liberated from the "inarticulate and unconscious" state of feeling into the world of thought, how can he possibly attain the objective vision necessary to recognize, let alone condemn his family's blindness? By refusing to attribute to Bigger the consciousness inherent in thought, the narrator relegates him to the inarticulate world that Bigger associates with blindness.

At times, the clash between Bigger as character and Bigger as symbol manifests itself in narrative double vision:

> He lay on the cold floor sobbing; but really he was standing up strongly with contrite heart, holding his life in his hands, staring at it with a wondering question. He lay on the cold floor sobbing; but really he was pushing forward with his puny strength against a world too big and too strong for him. He lay on the cold floor sobbing; but really he was groping forward with fierce zeal into a welter of circumstances which he felt contained a water of mercy for the thirst of his heart and brain. (288)

As in the scene in which Bigger composes the kidnap note, the contest between material and metaphorical readings of Bigger's situation manifests itself in the narrative voice of the novel. The elaborate sentence construction juxtaposes the more straightforward description of Bigger's literal activity with the lyrical evocation of another, highly symbolic reality. In a recent article Joyce Ann Joyce argues that such intricate forms of linguistic variation operate in the novel to initiate a "lyrical ebb and flow that reflects the activity of Bigger's thoughts and actions."[11] Because she makes no distinction between "Bigger's thoughts" and the thoughts attributed to him by the narrator, Joyce fails to detect any tension generated by the placement of "contrasting ideas inside similar grammatical structures."[12] In fact, the sophisticated use of rhetoric that Joyce applauds in this passage succeeds largely in emphasizing the difference between the experienced world in which Bigger exists and the symbolic world to which the narrator turns to make meaning out of that existence. While the narrator's highly metaphorical account of Bigger's composition of the kidnap note contrasted with Bigger's simplistic language to undercut his authority as text maker, this passage works in the opposite way: the force of the material world dissolves the narrator's overinflated rhetoric. In the universe that Bigger's own voice substantiates, "a water of mercy for the thirst of his heart and brain" pales beside a pressing desire for a simple glass of milk. What Robert Bone describes as "the successful fusion of narrative and metaphorical levels in *Native Son*"[13] is in fact a rhetorical linking of contradictory world views that only partially obscures a major fissure in the narrative.

The "crazy prisoner" whom Bigger meets momentarily in prison emphasizes the tension between material and symbolic realities in Wright's text. This character's presence, though inexplicable in terms of plot, exposes to the reader the danger inherent in the narrator's misuse of "the subtle power of words." The paranoia of this frantic black scholar, who, in the words of one prisoner, "went off his nut from studying too much at the university" (318), is merely an extension of the confusion that defines the life of any black man whose language, values, and sense of reality are distorted by their subjection to the symbols that define and control the powerful white world. The continual "rewriting" of the black prisoner's reality within a white paradigm has fractured his very existence and upset his ability to distinguish between material and intellectual facts; he lives in constant fear that his ideas will be taken from him, as if they were so many potatoes or dollar bills: "He was writing a book on how colored people live and he says somebody stole all the facts he'd found" (318). While it is possible that the literal material on which his observations were noted might have been stolen, it is clearly not this kind of theft about which the prisoner is concerned. His statements to the other prisoners make it clear that he has not forgotten the "facts" which are to serve as the basis for his exposure of the horrors of oppression. While his facts may be intact, however, he is clearly anxious about their reception by the white authorities. By projecting that fear onto a physical plane, the scholar manages to convince himself that his facts are in danger of being "stolen" rather than denied; the overwhelming frustration of existing in a society where black truths have no concrete validity has led this man to confuse intellectual truths with material realities. While the narrator has converted the material acts of Bigger's existence into metaphorical truths, this crazy prisoner, whose "driving frenzy" threatens to "suck [Bigger] into its hot whirlpool" (318), reduces truths to physical realities capable of being stolen. In both cases, this material/metaphorical confusion destabilizes the world, as Bigger's response to his fellow prisoner demonstrates: "Finally, things quieted. For the first time since his capture, Bigger felt that he wanted someone near him, something physical to cling to" (319). Bigger's sudden need to assure himself of the reality of his own existence by embracing the object world reveals the deep threat constituted by the white world's ability to tear out the reality from beneath the black man's feet. Even as he searches desperately for "something physical to cling to," however, the experiential world in which Bigger exists is rocked haphazardly in the hands of a narrator intent on reshaping the world into the form of a symbolic universe.

Occasionally, however, Bigger the character breaks the mold into which his symbolic counterpart has been forced; the collision of his experiential world with the novel's symbolic universe threatens to destabilize the narrative vision. Under the glow of the "lurid objective light" of a white man's kitchen, Bigger the symbol melts into obscurity:

> He rested his black fingers on the edge of the white table and a silent laugh burst from his parted lips as he saw himself for a split second in a lurid objective light: he had killed a rich white girl and had burned her body after cutting her head off and had lied to throw the blame on someone else and had written a kidnap note demanding ten thousand dollars and yet he stood here afraid to touch food on the table, food which undoubtedly was his own. (175)

The strategic advance gained in an abstract linguistic world crumbles here in a moment of high irony. The experiential world in which Bigger exists cannot, as he recognizes with a laugh, be transformed with a single action, no matter how symbolic. Because we have grown accustomed to the narrator's symbolic rewriting of Bigger's actions, we, too, respond to this situation with ironic laughter. The distance between Bigger as character and Bigger as symbol continues to erupt as irony in the novel, despite the narrator's attempts to obscure it.[14]

While we may laugh along with Bigger as our symbolic vision is jolted by a moment of hard realism, the narrative's insistence on its symbolic mode has a serious impact on our understanding of Bigger. If we accept the narrator's "translation" of Bigger's consciousness, we come to view Bigger's violence as the symbolic prelude to his creation of new paradigms for self-expression; with our acceptance of this interpretive gloss, we as readers begin to measure Bigger's own actions and statements against the framework defined by the narrator. Both the narrator's own skillful use of language and his reading of Bigger's violence as a form of self-expression establish linguistic aptitude as central to the text. As a result, Bigger is indicted not only when his voice is mimicked in the narrative (as in the kidnap note episode) but every time he, as a character, attempts to articulate his thoughts. The symbolic linguistic gains which the narrator attributes to Bigger make his clumsy relationship with the master language more obvious each time he speaks.

In the attempt to comfort his family after his arrest, Bigger desperately "cast about for something to say. Hate and shame boiled in him against the people behind his back; he tried to think of words that would defy them, words that would let them know that he had a world and life of his own in spite of them. And at the same time he wanted those words to stop the tears of his mother and sister, to quiet and soothe the anger of his brother" (275). Despite his efforts, Bigger's words are as futile as his family's anger; his response (" 'Aw, Ma, don't you-all worry none. . . . I'll be out of this in no time' ") leaves his family "incredulous" and causes Bigger to reflect bitterly, "Maybe they would remember him only by those foolish words after they had killed him" (276). In juxtaposition with the narrator's sophisticated prose, Bigger's words are crude and simplistic; in comparison with the complicated insights which the narrator attributes to him, Bigger's response is naive. If the master language is the standard against which Bigger's exclamation is to be measured, his are indeed "foolish words." By participating in the master language and adopting a highly symbolic mode, the narrator provides no alternative standard with which to judge Bigger. Just as Mary and Jan appear ridiculous in their attempt to sing Negro spirituals, Bigger, too, cannot help but appear ridiculous when measured solely by his expertise in a language created by and for whites.

The presence of white influence in language is demonstrated by Bigger's exaggerated inability to use that language in the presence of his oppressors. When surrounded by whites, Bigger is deserted by any linguistic facility: "Listlessly, he talked. He traced his every action. He paused at each question Buckley asked and wondered how he could link up his bare actions with what he had felt; but his words came out flat and dull. White men were looking at him, waiting for his words" (287). Even though he is able to talk "listlessly," Bigger here fails completely in his attempt to communicate the reality of his experience. The power of the white stare reinforces the alienating potential of white language; although Bigger can speak the words of that language, he is unable to convey the reality of his own experience in a language game as hostile to him as the white authorities by whom he is surrounded.

The facility with which the narrator utilizes the master language is a sign of the degree to which he is implicated in the very system against which Bigger defines himself. Contrary to the claims of Judith Brazinsky, who calls upon "the brilliance of [*Native Son*'s] narrative method" to explain "how so gruesome a plot can be managed with any sympathy for Bigger,"[15] the narrator's sophisticated translation of Bigger's thoughts does not persuade Wright's reader to sympathize with Bigger. Instead, it sets up a tension between narrative expectation and literal circumstance that explodes in Bigger's face every time he attempts to speak. If the link between violence and articulation that the narrator establishes is a valid one, the ineffectual violence of Bigger's speech at the end of the novel is a sorry comment on the ultimate impact of his "monstrous crimes." In response to an overwhelming desire to communicate with Max, Bigger

> summoned his energies and lifted his head and struck out desperately, de-termined to rise from the grave, resolved to force upon Max the reality of his living.
> "I'm glad I got to know you before I go!" he said with almost a shout; then was silent, for that was not what he had wanted to say. (386)

The intricate philosophical conclusions attributed to Bigger in the narrator's sophis-ticated voice establish a standard of measurement governed by the assumption of intellectual eloquence; because Bigger himself has not been schooled in the rhetoric of white English, his desperate attempts to communicate are received by the reader primarily as signs of linguistic ineptitude.

Book 3, which focuses on Bigger's trial and introduces the character of Max, is frequently cited by critics as the point at which the novel lapses into mere rhetoric. In "The Social Significance of Bigger Thomas," Dan McCall articulates a criticism of *Native Son* that has not been effectively challenged by contemporary scholars:

> In the first two parts of the book . . . we were not seeing Bigger as an object, we were participating with him as a subject. . . . In the last section we are no longer in Bigger's mind. . . . That is what is wrong. It is an "interpretation." . . . The third section of the book, all the rhetoric in the courtroom, is the archi-tectural equivalent of the local failures all through the book sentence by sentence, in the unnecessary adverbs and stereotypic figures of speech.[16]

On the one hand, McCall distinguishes book 3 from the earlier books for its interpretive quality; on the other hand, he cites it as an extension of what he sees as frequent stylistic failures throughout the novel. If, as I have demonstrated, those "stylistic failures and stereotypic figures of speech" are part of the narrator's attempt to define Bigger in symbolic terms, is it not possible that the "rhetoric" of book 3 (and Max's speech in particular) is merely a doubling of the narrative voice that more obviously exposes the limitations of its symbolic generalizations?

Although his perspective is a sympathetic one, Max's story of Bigger's life is no less limited than the stories generated by the media and the frightened white populace. Max, too, approaches Bigger not as an individual but as a symbol:

> "A man's life is at stake. And not only is this man a criminal, but he is a black criminal. . . . The complex forces of society have isolated here for us a symbol, a test symbol. The prejudices of men have stained this symbol, like a germ stained for examination under the microscope. The unremitting hate of men has given us a psychological distance that will enable us to see this tiny social symbol in relation to our whole sick social organism." (354)

As critics such as Donald Gibson recognize, Max's position, though it contradicts that of the shortsighted majority, errs because it rests on a highly symbolic epistemology.[17] In Max's mind, Bigger is not an individual but a "mode of life," created and shaped entirely by a powerful white elite. Claiming that Bigger springs from a " 'soil prepared by the collective but blind will of a hundred million people,' " Max implores, " 'I beg you to recognize human life draped in a form and guise alien to ours, but springing from a soil plowed and sown by all our hands' " (358).

Max functions in the plot exactly as the narrator's presence functions in the novel; the limitations of Max's speech expose to the reader the unreliability of the narrative voice through which Bigger's consciousness has been articulated throughout the work. Like the narrator, Max possesses a full command of white language and an understanding of abstraction; like the narrator, he uses the power of rhetoric to persuade the audience (whether it be reader or court) of the efficacy of his interpretation of Bigger. The ease with which Max's voice usurps the role of the narrator has led many critics to ignore the limitation of Max's speech and evaluate it as Wright's rhetorical plug for Bigger. In fact, however, Max's voice does not merely resemble the narrator's. While the pure rhetorical structuring of Max's speech temporarily assumes narrative control of the novel, Max reiterates the narrator's phrases and conclusions about Bigger with haunting similitude. The striking likeness between the contents of Max's speech and the conclusions drawn throughout the novel by the narrator is so blatant as to fail miserably as the kind of political plea that many critics have assumed it to be. Rather than authorizing the speaker as orator or politician, the lawyer's speech functions to deconstruct the very rhetoric that it employs; Max's adoption of the narrator's style, use of his images and reiteration of his conclusions underscores the limitations of the perspective shared by both.[18]

In his speech, Max describes Bigger's distance from those around him with imagery that is clearly drawn from the idea of the "curtain" used so extensively by the narrator. " '[T]he accidental nature of [Bigger's] crime,' " Max tells the court, " 'took the guise of a sudden and violent rent in the veil behind which he lived' "

(361). The idea of the omnipresent veil behind which Bigger hides clearly echoes the narrator's constant association of Bigger's existence with the image of a wall separating him from reality: "So he held toward them an attitude of iron reserve; he lived with them, but behind a wall, a curtain" (14). Having rent that veil or curtain, Max tells the court, Bigger claims the murder as "the first full act of his life; it was the most meaningful, exciting and stirring thing that had ever happened to him. He accepted it because it made him free, gave him the possibility of choice, of action, the opportunity to act and to feel that his actions carried weight" (364). Once again, then, Max echoes the narrator's commentary in very explicit terms; earlier in the novel, we were told that Bigger's acts "made him feel free" (179), that they "were the most meaningful things that had ever happened to him" (225), that for the first time, "his whole life was caught up in a supreme and meaningful act" (111).

In the process of narrative translation, Bigger's murders are often described as forms of creation: "To live, he had created a new world for himself, and for that he was to die" (264). Using not only a similar idea but very similar terminology, Max remarks of the murder, " 'It was an act of creation!' " (366). He goes on to say, " 'This Negro boy's entire attitude toward life is a crime! . . . Every time he comes in contact with us, he kills! . . . Every thought he thinks is potential murder' " (214). The sense of repetition that the reader may have intuited earlier is by this point overwhelmingly obvious; Bigger, the narrator tells us, "committed rape every time he looked into a white face" (214). In retrospect, the narrator's repeated assess-ments of Bigger's situation emerge as more than mere foreshadowings of Max's speech; they are, in fact, previews: "He had killed many times before, only on those other times there had been no handy victim or circumstance to make visible or dramatic his will to kill. His crime seemed natural; he felt that all of his life had been leading to something like this" (101). By the point at which Max concludes his speech, his voice and commentary are practically indistinguishable from the narra-tor's: "What does matter is that he was guilty *before* he killed! That was why his whole life became so quickly and naturally organized, pointed, charged with a new meaning when this thing occurred" (369).

Although Bigger tells Max that his murder somehow set him free, he com-municates none of the other phrases or ideas that Max adopts from the narrative itself; the notion that Bigger distances himself by hiding behind a veil or curtain, the idea that the murders were the most meaningful things that had ever occurred to him, that violence was in fact an "act of creation," that Bigger was guilty of crime each time he looked at a white person—these conclusions and many of the actual words and phrases used by Max are borrowed directly from the narrative, a narrative to which he as a character had no access. Surely Wright, creator of Max's skillful rhetoric and source of the complex narrative style lauded by critics, could have assumed a more sophisticated strategy had he wanted to reinforce the substance of an argument made earlier in the novel. Those who cite Max's speech as an example of Wright's overwhelming political didacticism surely do injustice to Wright's technical skill if not to his political viewpoint. In fact, Max's speech is more than a clumsy repetition of conclusions to which the reader has already been exposed; the obvious limitations of Max's epistemology provide the reader with an interpretive gloss that calls attention to the limitations of the symbolic outlook shared by the narrator and Max. Ultimately, as Wright remarks in "How 'Bigger' Was Born," Bigger's character is "more important than what any person, white or black, would say or try to make of him, more important than any political analysis designed to explain or deny him, more important, even, than my own sense of fear, shame, and diffidence" (xxiii).

Max's appearance represents the bodily intrusion of the narrator's symbolic perspective into Bigger's world. In the novel's final scene, Bigger confronts his manipulator in a last attempt to overcome his own inability to communicate. As he interacts with Max, Bigger finally expresses the sophisticated understanding of linguistic workings that the narrator has attributed to him since the murder. After attempting and failing to communicate, Bigger listens to yet another long-winded rhetorical speech in which Max addresses complicated philosophical issues but ignores Bigger's most basic questions. Speaking in the language of symbolic abstractions that he shares with the narrator, Max avoids the issue of Bigger's death: " 'But on both sides men want to live; men are fighting for life. Who will win? Well, the side that feels most, the side with the most humanity and the most men.' " This time, however, Bigger no longer proves the passive and self-denigrating audience that Max has come to expect: "Max's head jerked up in surprise when Bigger laughed. 'Ah, I reckon I believe in myself. . . . I ain't got nothing else. . . . I got to die' " (391). With Bigger's laugh, the delicate, philosophical world that Max (and the narrator) have constructed around the skeletal framework of Bigger's actions comes tumbling down like Wittgenstein's house of cards, felled by one breath of the man who committed those actions, who knows he is to die, who stands firmly on the ground beneath him. Speaking from the force of the concrete, material world, Bigger makes sense of his act in the only way he knows how:

> "What I killed for must've been good!" Bigger's voice was full of frenzied anguish. "It must have been good! When a man kills, it's for something. . . . I didn't know I was really alive in this world until I felt things hard enough to kill for 'em. . . . It's the truth, Mr. Max. I can say it now, 'cause I'm going to die. I know what I'm saying real good and I know how it sounds. But I'm all right. I feel all right when I look at it that way." (392)

Max's response to Bigger's words is to step back in "terror," to "back away from him with compressed lips." While Bigger has failed in attempt after attempt to express himself, Max's shocked silence reflects the success of the prisoner's final communication. Knowingly or unknowingly, Bigger has adopted Max's conclusions but changed their reference, adopted his language but changed the language game. The words that Bigger speaks are taken directly from Max's courtroom argument; by removing those words from their symbolic context and citing them as literal justification for his acts of murder, however, Bigger exposes their most basic

signification and horrifies their creator.[19] Bigger himself has finally become adept at
the storytelling competition that governs the political world and the novel itself; for
the first time, perhaps, he tells the story "like he wanted it." Ironically, it is Max who
is now alienated from the very language he speaks; as he retreats from the cell and
the novel, his groping actions are compared to those of a blind man, a man
deprived of all traditional points of reference. Bigger at last becomes author and
narrator of his own text, driving from the novel the voices that would overwhelm
his own.

In many respects *Native Son* is a novel about the insufficiency of novels, a story
about the insufficiency of words. In "Black Words and Black Becoming," Frank D.
McConnell suggests that

> Negro fiction—including the novel, tale, and autobiography—operates on a
> level of energy which is itself a criterion of the bourgeois novel form and of
> "novelistic" forms of understanding in general. . . . For not only the plot, but the
> language itself of the economic and social world, generating and generated by
> the novel, is available to the American black writer only as an acquired form,
> just as his existence in that social world is an acquisition rather than a birthright.
> And this means that its conventions can be employed only insofar as they are
> simultaneously tested.[20]

In *Native Son* the narrator's manipulation of the "magical disguise" of language
exposes the linguistic and formal conventions that the text simultaneously em-
ployees. The novel, then, tells not one story but many; most important, it reveals
the assumptions on which stories are made. In contemplating his own task as a
philosopher, Ludwig Wittgenstein addresses the implications of such a radical linguistic critique: "Where does our investigation get its importance from, since it
seems only to destroy everything interesting, that is, all that is great and important?
(As it were all the buildings, leaving behind only bits of stone and rubble.) What we
are destroying is nothing but houses of cards and we are clearing up the grounds
of language on which they stand."[21]

NOTES

[1] Ralph Ellison, *Shadow and Act* (New York: Random House, 1964), 24.
[2] For the Afro-American writing in what Ludwig Wittgenstein would call the "language-game" of the
white master, the split between sign and signifier that problematizes all linguistic discourse is exaggerated. "If language is to be a means of communication," Wittgenstein observes, "there must be agreement
not only in definitions but also in judgements" (*Philosophical Investigations* [New York: Macmillan, 1968],
88). Throughout, I choose to use Wittgenstein's terminology to describe the language games played by
Bigger, the narrator, and the white characters of *Native Son*. Wittgenstein's phrase is useful for my
purposes because it invokes the close association between a language and the context in which it is
created and used. While the black and white characters and the narrator of *Native Son* all speak and
write in English, their differing relationships to the master language define the language games within
which they operate as distinct. The English spoken by a white intellectual reflects a facility with the
language that is usually a sign not only of education but of his/her unmediated access to the world view
underlying the master language itself. Bigger's language game, on the other hand, is defined both by his

linguistic clumsiness and, more important, by his exclusion from the culture that shapes the meaning of the words with which he is forced to communicate. Wright's continual reiteration of the words "black" and "white" as descriptive adjectives in the novel is one way in which he calls attention to the ideological nature of even the simplest components of the master language.

3 Graham Clarke, "Beyond Realism: Recent Black Fiction and the Language of 'The Real Thing,' " *Black American Literature Forum* 16.1 (1982): 43.

4 Ibid., 43.

5 My revisionary reading of *Native Son* may raise the issue of authorial intention, especially in light of the fact that Wright's own comments about the novel in "How 'Bigger' Was Born" appear to substantiate the viewpoint of those critics who do not see the narrative voice of the novel as problematic. In that essay, Wright claims, "I tried to write so that, in the same instant of time, the objective and subjective aspects of Bigger's life would be caught in a focus of prose" (*Native Son* [New York: Harper & Row, 1940], xxxi). Throughout the novel, Wright remarks, "there is but one point of view: Bigger's" (xxxii). Because my argument documents the split in narrative focus and the fracture of point of view in the novel, some would argue that it contradicts Wright's own vision of *Native Son*.

While authorial intention is in and of itself a vexed issue the problematics of which I will not address here, Wright's own intentions are, in this case, not nearly so clear-cut as the often quoted passages from his commentary would lead us to believe. Wright's essay on *Native Son* is itself an ambiguous text which, while it makes the more obvious assertions about focus and point of view represented above, also displays a radical ambivalence about language. "As I wrote," Wright remarks in "How 'Bigger' Was Born," "for some reason or other, one image, symbol, character, scene, mood, feeling evoked its opposite, its parallel, its complementary, and its ironic counterpart. Why? I don't know" (xxxiii). Given what Wright describes in his autobiography as the inability of the culturally dominant language to express coherently his own thoughts and feelings, his apparently inexplicable tendency to invoke the "ironic counterpart" of his every word and metaphor is completely intelligible. "We shared a common tongue," he says of blacks and whites, "but my language was a different language from theirs" (*American Hunger* [New York: Harper & Row, 1977], 13). Tellingly, his own entrance into the world of Western art is accompanied, not by an expression of his hope to achieve a unified and coherent vision through words, but with a recognition of white language's limited ability to speak for him: "Humbly now, with no vaulting dream of achieving a vast unity, I wanted to try to build a bridge of words between me and that world outside, that world which was so distant and elusive that it seemed unreal" (*American Hunger*, 135). Given this autobiographical gloss, it is easy to see how Wright's seemingly definitive statements about the clear focus and point of view in his own prose may dissolve into a recognition that every image in his work is not without its ironic counterpart. While the standard criticisms of *Native Son* adopt Wright's rhetoric of direction, my own reading of the novel takes as its model the "ironic counterpart" of Wright's apparent struggle for unity and focus.

6 Wright, *Native Son*, 286. All subsequent references to *Native Son* will be cited by page number in the text.

7 See, for example, Robert James Butler, "The Function of Violence in Richard Wright's *Native Son*," *Black American Literature Forum* 20.1–2 (1986): 9–25. "Although Bigger Thomas's acts of violence may appear as monstrous," Butler states, "Bigger is always presented by Wright in complexly human terms" (23). See also Jerry H. Bryant, "The Violence of *Native Son*," *Southern Review* 17.2 (1981): 303–19. Throughout the novel, Bryant concludes, "We see from Bigger's point of view" (318).

8 In "The Clue Undetected in Richard Wright's *Native Son*" (*American Literature* 57.1 [1985]: 125–28), Doyle W. Walls also comments upon the diction that marks the origin of Bigger's correspondence in the Black Vernacular. Although he recognizes that "the white men did not know Bigger's language" (128), Walls does not extend his scrutiny to the problematic language of the novel's narrative voice.

9 In Derridian terms, the presence of the narrator's "supplement" exposes a corresponding absence; the supplement "is not simply added to the positivity of a presence, it produces no relief, its place is assigned by the mark of an emptiness. Somewhere, something can be filled up of itself, can accomplish itself, only by allowing itself to be filled through sign and proxy" (145). For a further discussion of the "supplement," see Jacques Derrida, *Of Grammatology*, trans. Gayatri Chakravorty Spivak (Baltimore: Johns Hopkins University Press, 1976).

10 Benjamin Lee Whorf, *Language, Thought, and Reality* (Cambridge: MIT Press, 1956), 256.

11 Joyce Ann Joyce, "Style and Meaning in Richard Wright's *Native Son*," *Black American Literature Forum* 16.3 (1982): 113.

12 Ibid., 114.

[13] Robert Bone, *The Negro Novel in America* (New Haven: Yale University Press, 1965), 147.

[14] In "Bigger Thomas Reconsidered: *Native Son,* Film, and *King Kong*" (*Journal of American Culture* 16.1 [1983]: 84–95), Harold Hellenbrand points to the way in which *Native Son* offers an implicit critique of the symbolic mode. "Repeatedly," Hellenbrand states, "Wright suggests that to picture is often to oversimplify and to ignore the human life beneath the image" (94). Although he does not apply his conclusions to the novel's narrative voice, Hellenbrand's remarks lend themselves well to such an application. Throughout the novel, Hellenbrand observes, "Bigger remains an outsider, a spectator, to the 'symbols and images' of society. They never have expressed his thoughts and feelings properly" (94).

[15] Judith Giblin Brazinsky, "The Demands of Conscience and the Imperatives of Form: The Dramatization of *Native Son,*" *Black American Literature Forum* 18.3 (1984): 107.

[16] Dan McCall, "The Social Significance of Bigger Thomas," rpt. in Native Son: *A Critical Handbook,* ed. Richard Abcarian (Belmont, CA: Wadsworth, 1970), 190–91.

[17] In "Wright's Invisible Native Son" (in *Twentieth-Century Interpretations of* Native Son, ed. Houston A. Baker, Jr. [Englewood Cliffs, N.J.: Prentice-Hall, 1972], 96–108), Gibson claims, "Max is not really thinking about Bigger the existential person, the discrete human entity. . . . Max is talking about a symbol, a representative figure" (100).

[18] In "The Conclusion of Richard Wright's *Native Son*" (*PMLA* 89 [1974]: 517–23), Paul N. Siegel points out what he describes as "recurring themes and images in the novel that [Max's] speech brings together." Rather than recognizing Max's speech as another version of the narrator's symbolic interpretation of Bigger, however, Siegel falls in line with those who claim that the speech "repeats too obviously what has already been said."

[19] In "Richard Wright's Inside Narratives" (in *American Fiction: New Readings,* ed. Richard Gray [Totowa, N.J.: Barnes & Noble, 1983], 200–21), A. Robert Lee defines what he sees as Wright's task as a novelist. "To 'build a bridge of words' between himself and America," Lee states, "must indeed in the light of [Wright's] background have seemed an unreal notion. For in claiming the right to use words to his own design Wright not only gave notice of his chosen path as a writer, he also affirmed that he intended nothing less than to take on and beat at its own game the white-run and proprietary world accustomed as if by ancient decree to doing the very defining of reality" (201). While Lee does not explore the parallel between Wright's artistry and Bigger's storytelling, Bigger accomplishes the very task that Lee defines as crucial to Wright's enterprise when he, as a character, resignifies the symbolic labels pinned upon him by the narrator and Max.

[20] Frank D. McConnell, "Black Words and Black Becoming," *Yale Review* 63.2 (1973): 195–96.

[21] Wittgenstein, 48.

Valerie Smith

ALIENATION AND CREATIVITY IN *NATIVE SON*

The criticism of Wright's work commonly notes that his prose writings center on the figure of the outsider; the novelist focuses on protagonists who either cannot or will not conform to the expectations that figures of authority, whether black or white, impose on them. What concerns me about Wright is not so much that his protagonists are all rebel-victims or outsiders. Rather, I am interested in the strategies his characters use to come to terms with their isolation and their sense of the discontinuity of their lives. My analysis of *Native Son* demonstrates that for Bigger Thomas, the protagonist, as for the autobiographical Richard, learning to tell his own story gives him a measure of control over his life and releases him from his feelings of isolation. Bigger is an uneducated criminal, a far cry from young Richard Wright—the brilliant, sensitive, rather self-righteous budding artist. But both young men are able to heal the discontinuities of their lives by learning to use language to describe themselves.

From the beginning of the novel Bigger's alienation from his oppressive environment is evident. His family and friends—poor, frustrated, brutalized—are tantalized by the promise of the American Dream, a narrative of limitless possibilities that will never be theirs. To mitigate their frustration, Bigger's family and friends all participate in some kind of communal activity. His mother finds consolation in religion, his friends and his girlfriend, Bessie, in drinking. Neither of these particular techniques of evasion satisfies Bigger, although he too seeks a way of alleviating his sense of marginality. As the narrator remarks, "He knew that the moment he allowed himself to feel to its fullness how they lived, the shame and misery of their lives, he would be swept out of himself with fear and despair."[1]

On occasion Bigger avoids his "fear and despair" by blocking out another person's presence. When his family reminds him of their suffering, for example, "he shut their voices out of his mind" (p. 13). When tempted to consider ways of

From *Self-Discovery and Authority in Afro-American Narrative* (Cambridge, MA: Harvard University Press, 1987), pp. 75–87.

escaping his situation, he "stopped thinking" (p. 16) in order to avoid disappoint-
ment. And when at first the Daltons, his white employers, make him feel uncomfortable, Bigger wishes earnestly to "blot" out both himself and "the other[s]" (pp.
49–50; 70).

As his confrontation with his friend Gus shows, Bigger also tries to avoid his
own suffering by displacing his self-hatred onto other people. Gus and Bigger argue
violently over whether to rob a white-owned store. Bigger fears the consequences
both of perpetrating a crime against a white person and of admitting that timidity
to his friends. Unable to express his own trepidation, he assaults Gus when he
appears reluctant. Bigger recognizes his own fear in Gus's hesitation, and attacks
Gus in an effort to destroy it.

Bigger participates in various activities with his friends that insulate him from his
fears and insecurities. They rob other black people because they know that to do
so will not bring punishment. Moreover, they imagine themselves the protagonists
of alternate plots that coincide with the American myth in a way that their own lives
do not. When they "play white," for instance, they pretend to be millionaires or
public officials, and momentarily forget their own powerlessness. Likewise, they live
vicariously through the movies they see. Yet despite this ostensible camaraderie
and the lure of fantasy, Bigger is alienated from his friends, for he fears acknowl-
edging his feelings either to himself or to other people. In the words of the narrator:
"As long as he could remember, [Bigger] had never been responsible to anyone.
The moment a situation became so that it exacted something of him, he rebelled.
That was the way he lived; he passed his days trying to defeat or gratify powerful
impulses in a world he feared" (p. 44; emphasis mine).

In order to emphasize Bigger's passivity and fear of articulation in the early
sections of the novel, Wright relies on an omniscient narrative presence to tell his
reader what Bigger thinks. Since Bigger does not allow himself to think, to act, or
to speak directly and openly, the narrator tells us the things Bigger cannot admit to
himself, such as his reason for attacking Gus.

Bigger's fear of articulation is also shown in his response to the way strangers
talk to him. Bigger is terrified by the Daltons when he arrives at their home. On the
surface he seems to be intimidated by their wealth and power. But in fact his
disorientation results from his inability to understand their language. When Mrs.
Dalton suggests how the family should treat him, she uses a vocabulary that Bigger
finds unintelligible and that ironically undercuts the very point she is trying to make:
" 'I think it's important emotionally that he feels free to trust his environment,' the
woman said. 'Using the analysis contained in the case record the relief sent us, I
think we should evoke an immediate feeling of confidence' " (p. 48). Unaccustomed
to this kind of speech, Bigger finds her vocabulary threatening: "It made him uneasy,
tense, as though there were influences and presences about him which he could
feel but not see" (p. 48).

In several ways Bigger's killing of Mary Dalton transforms his personality. The
murder, which Bigger has not planned, is ostensibly inadvertent; nevertheless, on a

more profound level it is fully intended. Bigger has wanted to "blot" Mary out whenever she has made him feel self-conscious and disoriented. Her murder is therefore important to Bigger because it enables him to complete an action he has willed:

> *He* had done this. *He* had brought all this about. In all of his life these two murders were the most meaningful things that had ever happened to him. He was living, truly and deeply, no matter what others might think, looking at him with their blind eyes. Never had he had the chance to live out the consequences of his actions; never had his will been so free as in this night and day of fear and murder and flight. (pp. 224–225)

The murder is also profoundly significant because it forces Bigger to confront the fear of the unknown, which has plagued him throughout his life. He and his friends never rob Blum, the white storekeeper, because for them, to commit a crime against a white person is to enter a realm of terror, an area variously referred to by the narrator as "territory where the full wrath of an alien white world would be turned loose upon them" (p. 18), a "shadowy region, a No Man's Land, the ground that separated the white world from the black" (p. 67). It is this unexplored danger zone that Bigger fears and that he persists in avoiding until he kills Mary Dalton. Once he has committed this action, he advances into this gray area, this "No Man's Land"; he realizes that at least initially this trespass has not destroyed him. Indeed, the knowledge that he continues to exist even after he has looked at the heart of darkness empowers him to achieve levels of action and articulation that he had formerly been unable to attain. Having been forced to look directly at that which had frightened him the most, Bigger now begins to liberate himself from the fear that haunts him. Although the murder makes him first a fugitive from and then a prisoner of justice, it initiates the process by which he ultimately comes to understand the meaning of his life.

Because the murder makes Bigger less fearful of the truth, it enables him to understand his environment more clearly. He becomes more analytical, and instead of blotting out his perceptions, he begins to make fine discriminations. Over breakfast on the morning after the murder, for example, he looks at his family as if with new eyes. He sees in his brother's blindness "a certain stillness, an isolation, meaninglessness" (p. 103). He perceives the nuances of his mother's demeanor: "Whenever she wanted to look at anything, even though it was near her, she turned her entire head and body to see it and did not shift her eyes. There was in her heart, it seemed, a heavy and delicately balanced burden whose weight she did not want to assume by disturbing it one whit" (p. 103). And he sees his sister's fear as if for the first time: she "seemed to be shrinking from life in every gesture she made. The very manner in which she sat showed a fear so deep as to be an organic part of her; she carried the food to her mouth in tiny bits, as if dreading its choking her, or fearing that it would give out too quickly" (p. 104).

Moreover, Bigger begins to look at his own life more contemplatively. He interprets what and how his life means by trying to assign value to his past actions. He concludes that the murder was a creative gesture because it has enabled him to refashion his life: "His crime was an anchor weighing him safely in time" (p. 101). In addition, he consciously decides to accept responsibility for an action that might be considered accidental:

> Though he had killed by accident, not once did he feel the need to tell himself that it had been an accident. He was black and he had been alone in a room where a white girl had been killed; therefore he had killed her . . . It was no longer a matter of dumb wonder as to what would happen to him and his black skin; he knew now. The hidden meaning of his life—a meaning which others did not see and which he had always tried to hide—had spilled out. (p. 101)

Bigger's immediate response to the murder demonstrates the extent to which it has liberated him and sharpened his vision. Before the murder Bigger's imagination was inhibited by his fears; he generally preferred not to think. Immediately afterward, however, instead of blocking out the fact of the murder, he confronts and verbalizes it. He has a momentary impulse to run away, but he denies it. Instead of lapsing into his characteristically evasive behavior, he begins to plan his defense with a previously unrevealed freedom of mind. It would have been simple for Bigger to follow his first instincts and choose the more passive way out. Earlier in the evening he had been directed to take Mary's trunk to the basement before going home for the night. He could have proceeded as if nothing had gone wrong. He could have taken the trunk to the basement, put the car in the garage, and gone home. Instead, he decides to destroy the body and implicate Mary's boyfriend, Jan. Rather than choosing the path of least resistance, Bigger creates an elaborate story in order to save himself.

By identifying Jan (indirectly) as the kidnapper and burning Mary's body, Bigger actually seeks to return to and change the past. In a sense, it is as if Bigger takes the pen from Wright and rewrites his story into the tale he wants it to be. Bigger removes himself from the role of the protagonist and changes the nature of the crime to a kidnapping. He tries to create a substitute reality—that is, a fiction—to replace the one that threatens to destroy him. The extent of Bigger's investment in the story he creates is demonstrated in the way he embellishes it. He keeps searching for a better story, not merely the tightest excuse he can find: "[S]uppose he told them that he had come to get the trunk?—That was it! The *trunk!* His fingerprints had a right to be there . . . He could take the trunk to the basement and put the car into the garage and then go home. *No!* There was a better way. . . . He would say that Jan had come to the house and he had left Jan outside in the car. But there was still a *better way!* Make them think that Jan did it" (p. 87).[2] The larger significance of Bigger's fiction making and its similarity to young Richard's impulse to write reveals itself if we consider that he has suffered throughout his life from other people's attempts to impose their fictions—stereotypes—on him. Precisely because whites insist on seeing Bigger as less than human, he cannot enjoy the privileges that should be his. Dalton, who is sufficiently myopic to believe that he can be at once a slumlord and a philanthropist, fails to recognize Bigger (or any black person) as fully human. Instead, to him black people are objects of charity easily placated with ping-pong tables. His wife responds to Bigger as if he were a sociological case study. And although Mary and Jan pride themselves on their radical politics, they never really see Bigger either. They treat him as if he and his people were curiosities. They sing spirituals and use black colloquialisms in order to exhibit their familiarity with what are to them exotic artifacts. They insist on eating with Bigger at a black-owned restaurant, oblivious to the discomfort that may cause him. That Jan and Mary use Bigger as a means of access to certain experiences, with no awareness of his feelings, shows that they too see Bigger as their own creation, not as what Bigger himself actually is.

Bigger's misrepresentation in court and in the press epitomizes his lifelong struggle against other people's fictions. Buckley, the State's Attorney, considers him to be violent and subhuman and prosecutes him according to collectively held stereotypes of black male behavior. To him the specific details of Bigger's case are uninteresting, irrelevant. Bigger is guilty of one count of second-degree murder (Mary's) and one count of first-degree murder (Bessie's). The State's Attorney, however, considers Bessie's murder significant only insofar as it provides evidence that he can use to reconstruct Mary's death. He successfully prosecutes Bigger for raping Mary on the assumption that black men are driven to possess white women sexually. Moreover, he assumes that Bigger killed Mary to hide the fact that he had raped her. The press similarly denies Bigger's individuality, referring to him with such epithets as "jungle beast" and "missing link" (p. 261). Indeed, the journalists insist that Bigger, a black man, could not be smart enough to have committed his crimes without the assistance of white co-conspirators. They argue that communists helped him plot his crime, because "the plan of the murder and kidnaping was too elaborate to be the work of a Negro mind" (p. 229).

Bigger's complex defense signals his ability to articulate a story about himself that challenges the one that others impose on him. But his story has its limitations and does not accomplish all that Bigger intends. At this stage in his life, he, like the young Richard Wright, recognizes that language has power, but he does not yet know how to use it.

In his naiveté Bigger patterns his tale on pulp detective fiction (p. 87). The story, based on poorly written models, depends on too many narrative inconsistencies. Bigger does not, for example, remember that Jan left him and Mary in order to go to a party and will therefore have an alibi. What is perhaps more important, however, is that Bigger's first story (like the ex-colored man's narrative) fails him because he uses it as a technique of evasion. Although his experience has helped him face his situation, he uses his story to help him escape it.

As I have pointed out, during the period when Bigger is most timid and self-protective (before he arrives at the Dalton home), his consciousness is most restrained, and Wright relies on an omniscient narrator to explain his character's thoughts and motivations. As Bigger's imagination and emotions spring to life, ironically after he kills Mary, Wright relies increasingly on free indirect discourse. In other words, as Bigger's capacity to understand and express himself increases, Wright allows him to speak for himself. Even though Bigger is terrified by the thought of seeing Mary's bones, for example, he can at least acknowledge his fear; he has moved beyond the point of denying his trepidation. As a result, Wright presents his consciousness by approximating Bigger's thoughts:

> He stood a moment looking through the cracks into the humming fire, blindingly red now. But how long would it keep that way, if he did not shake the ashes down? He remembered the last time he had tried and how hysterical he had felt. He must do better than this. . . . For the life of him, he could not bring himself to shake those ashes. But did it really matter? No. . . . No one would look into the bin. Why should they? (p. 161)

Similarly, Bigger comprehends the significance of his inability to retrieve his money from Bessie's dress pocket after he has thrown her down the air-shaft: "*Good God! Goddamn, yes, it was in her dress pocket! Now, he was in for it. He had thrown Bessie down the air-shaft and the money was in the pocket of her dress! What could he do about it? Should he go down and get it? Anguish gripped him. . . . He did not want to see her again. . . . Well, he would have to do without money; that was all*" (p. 224).

As long as Bigger is a fugitive from the law, he thinks quickly and improvises plans to remain free. When his capture is imminent and Bigger realizes that his future will be even more closely confined than his past, his earlier fears descend on him again and he resumes his former passive, evasive behavior. When his pursuers corner him, Bigger gives up his sense of wholeness and returns to his earlier unresponsiveness. Gradually he steps outside of himself, watching his capture as if from behind a curtain and then ignoring it as if he is standing behind a wall (p. 250). As his captors drag him downstairs, he completes this dissociation by forcing himself to lose consciousness.

Bigger tries but fails to pass his final days in this unresponsive condition. At first he refuses to eat, to drink, to smoke, to resist, and "steadfastly [refuses] to speak" (p. 254). He tries to avoid thinking and feeling as well, because he assumes that his one leap of faith has caused his defeat: "Why not kill that wayward yearning within him that had led him to this end? He had reached out and killed and had not solved anything, so why not reach inward and kill that which had duped him?" (p. 255). When he is bombarded with faces and with the reality of his situation, Bigger faints at his inquest. But when he regains consciousness a second time, his recently acquired sense of himself (the narrator calls it "pride," p. 259) returns, and Bigger begins to rebuild that bridge of words that once connected him with other people. He insists on reading a newspaper because he cannot understand his position until he knows what others are saying about him. More important than his reading, however, are the conversations Bigger has with Jan, Buckley, and Max, the attorney from the Labor Defenders who is in charge of Bigger's defense. Each interview or exchange teaches him something about communication and about himself.

In his conversation with Jan, Bigger conquers his fear of self-scrutiny. Indeed, in his subsequent conversations he attempts to use language to make himself understood with the same clarity he achieves with Jan. By admitting that he and Mary had humiliated Bigger inadvertently, and by offering to help him, Jan enables Bigger to overcome his defenses. His words take Bigger outside of himself and allow him to feel his humanity.

This conversation restores and heightens Bigger's faith in the power of language. Because of this exchange, Bigger does not retreat from his family when they visit him. Instead, he searches for the right words both to comfort them and to defy the authorities. His first attempt to speak to them is unsatisfactory: he tries to dismiss cavalierly the extremity of his situation. But his conversation with Jan has impressed upon Bigger the necessity of candor; Bigger retracts these defensive comments, replacing them with words that express his resignation.

His confession to Buckley teaches Bigger an additional lesson about the necessity of articulation. Buckley's interrogation consists essentially of a series of true-or-false questions. He accuses Bigger of numerous crimes and tries to make him confess to them. Because Buckley seems so eager to pin offenses on him that he never committed, Bigger is forced to defend himself and tell his story as it happened. The effect of articulating this story to a hostile listener drains Bigger; he fears that he may have made himself excessively vulnerable by telling his enemy the truth. But as the narrator suggests, the ostensible ordeal of telling his story actually propels Bigger on to a higher level of self-knowledge:

> He lay on the cold floor sobbing; but really he was standing up strongly with contrite heart, holding his life in his hands, staring at it with a wondering question. He lay on the cold floor sobbing; but really he was pushing forward with his puny strength against a world too big and too strong for him. He lay on the cold floor sobbing; but really he was groping forward with fierce zeal into a welter of circumstances which he felt contained a water of mercy for the thirst of his heart and brain. (p. 288)

If Bigger's confession to Buckley is important because it enables him to tell what really happened, his confession to Max in a parallel scene is important because it enables him to tell why it happened. Talking to Max allows Bigger to understand for the first time the complex feelings he had for Mary. The search for the appropriate words is a painful and gradual one for him; remembering Mary triggers "a net of vague, associative" memories of his sister. And ultimately, he gives up "trying to explain" his actions logically and reverts "to his feelings as a guide in answering Max" (p. 324). But as he traces his thoughts and anxieties, Bigger becomes conscious for the first time of certain feelings, and he expresses to Max emotions that had been intensely private. For example, during this conversation he first understands the relationship between the frustration he has always felt and his violence toward Mary. Moreover, on this occasion he admits to someone else that he lost control of himself at the moment he killed Mary. Most important, he is able to explain the value of the murder: that it freed him from his lifelong fears. While Bigger felt helpless and betrayed after confessing to Buckley, explaining himself to Max gives him an enormous sense of relief. That "urge to talk" had been so strong within him that he had felt "he ought to be able to reach out with his bare hands and carve from naked space the concrete solid reasons why he had murdered" (p. 323). Telling his story helps him understand those reasons and grants him a "cool breath of peace" that he had never known before (p. 332).

Wright's protagonists tend to fit a particular mold. Fishburn notes that the protagonists of Wright's later writings are all patterned after his autobiographical identity: "The young Richard Wright, like all his later heroes, must wrench his identity from a hostile environment; neither Wright nor his heroes have the comfort of being accepted by their own race. All are aliens among both the whites and the blacks."[3] And in "Self-Portraits by Richard Wright," John M. Reilly comments that in Black Boy and "The Man Who Lived Underground," "a common viewpoint is that of the outsider in defensive flight from forces in the environment that threaten the personality."[4]

Certainly Bigger suffers alienation from blacks and whites in the way that the autobiographical persona of Black Boy and American Hunger does. I would suggest a further parallel, however: like this other protagonist, Bigger comes to understand the power of language as a means of creating an identity for himself in an alien environment. Young Richard achieves the greater success; his talent for writing liberates him from the oppression of both the black and the white communities. But Bigger develops the capacity to use language as a way of confronting directly the truths of his own experience. Although it does not save him from electrocution, the capacity to explain himself to others provides him with an awareness of what his life has meant.

NOTES

[1] Richard Wright, Native Son (New York: Harper and Row, 1966), p. 13. Subsequent references are to this edition and will be cited in the text.
[2] Robert Bone argues as well that Bigger's kidnap note demonstrates his creative capacity. See his pamphlet Richard Wright (Minneapolis: University of Minnesota Press, 1969), p. 21.
[3] Katherine Fishburn, Richard Wright's Hero: The Faces of a Rebel-Victim (Metuchen, N.J.: Scarecrow Press, 1977), p. 7.
[4] John M. Reilly, "Self-Portraits by Richard Wright," The Colorado Quarterly, 20 (1971), 45.

Alan W. France

MISOGYNY AND APPROPRIATION IN *NATIVE SON*

In his essay "How 'Bigger' Was Born," Richard Wright reminds the reader of *Native Son* that the novel's point of view has been restricted to the horizon of its protagonist:

> because I had limited myself to rendering only what Bigger saw and felt, I gave no more reality to the other characters than that which Bigger himself saw.... Throughout there is but one point of view: Bigger's. (xxxii)

Poststructural literary criticism has at last rebelled against this kind of authorial control over texts and has endorsed a policy of expropriation: readings of literary works need no longer by synonymous with divination of authorial intention. Holding up the author's intention as the sole legitimate code for interpreting the work may be seen, therefore, as propaganda masking and muzzling an absent reality. The repressed absences are now empowered to challenge the inscribed, privileged interpretation of the work and to demand an equal voice in its dialogical world.

To change the figures, it is as if the maker had arranged an object of his art, half exposed, in wet plaster. With the fetish of ownership gone, we viewers are entitled, indeed required, to become participants in interpreting and evaluating the art of the work. This means that criticism must now break the work out of its authorial mold and examine the heretofore hidden impression made by its buried underside. In reading works of the patriarchal canon, this concealed impression can be conceived as a female mold that forms the work by its resistance but is absent from it.

The exposed presence of *Native Son* is the dialectical struggle between Bigger Thomas' desire for freedom and dignity, on the one hand, and the inhuman, oppressive degradation of racism used as a weapon of domination by the white propertied elite, on the other. This much of the meaning has been authorized by inscription into text; it has been exposed by the author to the study of critics and

From *Modern Fiction Studies* 34, No. 3 (Autumn 1988): 413–23.

scholars for the past four and a half decades. It is now time to break open the author's cast and to examine the previously concealed contours, shaped by the absent Other.

When the text is read as one would read the black and white negative of a photograph, what immediately becomes apparent is a *second* dialectical struggle underlying the authorized one: the struggle to appropriate (and thus dehumanize) women by reducing them to objects of male status conflict, to what Hélène Cixous calls "The Realm of the Proper," which "functions by the appropriation articulated, set into play, by man's classic fear of seeing himself expropriated" (Moi 112). From underneath, *Native Son* is the story of a black man's rebellion against white male authority. The rebellion takes the form of the ultimate appropriation of human beings; the rape-slaying, which is also the ultimate expropriation of patriarchal property, the total consumption of the commodified woman.

Even feminist critics of Wright's work, while noting its strains of violence and misogyny, have not opened the text sufficiently to reveal its submerged underside. Sherley Anne Williams, for example, observes Wright's tendency to portray black women as treacherous and traitorous and to present their suffering as, primarily, "an affront to the masculinity of black men" (406). Williams, nevertheless, fails to challenge Wright's authority over the interpretation of female characters in *Native Son*: "We excuse these characterizations [of women]," she writes, "because of the power of Wright's psychological portrait of Bigger; this is Bigger's story" (397). It is time now to revoke these privileges accorded to Bigger and to recover the radical alterity in the text that reduces women to property, valuable only to the extent they serve as objects of phallocentric status conflicts. If read as the negative polarity of the text, this process of male reification and appropriation pervades the work.

In the initial episode of *Native Son,* Bigger kills a huge rat while his mother and sister, Vera, cower and scream on the bed in fear. This emblematic act occupies the surface of the novel's first six pages. The rat, an omnivorous, disease-bearing pest, fairly represents the socioeconomic system under which Mr. Dalton squeezes his fortune out of the ghetto. The killing of the rat represents, perhaps, Bigger's one chance to protect his mother and younger siblings as the patriarch of the Thomas family. The text urges us specifically to make this latter interpretation when its omniscient narrator tells us:

> He [Bigger] hated his family because he knew that they were suffering and that he was powerless to help them. He knew that the moment he allowed himself to feel to its fullness how they lived, the shame and misery of their lives, he would be swept out of himself with fear and despair. (13)

In this passage we are asked to privilege Bigger Thomas' feeling of powerlessness caused by the family's living conditions over the actual physical suffering that those conditions impose on the family. The text, that is, points to Bigger's status deprivation as the real significance of economic and social oppression.

In this initial episode, Bigger experiences his killing of the rat not with the pride of one who alleviates his family's distress, if only partially and temporarily, but with the giddy exultation of one glorying in the rare and momentary dominance that killing an adversary confers. Bigger uses the occasion of conquest to lord it over the dependent females of his family.

The phallocentricity of this scene is created first of all by Bigger's threatening his sister with the crushed and bloody carcass of the rat. The threat to Bigger (and the phallic suggestiveness can here be noted in his name) is indicated by a suggestively vaginal "three-inch rip" in his pant-leg. Bigger crushes the rat's head with his shoe while "cursing hysterically: You sonofa*bitch!*" The italics further suggest a reading of the episode as a struggle for phallic dominance with overtones of castration anxiety. In the economy of male aggression, Bigger's killing of the rat converts it into an object "over a foot long" that now becomes a weapon in his hands. As victor in a battle that the text compels us to see in overtly sexual terms, Bigger attempts to exact the maximum abasement of those whose subordination he has won by right of conquest. When Vera begs him to throw the rat out, "Bigger laughed and approached the bed with the dangling rat, swinging it to and fro like a pendulum, enjoying his sister's fear" (11). It is not the conquest over the rat, *qua* rat, in which Bigger most exults. Rather, he enjoys the dominance over the women that violent conquest has conferred on him.

Nor is it merely the physical destruction of the rat—its reduction to symbolic phallus—that allows him dominance over the women: it is their own contemptible weakness, that which denies them utterance of the words of the novel's epitaph from Job: "My stroke is heavier than my groaning" (6). From the very beginning of the text, narrative instructions make clear that the absent phallus is the source of shame as well as weakness. The mother calls to the sons as she stands in her nightgown in the single-room apartment, "Turn your heads so I can dress" (7). Bigger and his brother, Buddy, "kept their faces averted while their mother and sister put on enough clothes to keep them from feeling ashamed...." And this aversion of the eyes is "a conspiracy against shame" (8). From the very outset of the novel, therefore, the text's psychodynamics are polarized sexually: Bigger and other male characters continue the violent struggle, presaged by the killing of the rat, for the appropriation or continued enjoyment of—the narcissistic desire for—status. Women, as characters in *Native Son,* are objects of this appropriation; they are at the same time desired as objects but contemptible in their weakness and passivity.

The woman, as displaced Other, is characterized as blind and weak. Mrs. Dalton is literally sightless; but to Bigger, all the characters who are not conscious of the predatory economy in which they are immersed are blind. It is, in fact, the killing of Mary Dalton that makes Bigger aware of the general blindness. After Mary's murder, he notices that those around him "did not want to see what others were doing if that doing did not feed their own desires." The corollary is that "if he could see while others were blind, then he could get what he wanted and never be caught at it" (102). Mrs. Thomas' religion and Bessie's drinking blind and weaken these women, arousing Bigger's abhorrence: "He hated his mother for that way of hers which was like Bessie's. What his mother had was Bessie's whiskey, and Bessie's whiskey was his mother's religion" (226).

The text's denial of misogyny and appropriation of women most nearly bursts free from its self-authorized interpretation at three points of crisis that share to different degrees the ultimate patriarchal sentence on women, the rape-slaying. Although the negative polarity of female subjugation exists systematically through-out, it is most clearly visible at these cataclysms of phallic aggression and appro-priation. We must look, therefore, in some detail at Bigger's symbolic rape-slaying of Gus, the partially effected rape and the murder of Mary Dalton, and the overt rape-killing of Bessie Mears.

The initial rape of the novel is a public act, performed in front of male peers. It presents the brutal subjugation of another male, Gus, by means of sexually symbolic violence. After Gus throws off his initial unprovoked attack, Bigger ("as graceful as an animal leaping") trips him and jumps "on top of him, with the knife open and ready"; Gus is completely in Bigger's power: he speaks "in surrender" and looks at his assailant "pleadingly" (40). The dominant male forces the subordinate to perform an act of ritualistic sodomy:

> Bigger held the open blade an inch from Gus's lips.
> "Lick it," Bigger said, his body tingling with elation.
> Gus's eyes filled with tears.
> "Lick it, I said! You think I'm playing?" (40–41)

This formulaic sodomy is aggravated by Bigger's threat to cut out Gus's navel, an act of disembowelment that, in addition to being murderous, seems clearly to have anal signification. Gus is able to escape before suffering any further violence, symbolic or otherwise, but Bigger is not finished with his knife. He challenges Doc's proprietary authority (signified by the gun) by slicing the felt of Doc's pool table.

The novel's narrative warrant attempts to control the interpretation of the foregoing events by making the assault on Gus a displacement of fear, Bigger's fear of holding up Blum's store: "He hoped the fight he had had with Gus covered up what he was trying to hide"; but the next sentence betrays the phallocentric struggle for domination going on beneath the text's narrative surface: "At least the fight made him feel the equal of them [fellow gang members]. And he felt the equal of Doc, too; had he not slashed his table and dared him to use his gun?" (43).

The underlying system of sexual terrorism breaks through both preceding interpretations, however, and casts Bigger's unprovoked assault of Gus (rendered "fight" in the narrative) in terms of phallic aggression. After it was over, we read that Bigger "stood for two whole minutes staring at the shadow of a telephone pole" and then "stumbled violently over a tiny crack in the pavement" (43). He has triumphed and humiliated the subordinate male; but instead of feeling elated, he feels remorseful and depressed. The symbolic rape-slaying of another male has disrupted the gang by reducing a member to the level of a woman. This process is analogous to the "ideology of rape" that Susan Brownmiller finds in male prison culture. It is "a product of the violent subculture's definition of masculinity through physical triumph, and [in prison] those who emerged as 'women' were those who were subjugated by real or threatened force" (Brownmiller 295). The symbolic "feminization" of Gus has rendered the gang ineffective as a unit for action (armed robbery here) and thereby further isolated Bigger. It is in this sense that Bigger may be said to have "stumbled over a tiny crack."

The struggle to establish dominance over another male by violent sexual aggression gives way in the second half of Book One to Bigger's appropriation of Mary Dalton, first attempted by rape and then accomplished by murder. The word "rape" is used here not merely in a figurative or approximate sense. In many jurisdictions, sexual penetration of a woman too intoxicated to be able to consent to the act constitutes a rape. But what happens to Mary Dalton in the minutes preceding her death suggests the term rape-slaying in a more direct way. In the course of the narrative, the text keeps its curtain of authority drawn over the events it relates. But later, when Bigger is telling Bessie about the fateful events, there is less certainty. "Had he raped her?" he ponders: "Yes, he had raped her. Every time he felt as he had that night, he raped" (213–214). This admission is quickly retracted by the broadening of the term into a metaphor for the struggle against white society ("Rape was what one felt when one's back was against the wall . . ."). Nevertheless, the narrative questions its own authorial interpretation here as it does elsewhere.

The circumstances surrounding Mary's death are further made problematic when Mrs. Dalton appears at Mary's bedroom door: we are assured that Bigger "*knew* that if Mary spoke she [Mrs. Dalton] would come to the side of the bed and discover him, touch him" (84, emphasis added). Yet Mary's failure to respond to her mother's call does indeed draw Mrs. Dalton to her daughter's bedside; and when she does enter the room, Bigger is able to match "each of her movements toward the bed" with a movement away from her. The silence of the text here, its refusal to explain why Bigger fails to discern one moment the very opportunity for escape that he in fact takes the next, is curious at the least. A more obvious subterfuge reveals itself when the narrative of Mary's suffocation is deconstructed. The text's authority for Mary's "accidental" death is the presence of Mrs. Dalton, "the white blur," that will catch Bigger in a situation prescripted for lynching. But the text itself calls into question the certainty of his being found out: he is not found out. If we remove the presence of Mrs. Dalton from the narrative of Mary's death and collapse the text, the following is what remains:

> She tossed and mumbled sleepily. He tightened his fingers on her breasts, kissing her again, feeling her move toward him. He was aware only of her body now. . . .
>
> He felt Mary trying to rise and quickly he pushed her head back to the pillow. . . . He held his hand over her mouth. . . . Mary mumbled and tried to rise again. Frantically, he caught a corner of the pillow and brought it to her

lips. . . . [H]e grew tight and full, as though about to explode. Mary's fingernails tore at his hands and he caught the pillow and covered her entire face with it, firmly. Mary's body surged upward and he pushed downward upon the pillow with all of his weight. . . . Again Mary's body heaved and he held the pillow in a grip that took all his strength. For a long time he felt the sharp pain of her fingernails biting into his wrists. . . .

He clenched his teeth and held his breath, . . . His muscles flexed taut as steel. . . . Then suddenly her fingernails did not bite into his wrists. . . . He did not feel her surging and heaving against him. Her body was still. (84–85)

This reading may be perceived as being too violent for credibility; yet Robert James Butler has used just such a technique recently to vindicate completely the authorial mandate, that is, the privileged dialectic, Bigger's struggle against a racist society. Butler concludes his restructuring of the passage above as follows:

After her "surging and heaving" (84) body finally relaxes and Mrs. Dalton leaves the room, Bigger orgasmically utters "a long gasp" (85). In the afterglow of this strange experience, he is depicted as "weak and wet with sweat" (85), listening for some time to his heavy breathing filling the darkness. (14–15)

This reading, nevertheless, manages to go the text one better in its own repression of the sexual dialectic. Mention of Mary's drunkenness is completely suppressed; Bigger's exploitation of her condition is described as his giving in "to his warmer, more humane feelings" (15); the fatal episode is said to begin "romantically with Mary's encouraging Bigger's sexual attentions and his reciprocating, [but] Mrs. Dalton's entry into the room abruptly turns their lovemaking into deathmaking" (14). The "erotic images" of the killing are said to be "ironic," although the yawning absence of a possessive pronoun in front of "deathmaking" conceals perhaps still greater irony. And the final disposal of Mary and Bessie is their reduction, in Butler's phrase, to "aspects of Bigger's radically divided self " (16).

In Book Two, the narrator will actually authorize an interpretation of Mary's death much like the one above, one inscribed by the removal of Mrs. Dalton from the text:

Though he had killed by accident, not once did he feel the need to tell himself that it had been an accident. . . . And in a certain sense he knew that the girl's death had not been accidental. He had killed many times before, only on those other times there had been no handy victim. . . . (101)

Thinking back on his murder of Mary, Bigger reflects with satisfaction (but without conscious irony at the juxtaposition of these crimes) that whites "might think he would steal a dime, rape a woman, get drunk, or cut somebody; but to kill a millionaire's daughter and burn her body?" It is the appropriation of the woman's body that thrills Bigger, arousing in him a "tingling sensation enveloping all his body" (108).

The elation Bigger feels seems directly proportionate to Mary Dalton's value as a commodity, her status as the property of a millionaire. Thus, her life is fungible in dollars. In the economy of the novel, Bigger's use and destruction of the woman amounts to his expropriation of $10,000 worth of Mr. Dalton's property. Later, the narrative reveals exactly how Bigger perceives this transaction: "The knowledge that he had killed a white girl they loved and regarded as their symbol of beauty made him feel the equal of them, like a man who had been somehow cheated, but had now evened the score" (155). Denied participation in capitalist commodity culture, the chance to "fly planes and run ships" (23), Bigger satisfies himself with the use (and destruction) of the Dalton's property in spite of his exclusion.

It is in Bigger's rape-murder of Bessie Mears, however, that the full misogynistic implications of the text are revealed. Before the discovery of Mary Dalton's remains, while the exaction of ransom is still possible, Bessie retains enough value for Bigger to risk the possibility that she might "snitch." After Bigger is found out, Bessie is of no further use to him; she has become disposable. Bigger's authorial apologist attempts to rationalize the inevitable disposal: "If she stayed . . . they would come to her and she would simply lie on the bed and sob out everything. . . . And what she would tell them about him, his habits, his life, would help them to track him down" (212). He must take her with him, "and then at some future time settle things with her, settle them in a way that would not leave him in any danger" (215). This final settlement takes place, appropriately, in an abandoned building which, like Bessie, has no further use nor value as property.

The rape and murder that follow are punctuated in the text by a veritable litany of narrative exculpations. Three times in two paragraphs: "He could not take her with him and he could not leave her behind. . . . He could not leave her here and he could not take her with him. . . . He could not take her and he could not leave her" (221–222). Yet he is on the run, has no idea himself where he is going, and so nothing Bessie could tell the police would help in his capture.

The identification of phallic aggression with death is completed by the rape and the murder that follow. Only the inscription of the text identifies the blunt instrument that "plunged downward . . . landed with a thud . . . lifted . . . again and again . . . in falling . . . struck a sodden mass that gave softly but stoutly to each landing blow . . . seemed to be striking a wet wad of cotton . . . the jarring . . . impact " (222) as the weapon of the murder and not the rape.

Before her death, Bessie comes to the realization that she has been used by Bigger, enjoyed as sexual property: "All you ever did since we been knowing each other was to get me drunk so's you could have me. That was all! I see it now" (215). In the context of their relationship, Bessie's rape-slaying comes to seem merely the last act in a long process of appropriation. During his conversation with Boris Max, Bigger admits the extent to which he perceives his proprietary interest to have gone: "I wasn't in love with Bessie. She was just my girl. . . . I killed Bessie to save myself. You have to have a girl, so I had Bessie. And I killed her" (326). Except for his knife and gun, Bessie is the only property Bigger has ever possessed. When her battered corpse is brought before the court as evidence in Bigger's murder trial, it is only textual authority that can maintain the reader's attention on the privileged theme, the black man's oppression by the white. Without that privilege, Bigger's "deeper sympathy" and his knowledge that Bessie "though dead, though killed by him, would resent her dead body being used in this way [to convict her murderer]" (307) are incredible.

The slippage of signification by which sexual penetration becomes confused with murder is nowhere more frighteningly out of narrative control than in the dialogue of the white men who are hunting Bigger:

> "Say, did you see that brown gal in there?"
> "The one that didn't have much on?"
> "Yeah."
> "Boy, she was a peach, wasn't she?"
> "Yeah; I wonder what on earth a nigger wants to kill a white woman for when he has such good-looking women in his own race. . . ." (243–244)

The implied phallic violence in the equation of "killing" and "having" women has clearly leaked into the narrative while it points its readers toward the white man's hunt for Bigger Thomas.

An even more chilling possibility is suggested by the Derridean tactic of "double writing," a process of "erasure which allows what it obliterates to be read, violently inscribing within the text that which attempted to govern it from without" (6). If the text can suppress, can it deceive? If it can omit and apologize, can it lie? Given Bigger's insistence on the liberating power of killing women, it is only with difficulty that the text can absolve him of the rapes and murders that Buckley, the State's Attorney, accuses him of in the course of the interrogation. Once the external authority of the text is superceded, the assurance evaporates that another man, not Bigger, raped and choked to death the woman on University Avenue, climbed in Miss Ashton's bedroom window and attacked her, killed Mrs. Clinton, raped the woman in Englewood, and attacked the girl in Jackson Park last summer (283–284). The normality, the ubiquity of phallic violence, largely erased from the text, can be vaguely but unmistakably perceived in Buckley's question: "Listen, start at the beginning. Who was the first woman you ever killed?"

The final attempts of the text to cover the repressed phallocentricity and to achieve some sort of rapprochement between Bigger and the white male society that oppresses him are almost comic against this backdrop of violence against women. Jan forgives Bigger for Mary Dalton's murder:

> "Though this thing [Mary's murder] hurt me, I got something out of it," Jan said, sitting down and turning to Bigger. "It made me see deeper into men. . . . I—I lost something, but I got something, too. . . . I see now that you couldn't do anything else but that; it was all you had. . . . " (267)

Obviously, Mary Dalton has become an absence, a silence that Irigaray believes patriarchal discourse always means when it inscribes "woman": "Women are
trapped in a system of meaning which serves the auto-affection of the (masculine)
subject" (122). Bessie, Mary, and the other victims that appear like bubbles on the
surface of the text are effectively silenced. The last words are uttered by Bigger
Thomas: "When a man kills, it's for something. . . . I didn't know I was really alive in
this world until I felt things hard enough to kill for 'em" (392).

Critics have only begun the process of "teasing out" (Johnson 140) this textual
silence that "serves the auto-affection" of men. One well-known reading maintains,
for example, that Native Son "forces us to experience the truth of what man does
to man" (Reilly 397). Another concludes accurately, if with what I hope can be
recognized by now as unintentional irony: "Jan Erlone forgives Bigger for killing the
girl he loves and conveys to the black youth his first sense of a white man's
humanity" (Magistrale 66).

It must be stressed that the pathos of Bigger Thomas' diminishment, the
stunting and warping effects of racial oppression that form the text's reigning
dialectic, is in no way reduced by reading the repressed dialectic, the violent and
phallocentric appropriation of women. Both belong to a system in which the Other
is marginalized and dehumanized. This system of ownership uses racism and sexism
to reduce the Other to objects of appropriation in the struggle over property
relationships that determine status. The centrality of these relations to the structure
of Native Son is suggested by the role inheritance plays. If the faithful family retainer,
Peggy, can be trusted, the Dalton's wealth was inherited from Mrs. Dalton's family.
Mr. Dalton acquired it, along with Mrs. Dalton, in marriage. Mary Dalton's earring,
which becomes the only identifying trace of her existence, was passed down to her
according to the very same patrilineal property arrangements by which her father
inherited the slum properties that bred her killer.

The misogynistic underside of the text, once exposed by wresting it from
authorial control, must become part of the critical reading of Native Son. Only in
this way can the interrelationship among patriarchal repression, racism, and capi-
talist culture be clearly understood. The novel grows out of this suppressed interrelationship in which value is conferred according to property arrangements, and
status is a phallic prerogative assigned by access to and ownership of commodities,
including women.

WORKS CITED

Brownmiller, Susan. *Against Our Will: Men, Women and Rape*. 1975. New York: Bantam,
    1976.
Butler, Robert James. "The Function of Violence in Richard Wright's *Native Son*." *Black
    American Literature Forum* 20 (1986): 9–25.
Derrida, Jacques. *Positions*. Chicago: U of Chicago P, 1981.
Irigaray, Luce. *This Sex Which Is Not One*. Trans. Catherine Porter. Ithaca: Cornell UP,
    1985.

Johnson, Barbara. "Teaching Deconstructively." *Reading and Writing Differently: Deconstruction and the Teaching of Composition and Literature.* Eds. C. Douglas Atkins and Michael L. Johnson. Lawrence: UP of Kansas, 1985. 140–148.

Magistrale, Tony. "From St. Petersburg to Chicago: Wright's *Crime and Punishment.*" *Comparative Literature Studies* 23 (1986): 59–70.

Moi, Toril. *Sexual/Textual Politics: Feminist Literary Theory.* New York: Methuen, 1985.

Reilly, John. "Afterword." *Native Son.* By Richard Wright. New York: Harper, 1966. 393–397.

Williams, Sherley Anne. "Papa Dick and Sister-Woman: Reflections on Women in the Fiction of Richard Wright." *American Novelists Revisited: Essays in Feminist Criticism.* Ed. Fritz Fleischmann. Boston: Hall, 1982. 394–415.

Wright, Richard. "How 'Bigger' Was Born." *Native Son.* 1940. New York: Harper, 1966. vii–xxxiv.

———. *Native Son.* 1940. New York: Harper, 1966.

CONTRIBUTORS

HAROLD BLOOM is Sterling Professor of the Humanities at Yale University and Henry W. and Albert A. Berg Professor of English at the New York University Graduate School. He is a 1985 MacArthur Foundation Award recipient, served as the Charles Eliot Norton Professor of Poetry at Harvard University (1987-88), and is the author of eighteen books, the most recent being *Poetics of Influence: New and Selected Criticism* (1988). Currently he is editing the Chelsea House series *Modern Critical Views* and *The Critical Cosmos,* and other Chelsea House series in literary criticism.

EDWARD MARGOLIES is Professor of English at CUNY, College of Staten Island. He is author of *Native Sons: A Critical Study of Twentieth Century Negro American Authors* (1968), *The Art of Richard Wright* (1969), and *Antebellum Slave Narratives: Their Place in American Literary History* (1975), and co-author of *Afro-American Fiction 1853–1976: A Guide to Information Sources* (1979; with David Bakish). He has also written on detective fiction and American popular culture.

EDWARD A. WATSON teaches in the Department of English at the University of Windsor in Windsor, Ontario. His most recent publication is *A Study of Selected English Critical Terms from 1650 to 1800: A Constellation* (1987). He has written several articles on English literature and criticism. In 1976 he published a book of poems, *Out of Silence.*

KENETH KINNAMON is Professor and Chair of the Department of English at the University of Arkansas. He is author of *The Emergence of Richard Wright: A Study in Literature and Society* (1972) and *A Richard Wright Bibliography: Fifty Years of Criticism and Commentary 1933–1982* (1988), and co-editor of *Black Writers of America: A Comprehensive Anthology* (1972; with Richard Barksdale).

DOROTHY S. REDDEN formerly taught in the Department of English at Douglass College, Rutgers University.

CHARLES DE ARMAN has written on Richard Wright and Toni Morrison in *Black American Literature Forum* and *Obsidian.* He is a librarian at the Motion Picture, Sound and Video Branch of the National Archives Library.

ROSS PUDALOFF teaches in the Department of English at Wayne State University. He has published several articles on American literature in *Bucknell Review, Mosaic, Genre,* and *Southern Literary Journal.*

ROBERT JAMES BUTLER is Associate Professor of English at Canisius College in Buffalo. He has published articles on Richard Wright in *Black American Literature Forum* and *Melus.*

TONY MAGISTRALE teaches in the Department of English at the University of Vermont. He is author of *Landscape of Fear: Stephen King's American Gothic* (1988) and of essays on American literature and popular culture. He has edited *The Shining Reader* (1989).

LAURA E. TANNER is Assistant Professor of English at Emory University. She has published essays on American drama and is currently completing a book on the representation of violence in twentieth-century fiction.

VALERIE SMITH is Associate Professor of English at Princeton University. She is author of *Self-Discovery and Authority in Afro-American Narrative* (1987).

ALAN W. FRANCE teaches in the Department of English at Louisiana State University. He has published articles in *Modern Fiction Studies* and *CCTE Studies.*

BIBLIOGRAPHY

Avery, Evelyn Gross. *Rebels and Victims: The Fiction of Richard Wright and Bernard Mala-mud.* Port Washington, NY: Kennikat Press, 1979.

Baker, Houston A., Jr. *Afro-American Poetics: Revisions of Harlem and the Black Aesthetic.* Madison: University of Wisconsin Press, 1988.

————. *Blues, Ideology, and Afro-American Literature: A Vernacular Theory.* Chicago: University of Chicago Press, 1984.

————. *The Journey Back: Issues in Black Literature and Criticism.* Chicago: University of Chicago Press, 1980.

————. *Modernism and the Harlem Renaissance.* Chicago: University of Chicago Press, 1987.

Bell, Bernard W. *The Afro-American Novel and Its Tradition.* Amherst: University of Massachusetts Press, 1987.

Bigsby, C. W. E. *The Second Black Renaissance: Essays in Black Literature.* Westport, CT: Greenwood Press, 1980.

Bloom, Harold, ed. *Richard Wright.* New York: Chelsea House, 1987.

————, ed. *Richard Wright's* Native Son. New York: Chelsea House, 1988.

Bone, Robert. *The Negro Novel in America.* New Haven: Yale University Press, 1958 (rev. ed. 1965).

Brazinsky, Judith Giblin. "The Demands of Conscience and the Imperatives of Form: The Dramatization of *Native Son.*" *Black American Literature Forum* 18 (1984): 106–9.

Brignano, Russell C. *Richard Wright: An Introduction to the Man and His Works.* Pittsburgh: University of Pittsburgh Press, 1970.

Bryant, Jerry H. "The Violence of *Native Son.*" *Southern Review* 17 (1981): 303–19.

Butler, Robert James. "Wright's *Native Son* and Two Novels by Zola: A Comparative Study." *Black American Literature Forum* 18 (1984): 100–105.

Campbell, Jane. *Mythic Black Fiction: The Transformation of History.* Knoxville: University of Tennessee Press, 1986.

Clarke, Graham. "Beyond Realism: Recent Black Fiction and the Language of 'The Real Thing.'" *Black American Literature Forum* 16 (1982): 43–48.

Cobb, Nina Kressner. "Richard Wright: Exile and Existentialism." *Phylon* 40 (1979): 362–74.

Cooke, Michael G. *Afro-American Literature in the Twentieth Century: The Achievement of Intimacy.* New Haven: Yale University Press, 1984.

Dixon, Melvin. *Ride Out the Wilderness: Geography and Identity in Afro-American Literature.* Urbana: University of Illinois Press, 1987.

Fabre, Michel. *The Unfinished Quest of Richard Wright.* Translated by Isabel Barzun. New York: Morrow, 1973.

————. *The World of Richard Wright.* Jackson: University Press of Mississippi, 1985.

Felgar, Robert. *Richard Wright.* Boston: Twayne, 1980.

Fishburn, Katherine. *Richard Wright's Hero: The Faces of a Rebel-Victim.* Metuchen, NJ: Scarecrow Press, 1977.

Gates, Henry Louis, Jr. *Figures in Black: Words, Signs, and the "Racial" Self.* New York: Oxford University Press, 1987.

————. *"Race," Writing, and Difference.* Chicago: University of Chicago Press, 1986.

———. *The Signifying Monkey: A Theory of Afro-American Literary Criticism.* New York: Oxford University Press, 1988.

Gayle, Addison, Jr. "Richard Wright: Beyond Nihilism." *Negro Digest* 18 (December 1968): 4–10.

———. *Richard Wright: Ordeal of a Native Son.* Garden City, NY: Doubleday, 1980.

Gibson, Donald B. *The Politics of Literary Expression: A Study of Major Black Writers.* Westport, CT: Greenwood Press, 1981.

———, ed. *Five Black Writers: Essays on Wright, Ellison, Baldwin, Hughes and LeRoi Jones.* New York: New York University Press, 1970.

Hakutani, Yoshinobu. "Creation of the Self in Richard Wright's *Black Boy.*" *Black American Literature Forum* 19 (1985): 70–75.

Hedgepeth, Chester, Jr. *Theories of Social Action in Black Literature.* New York: Peter Lang, 1986.

Hellenbrand, Harold. "Bigger Thomas Reconsidered: *Native Son,* Film and *King Kong.*" *Journal of American Culture* 6 (1983): 84–95.

Hoeveler, Diane Long. "Oedipus Agonistes: Mothers and Sons in Richard Wright's Fiction." *Black American Literature Forum* 12 (1978): 65–68.

Jackson, Blyden. *The Waiting Years: Essays on American Negro Literature.* Baton Rouge: Louisiana State University Press, 1976.

Joyce, Joyce Ann. *Richard Wright's Art of Tragedy.* Iowa City: University of Iowa Press, 1986.

Kent, George E. *Blackness and the Adventure of Western Culture.* Chicago: Third World Press, 1972.

Kinnamon, Keneth, et al. *A Richard Wright Bibliography: Fifty Years of Criticism and Commentary 1933–1982.* Westport, CT: Greenwood Press, 1988.

Klotman, Phyllis R. "Moral Distancing as a Rhetorical Technique in *Native Son:* A Note on 'Fate.'" *CLA Journal* 18 (1974–75): 284–91.

McCall, Dan. *The Example of Richard Wright.* New York: Harcourt, Brace & World, 1969.

Margolies, Edward. *The Art of Richard Wright.* Carbondale: Southern Illinois University Press, 1969.

Payne, Ladell. "A Clear Case: Richard Wright 1908–1960." In *Black Novelists and the Southern Literary Tradition.* Athens: University of Georgia Press, 1981, pp. 54–79.

Reed, Kenneth T. "*Native Son:* An American *Crime and Punishment.*" *Studies in Black Literature* 1 (Summer 1970): 33–34.

Reilly, John M. "Self-Portraits by Richard Wright." *Colorado Quarterly* 20 (1971): 31–45.

Roache, Joel. "'What Had Made Him and What He Meant': The Politics of Wholeness in 'How "Bigger" Was Born.'" *Sub-stance* No. 15 (1976): 133–45.

Sanders, Ronald. "Relevance for the Sixties: Richard Wright Then and Now." *Negro Digest* 18 (December 1968): 83–98.

Schraufnagel, Noel. "Wright and the Protest Novel." In *From Apology to Protest: The Black American Novel.* DeLand, FL: Everett/Edwards, 1973, pp. 19–32.

Sisney, Mary F. "The Power and Horror of Whiteness: Wright and Ellison Respond to Poe." *CLA Journal* 29 (1985–86): 82–90.

Stepto, Robert B. *From Behind the Veil: A Study of Afro-American Narrative.* Urbana: University of Illinois Press, 1979.

Tremaine, Louis. "The Dissociated Sensibility of Bigger Thomas in Wright's *Native Son.*" *Studies in American Fiction* 14 (1986): 63–76.

Tuttleton, James W. "The Negro Writer as Spokesman." In *The Black American Writer, Volume I: Fiction,* edited by C. W. E. Bigsby. DeLand, FL: Everett/Edwards, 1969, pp. 245–69.

Walls, Doyle W. "The Clue Undetected in Richard Wright's *Native Son.*" *American Literature* 57 (1985): 125–28.

Weixlmann, Joe, and Houston A. Baker, ed. *Black Feminist Criticism and Critical Theory.* Greenwood, FL: Penkevill Publishing Co., 1988.

Williams, Sherley Ann. "Papa Dick and Sister Woman: Reflections on Women in the Fiction of Richard Wright." In *American Novelists Revisited: Essays in Feminist Criticism,* edited by Fritz Fleischmann. Boston: G. K. Hall, 1982, pp. 394–415.

Wright, Richard. "I Bite the Hand That Feeds Me." *Atlantic Monthly* 155 (June 1940): 826–28.

ACKNOWLEDGMENTS

"Everybody's Protest Novel" by James Baldwin from *Notes of a Native Son* by James Baldwin, © 1955, renewed 1983, by James Baldwin. Reprinted by permission of Beacon Press.

"Black Boys and Native Sons" by Irving Howe from *A World More Attractive: A View of Modern Literature and Politics* by Irving Howe, © 1963 by Irving Howe. Reprinted by permission of Horizon Press.

"The World and the Jug" by Ralph Ellison from *Shadow and Act* by Ralph Ellison, © 1963 by Ralph Ellison. Reprinted by permission of Random House, Inc. and William Morris Agency.

"Racial Wisdom and Richard Wright's *Native Son*" by Houston A. Baker, Jr. from *Long Black Song: Essays in Black American Literature and Culture* by Houston A. Baker, Jr., © 1972 by the Rectors and Visitors of the University of Virginia. Reprinted by permission of the University Press of Virginia.

"Rebel and Streetman in Black Literature" by Sherley Anne Williams from *Give Birth to Brightness: A Thematic Study in Neo-Black Literature* by Sherley Anne Williams, © 1972 by Sherley Anne Williams. Reprinted by permission of Doubleday, a division of Bantam, Doubleday, Dell Publishing Group, Inc.

"Richard Wright: Individualism Reconsidered" by Nina Kressner Cobb from *CLA Journal* 21, No. 3 (March 1978), © 1978 by the College Language Association. Reprinted by permission.

"Being and Race" by Charles Johnson from *Being and Race: Black Writing since 1970* by Charles Johnson, © 1988 by Charles Johnson. Reprinted by permission.

How "Bigger" Was Born by Richard Wright, © 1940 by Richard Wright. Reprinted by permission of Harper & Row, Publishers, Inc.

"Native Son and Three Kinds of Revolution" (originally titled "Richard Wright: *Native Son* and Three Kinds of Revolution") by Edward Margolies from *Native Sons: A Critical Study of Twentieth Century Negro American Authors,* © 1968 by Edward Margolies. Reprinted by permission.

"Bessie's Blues" by Edward A. Watson from *New Letters* 38, No. 2 (Winter 1971), © 1971 by the Curators of the University of Missouri. Reprinted by permission of *New Letters* and the Curators of the University of Missouri–Kansas City.

"Native Son" by Keneth Kinnamon from *The Emergence of Richard Wright: A Study of Literature and Society* by Keneth Kinnamon, © 1972 by the Board of Trustees of the University of Illinois. Reprinted by permission of the University of Illinois Press.

"Richard Wright and Native Son: Not Guilty" by Dorothy S. Redden from *Black American Literature Forum* 10, No. 4 (Winter 1976), © 1976 by Indiana State University. Reprinted by permission.

"Bigger Thomas: The Symbolic Negro and the Discrete Human Entity" by Charles De Arman from *Black American Literature Forum* 12, No. 2 (Summer 1978), © 1978 by Indiana State University. Reprinted by permission.

"*Native Son* and Mass Culture" (originally titled "Celebrity as Identity: Richard Wright, *Native Son,* and Mass Culture") by Ross Pudaloff from *Studies in American Fiction* 11, No. 1 (Spring 1983), © 1983 by Northeastern University. Reprinted by permission.

"The Function of Violence in *Native Son*" (originally titled "The Function of Violence in Richard Wright's *Native Son*") by Robert James Butler from *Black American Literature Forum* 20, Nos. 1–2 (Spring–Summer 1986), © 1986 by Indiana State University. Reprinted by permission.

"Wright's *Crime and Punishment*" (originally titled "From St. Petersburg to Chicago: Wright's *Crime and Punishment*") by Tony Magistrale from *Comparative Literature Studies* 23, No. 1 (Spring 1986), © 1986 by the Board of Trustees of the University of Illinois. Reprinted by permission of The Pennsylvania State University Press.

"The Narrative Presence in *Native Son*" (originally titled "Uncovering the Magical Disguise of Language: The Narrative Presence in Richard Wright's *Native Son*") by Laura E. Tanner from *Texas Studies in Literature and Language* 29, No. 4 (Winter 1987), © 1987 by the University of Texas Press. Reprinted by permission of the publisher and author.

"Alienation and Creativity in *Native Son*" (originally titled "Alienation and Creativity in the Fiction of Richard Wright") by Valerie Smith from *Self-Discovery and Authority in Afro-American Narrative* by Valerie Smith, © 1987 by the President and Fellows of Harvard College. Reprinted by permission of Harvard University Press.

"Misogyny and Appropriation in *Native Son*" (originally titled "Misogyny and Appropriation in Wright's *Native Son*") by Alan W. France from *Modern Fiction Studies* 34, No. 3 (Autumn 1988), © 1988 by Perdue Research Foundation. Reprinted by permission.

INDEX

American Hunger, 101n.24, 150
American Negro Folktales (Dorson), 13
American Tragedy, An (Dreiser), 17, 20
Anderson, John M., 20
Anti-Semite and Jew (Sartre), 88
Argentina: and *Native Son's* filming, 91
Argosy All-Story Magazine, 91
Armstrong, Louis, 14
Atwater, Lee, 1
Autobiography of an Ex-Colored Man
    (Johnson), 14

Bakish, David, 101n.33
Baldwin, James, 6–7, 10–11, 20, 52–53, 73,
    76, 79; as compared to Wright,
    10; and Ralph Ellison, 8; on *Native
    Son's* violence, 73
Bayley, John: on Pynchon and Wright, 99
"Bessie's Blues #1," 56
"Bessie's Blues #2," 57
"Bessie's Blues #3," 58
"Beyond Realism: Recent Black Fiction
    and the Language of 'The Real
    Thing' " (Clarke), 127
Big Boy (*Uncle Tom's Children*), 83
"Big Boy Leaves Home," 17, 83, 92, 97;
    and Communist perspective, 17
"Bigger Thomas Reconsidered: *Native
    Son,* Film, and *King Kong*" (Hellen-
    brand), 142n.14
Bill of Rights, the, 35
Birdoff, Harry: and Wright, 91
Black, Hugo L., 38
Black Belt, the, 38
Black Boy, 8, 11–12, 19, 150; as auto-
    biography, 12; and its original title,
    101n.24
black folklore: and *Native Son,* 14
Black Thunder (Bontemps), 14–15
"Black Words and Black Becoming" (Mc-
    Connell), 140
blacks: and Hitler, 28; and Mussolini, 28;
    and post–Civil War freedom, 27.
    See also Native Son; Thomas, Big-
    ger; and Wright, Richard
"Bleeding Hearted Blues" (Smith), 55
Bluestone, George: on cinema and fic-
    tion, 99

Blum: holdup of, 154
Bone, Robert, 15, 18, 75–77, 80; on fu-
    sion of narrative and metaphor in
    Native Son, 133
Bontemps, Arna, 14–15
Book of Negro Folklore, The (ed. Bon-
    temps and Hughes), 14
"Bright and Morning Star," 15
Brown, Cecil, 103
Brownmiller, Susan: on male rape, 154–
    55
Bryant, Jerry: on Wright's use of violence,
    115n.1; and hatred of white soci-
    ety, 50
Buckley (the State's Attorney), 74, 111,
    147, 150
Burke, Kenneth, 61
Bush, George, 1
Butler, Robert James: on repression of
    sexual dialectic in *Native Son,* 156

Camus, Albert, 50; on Satan, 51
Chicago: and St. Petersburg, 118–19
Chicago Tribune, The, 38, 96
    cinema: and *Native Son,* 91; and the
        novel, 90, 99; and Wright, 91
Civil War, the, 26
Cixous, Hélène: on the appropriation of
    women, 152
Clarke, Graham: on *Native Son's* stylistic
    weaknesses, 127
Cleaver, Eldridge: on Bigger, 15
Clifton, Todd, 22
Cohn, David L., 75; on Wright, 73
Communism, 17, 34, 44, 64–65, 70, 73,
    106
"Concept of Dread, The" (Kierkegaard),
    88n.4
Cowley, Malcolm, 103
Crime and Punishment (Dostoevsky), 20;
    and *Native Son,* 117–25

Daiches, David: on Mary Dalton's mur-
    der, 103
Dalton, Mary, 20, 86, 149; and her mur-
    der, 15, 20, 46, 50, 55, 65, 68,
    107–10, 112, 128, 145–47, 150,
    153, 155–56, 159; her "parlor